INTO AFRICA

Also by Kenneth M. Cameron

Novels:

Our Jo

As George Bartram:

Fair Game
A Job Abroad
The Aelian Fragment
The Sunset Gun
Under the Freeze
Master of Secrets

Plays:

The Hundred and First
Papp

As editor:

Chronicles of a Second African Trip, George Eastman

INTO AFRICA

The Story of the East African Safari

Kenneth M. Cameron

Constable · London

First published in Great Britain 1990
by Constable and Company Limited
10 Orange Street London WC2H 7EG
Copyright © 1990 by Kenneth M. Cameron
ISBN 0 09 469770 1
Set in Linotron Ehrhardt 10½pt by
Rowland Phototypesetting Limited
Bury St Edmunds, Suffolk
Printed in Great Britain by
St Edmundsbury Press Limited
Bury St Edmunds, Suffolk

A CIP catalogue record for this book
is available from the British Library

For Patti

CONTENTS

	Illustrations	9
	Acknowledgements	11
	Prologue	13
1	Haya Safari!	15
2	Safariland	31
3	Big Men, Irresistible Magic	42
4	No Trip for a Woman	63
5	Lions and Champagne	79
6	Lasso, Trap, and Balloon	95
7	Three Unforgettable Weeks	105
8	Kag	117
9	That Glorious Madness	133
10	An Expensive Luxury	158
11	Quite Simply the Whip	173
12	Zoo Africa	185
	Notes	197
	Bibliography	209
	Index	221

ILLUSTRATIONS

Map of the safariland of East Africa (drawn by John Mitchell)   page 14

between pages 60 and 61

H. M. Stanley
Stanley's historic meeting with Livingstone
The safari winding its way like a snake
Theodore Roosevelt's safari of 1909
For Africans, safaris were often hard work
Their pay was about 3 pence a day
Rhinos often broke up the line of march
The Boer ox-wagon
A rig that anticipated the shooting-car
The motor car changed the safari for ever
Motor car progress might be slow in the rains
The bush outfit in embryo
The Burberry 'veldt coat'
The bush outfit in 1910
London tailors created fashionable safari clothes
Clothes make the sportsman
Colonial outfits in 1914
Two hats are better than one
Newland and Tarlton's yard, Nairobi
The white hunter, R. J. Cuninghame
Denys Finch Hatton
The white hunter of Hollywood: from *The Nylon Safari* by R. M. Cloete
Camp was a few square feet of Europe
What a storm can do to a strong tent
A tent for all seasons in 1912
A tent in the twenties
All the comforts of home in the bush

between pages 156 and 157

Women often coped with safari better than men
Women's safari fashion: from *The Nylon Safari* by R. M. Cloete
The Big Five: buffalo, elephant, lion, rhino, and leopard
A hippo charging at Roosevelt's boat
Following a buffalo into reed and mud
A python was very rare
Hippo shooting
Giraffe skins drying
'A typical sportsman's Kenya bag'
A taxidermy and outfitting advertisement
The first step in building a piano
Elephant tusks, skull and skin being carried to the railway
The white professional and his ivory
An ivory factory in Hamburg
Sex and safari were often linked: from *The Nylon Safari* by R. M. Cloete
'Buffalo' Jones
Shooting a buffalo with a percussion rifle
A double rifle
Big game cartridges
Somali modes of carrying rifles
A Masai warrior
A Masai on safari
Black and white on safari
A safari headman
A safari worker at play
African trackers
A 'shari' with the chief
Cutting up an elephant

The Nylon Safari by R. M. Cloete, from which three pictures were taken (see above), was published by Riverside Press, Cambridge, Massachusetts in 1956. The pictures are reproduced by permission of Houghton Mifflin, Boston.

ACKNOWLEDGEMENTS

M ANY people and institutions have helped in preparing this book. For their kindness and help, I should like to thank the following individuals: John Bisley of Gametrackers, Nairobi; Patricia Gallahan; Professor Robert G. Gregory; Admiral Sir Nigel Henderson and Lady Henderson; Robert Kolker; Mrs B. Leigh; Paula McGehee of GAMECOIN; Patrick O'Connor; Kenhelm Stott; and Chuck Vaughan. The following institutions gave invaluable research aid: the American Museum of Natural History; the Chicago Historical Society; the International Museum of Photography at George Eastman House; the Manuscript Collection, the Film Division, and the African Office of the Library of Congress; the Houghton Library of Harvard University; the McKeldin Library of the University of Maryland; the Royal Commission on Historical Manuscripts; the Rare Books and Special Collections Division of the University of Rochester; Rhodes House Library, Oxford; the Arents Research Library of Syracuse University; and the Osa and Martin Johnson Safari Museum.

I am grateful to the following for granting permission to quote: the American Museum of Natural History; Mark G. E. N. Buxton; the Earl of Winchelsea; Exposition Press, publishers of *East African Safari* by Ruth Lothrop; Faber and Faber Ltd., publishers of *East Africa Journey* by Margery Perham; Martin Henderson; the Osa and Martin Johnson Safari Museum; the Kenya National Archives; Methuen and Company, publishers of *Speak to the Earth* by Vivienne de Watteville; John Murray (Publishers) Ltd., publishers of *African Adventure* by Dennis Lyell; Mrs Bryan Patterson; and George N. Rainsford.

Finally I should like to apologize to those holders of copyright whom, despite diligent search, I was unable to locate to request permission to quote. These include the literary heirs of Edmund Heller; Sir Alfred Pease; May French Sheldon; Frederick Courtney Selous; and Leslie and Jessie Tarlton.

PROLOGUE

Dawn

S OMETIMES a thin edge of silence is inserted between the East African night and the coming of day, but often the night's sounds and the day's overlap and merge, and it is only the change from the dark noise of violence to an illusory peace that marks the coming of the sun. The night, its sounds made menacing by darkness, is the time of predation, the lion's profound roar and the hyena's rising whoop and cackle. Approaching day brings birdsong – first a single dove's cool piping, then another's, and, even before light fills the sky, the mingled, never discordant calls of a hundred other birds.

It is dark inside the tent. Above your closed eyes, strange stars blaze like the lights of a fantastic city, but the tent is made of closely woven green canvas, and it is lined with red cloth, and yet another layer of canvas rides above it; you do not see the stars. The tent is an image of the night, the night given shape and familiarity, but inside it is utterly black, and the hurricane lamp that has burned with its wick turned low all night beyond the lowered flaps is invisible. As the night wanes, you sense no coming of the light, but you wake none the less, your body remembering already its new cycle. Alert, you lie with eyes opened against the tent's blackness and listen for the sound you think has wakened you, and, hearing then a zebra honk like a high-pitched donkey out on the plain, you tell yourself it was this, and you wait for the lion's gutturals.

Yet you doze before the next sound comes, and half in sleep you hear a hyena to your right, not so close as to threaten you; it repeats four times its locating cry, which rises from a baritone to a shrill falsetto and stops as if cut with a knife. Another answers from far away to your left, the call the same, and you sleep; and you wake now only when a low voice murmurs *Hodi* just outside the tied tent flap and then does not wait for the requested permission but continues, even as black fingers are untying the stiff canvas, 'Tea for morning, memsahib-bwana . . .'

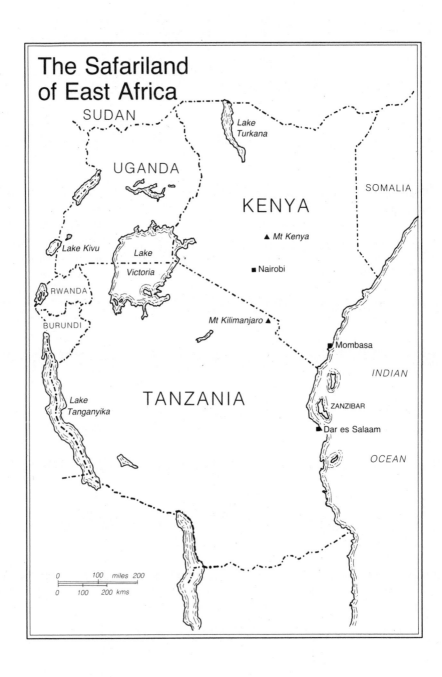

The Safariland
of East Africa

SUDAN

Lake
Turkana

UGANDA

SOMALIA

KENYA

Lake Kivu

Lake
Victoria

▲ Mt Kenya

■ Nairobi

RWANDA

BURUNDI

Mt Kilimanjaro ▲

■ Mombasa

INDIAN

Lake
Tanganyika

TANZANIA

ZANZIBAR

■ Dar es Salaam

OCEAN

| 0 | 100 | miles | 200 |
| 0 | 100 | 200 kms | |

1

HAYA SAFARI!

Beginnings to 1900

THE safari winds slowly through the long grass of history, perceived at a great distance as an indistinct scratch on the landscape, then a dotted line like slow-moving ants. There are no individuals yet, only these dots – perhaps they are heads, or burdens carried on heads, sticking up above the grass. It is only a few years after the death of Christ, but the burdens are the same as they will be for 1800 more years: ivory, rhinoceros horn, oil.

As the line creeps closer, we see its sinuous shape before we see the shape of men: it is a snake, one with a small head and a long, a very long, body. And now, as details emerge, we see them: 'two or three Arab merchants . . . with their half-caste hangers-on, a body of armed slaves, and the long string of porters . . . with the scarlet flag of the Sultan [of Zanzibar] at their head'. It is 1000 years after Christ – or 1500, or 1800. The porters are probably slaves, although a profession of porterage has grown up, with twin centres in Zanzibar and certain inland areas, especially Unyamwezi south of what Europeans call Lake Victoria. The trade is still in ivory, horn, and oil, but now there is also a vigorous trade in slaves to places as far away as Arabia, India, and China.

The Islamic Arabic trekkers who are the heads of the snake also have their centres at the island of Zanzibar and at inland towns like Ujiji, where fortified stone houses give them protection and companionship. They may go inland for a couple of years, trading cloth and beads and small tools and, of late, crude guns. On the coast, Islamic towns, even Islamic city-states, have sprung up – Lamu, Pembe – and contact has created a new language and a new black culture, both called Swahili. Fewer in number but none the less important are East Indians, 'banyans', who have settled in these coastal towns and Zanzibar. They are the merchant go-betweens for the Indian trade, which plies the ocean along regular sea routes in huge sailing dhows.

But now the snake is closer still, and, as the safari swings towards 1850, through history's telescope we recognize change: copal, animal hides, beeswax are carried, and the trade itself is shifting 'from its traditional Indian Ocean trading partners to Europe . . .' The cotton cloth called 'merikani' (from America) has become an important item; it will help to destroy an indigenous cloth industry.

And the business of slaving is more vigorous than ever.

And the armed guards, *askaris* in Swahili, are more prominent, their guns better. As recently as the time of America's and France's revolutions, a dangerous new force has appeared in East Africa – the tightly organized Masai. But not only fear of the Masai gives this increasingly militarized look. It is also a consequence of success: more traders, more safaris, more slaves. The trade is reaching out, penetrating deeper into Africa, and from Zanzibar routes lead to the shore of Lake Tanganyika, up across Masailand to the snow-covered mountains of Kilimanjaro and Kenya. And the Europeans, who have since the eighteenth century decided that slavery is an abominable thing, have come.

And now the snake is close, and for the first time it has a European head. It flies a European flag along with the scarlet of Zanzibar. We see, with the naked eye now it is so close, European gear on the porters' heads – tents, guns, tools, whisky, boots, beds. But all the rest of the snake is still black: the faces under the loads are black; the hands that point, that grasp the muskets, that carry and cook, are black. The snake is so close now that we can see that some of the figures are women, and they are black; some are children, and they are black. So the white head is leading into the near-present a black snake over black routes that began when white Europe was a barbarian unknown.

David Livingstone was one of the great figures in the European penetration of southern and eastern Africa – and one of the first to lead a caravan into what is now East Africa. Missionary, explorer, fervent anti-slaver, he gave his life to a vision and died pursuing it. His early African experience had been south of the Zambezi River, but in his final years he moved north into East Africa.

The missionary is often at least symbolically the outrider for the expansionist, and Livingstone, before Cecil Rhodes ever saw Africa, was opening up part of the great manipulator's Cape-to-Cairo route. While he explored the north of what would become Rhodesia, two other Englishmen, Richard Burton and John Hanning Speke, were using the Zanzibar trading routes to become the first Europeans to look at Lakes Tanganyika and Victoria (1857–9); then Speke and a new companion, James Grant, headed a caravan to gather evidence that Victoria was the source of the Nile (1861–3).

It was obligatory at the time to call these experiences 'discoveries'. Burton and Speke 'discovered' Tanganyika and Victoria, but it now seems puzzling – absent cultural chauvinism – that somebody was said to discover lakes on which thousands of people had been living for centuries, one of them the site of a major trading centre. But Europe was flexing its cultural muscles, here in the name of humanitarianism, there in the name of materialism. Livingstone and Speke believed that intertribal warfare (much overestimated by them) and slavery 'could only be prevented by a European administration'; Rhodes would say that 'the conquest of Africa by the English nation is a practical question'. 'Discovering' things meant that the things had been unknown to *civilized* (i.e., European) people – and with discovery often went a claim to ownership. Thus, both romantic yearning for the unknown and political expediency made this the period of the great controversy over discovering the source of the Nile, a controversy so bitter and so publicized that it divided Burton and Speke, probably led to Speke's death, and made their names and that of Samuel Baker household words.

And it raised one other name above even theirs: Henry Morton Stanley. He 'found' Livingstone, proved the source of the Nile, and made three stupendously famous African journeys, which became the stuff of not merely dreams, but also of the very European idea of Africa – and of the African safari.

In 1866, Livingstone began what was to be his last journey, which would end with his death in 1873 west of Lake Tanganyika in what he called 'Inner Africa'. This time he started well north of the Zambezi on the Rovuma (now the border between Mozambique and Tanzania) in what Alan Moorehead called a 'half-mystical' final effort that included hope of finding the Nile source, of ending slavery, of doing God's work – of finding 'a divine pattern in the geography of the river'. As it turned out, he made a disastrous head to the snake; it promptly fell apart, porters deserting, others drifting away, and by the late 1860s he was thought dead or lost. Thus, Livingstone – idealistic, benign, muddled – gave opportunity to Stanley, who 'found' him. Stanley's 1871 expedition from Zanzibar to the Arab trading centre of Ujiji on Lake Tanganyika allowed Stanley to write *How I Found Livingstone* and to become the great African expert, the man called upon to find lost African things – the source of the Nile, the Emin Pasha force.

After Stanley's first journey, others followed quickly; 'discovery' was turning, inevitably, into rivalry. Lovett Cameron crossed Africa via Ujiji in 1873; Stanley made his second journey in 1875–7; a very young Joseph Thomson took command of an expedition in 1879; Germany's Carl Peters marched for *Gott und Deutschland* in 1884, the same year that Thomson made his more famous second journey through the much-feared Masailand of what is now Kenya. Between 1888 and 1890, Stanley, Peters, and the Hungarian Count Teleki made what were arguably the last journeys of real exploration (Stanley's a violent disaster – passing 'through the jungle like a scourge, leaving a trail of burnt villages and perforated corpses' – that paradoxically made him 'Stanley Africanus', the toast of England).

By 1890, the East African map was transformed. England and Germany had signed a territorial agreement, and imperialism was giving way to mercantilism as the first private companies tried to open the interior. The Sultan of Zanzibar had been bypassed, and the point of entry had shifted north from Zanzibar to Mombasa and a new town called Dar es Salaam. Slavery was outlawed and trade was redirected.

The safari snake, however, crawled on. Now European administrators, engineers, and adventurers made its head. For the final decade of the century, it followed many of the old routes, but with new intents and new leaders: the loner Arthur Neumann, elephant hunter extraordinary; the officials F. D.

Lugard and Frederick Jackson; the traveller-sportsmen John C. Willoughby, Harry Johnston, Astor Chanler, Arthur Donaldson Smith, and Lord Delamere; and that remarkable woman, May French Sheldon.

By century's end, all of Africa was claimed. The map had been filled in. The Arab traders were vanishing. Safari travel, however, remained the only possibility in a vast land of distance and danger. The snake was now about to undergo a transformation, however, to shed one skin for a brilliant new one: recreation in place of work. The experience of these first European heads would make the transformation possible.

They began at exotic, fragrant, horrible, hot, quaint, delightful, damnable Zanzibar, 'the Bagdad, the Ispahan, the Stamboul . . . of East Africa'. Grant found himself both charmed and appalled by it – a frequent European ambivalence to Africa even now. The whole island smelled of cloves, and the winding streets, 'too narrow for carriages', were lined with Indian shops whose owners 'rose as we passed'. Alcohol was available in every street, it seemed, with more unfamiliar things like *khat* and *bhang*; the heat could be oppressive, and reminders of the slave trade could not be ignored.

Yet Zanzibar had to be borne: Grant spent 39 days there in 1860; as late as 1888, Willoughby was 35 days out from England before he ever got inland. Thomson was even more leisurely, taking four months for the usual calls on the Sultan and the British Consul, the hiring of porters, and, in his case, the learning of Swahili.

You could not simply sail to the coast and start walking. The Sultan's approval was essential, then the co-operation of Arab traders. Porters had to be got, always a tormented and maddening process. No matter how much gear and trade goods had been brought from Europe, more were required; seemingly endless bargaining and finagling, annoying to many Europeans, had to be done. Indian and Arab merchants, veterans of a culture of bargaining, had to be dealt with despite European racial feeling. *Baksheesh*, the oil for rusty hinges, had to be paid.

For what was being contemplated was a huge undertaking. Exploratory safaris were long: Stanley was more than a year getting from Zanzibar to Ujiji; Teleki was almost two years to the day going to Lake Turkana (Rudolf) and back; Speke was out 21 months with Burton and 29 with Grant. Preparations were like those of an army going on the march: Teleki and von Hohnel had 470 porter-loads of gear and goods; Peters had ten tons of material. Stanley on his first (and simplest) trip considered he needed 'what a ship must have when about to sail on a long voyage.' Broken down into porter-loads, one such safari's supplies included:

Tents and camp goods, 65 loads
Powder and arms, 35
Preserved food, 44

Medicines, rockets, axes, etc., 16
Cables for crossing rivers, 2
Rice, 5
Brandy, wine and vinegar, 4
Fabric (for trade), 80
Beads (for trade), 100
Wire (for trade), 80
An iron boat and a canvas boat, 22

The seemingly disproportionate amount of trade goods was motivated by the same notion as the large amount of arms – lots of carrots and lots of sticks. 'Beads stand for copper coins . . . cloth measures for silver, wire is reckoned as gold'. Beads, cloth, and wire were the currency of Africa, with which essential food was bought and with which the loathsome *hongo* – tribute or toll – was paid at every invisible border. Teleki took 600 40-yard pieces of white *merikani*, 250 blue and 100 red, as well as iron, brass, and copper wire, and tin, lead, 'fine wire . . . [trinkets] and naval and cavalry sabres'.

He also took, however, 800 lb of gunpowder and thousands of percussion caps. Burton 'provided ammunition for two years – ten thousand coppercaps . . . , forty boxes . . . containing ball, grape, and shot, six fire-proof magazines, and two small barrels of fine powder . . . together with four ten-pound kegs of a coarser kind for the escort'. Stanley took 'enough guns, powder, and ball to be able to make a series of good fights if necessary'. The military aspect of the Arab caravans was thus maintained. John Petherick, a trader and traveller early into Sudan from the north, in 1856 took mostly 'old flintlock muskets' for his men, but he had first-rate revolvers and a repeating rifle for himself. This distinction – best guns for the Europeans, inferior guns for the askaris and porters – was universal and expressed the distrust that marked most expeditions. Cap-and-ball was being replaced during this period by cartridge arms; therefore, obsolete flintlocks were often given to the porters, cap-and-ball to the askaris, with cartridge (repeating) guns kept by the Europeans. Speke had 50 carbines provided by the Indian government, which were to be used for defence and given to his best men at expedition's end; Stanley had a Winchester and a Henry repeating (cartridge) rifle, 2 Starr carbines and a Jocelyn, 2 revolvers, 6 single pistols, a double smooth-bore breech-loader, and an 8-bore (8-gauge in America) 'elephant rifle' – along with 24 flintlocks for his askaris.

Thomson held off distributing weapons until he had sailed from Zanzibar to the coast, and then his men were armed with a mixture of flint guns, 20 'old Enfield rifles' picked up at Zanzibar, and 30 outdated Snider carbines; each white, however, had an express rifle, a shotgun, and a revolver. Teleki and von Hohnel armed their men with 200 muzzle-loaders, 80 obsolete Werndl single-shot carbines, and 12 Colt repeaters, but they gave their personal bodyguard bolt-action rifles. Furthermore, the bodyguard was tribally distinct from the rest of the safari, on the advice of Burton, so that their loyalty would be to the Europeans.

This unease with Africa ran very deep. To be sure, caution was justified, but, as Stanley and Peters were to show, such preparation for battle was itself an urge to battle. Peters on his second journey took 'my little bush-piece [cannon] with one hundred rounds of grapeshot and the same number of bombshells', as well as 100 muzzle-loaders and 50 breech-loaders and other, better, weapons. This was a shift from defensiveness to offence; in Peters's case it was a move from unease with Africa to conquest of Africa. Stanley was to recommend a thousand rifles to enter Masai country; as late as 1895, Frederick Jackson was suggesting 25 rifles to go within 50 miles of Kilimanjaro, 80–100 to go beyond Lake Baringo. The gun became both cause and effect of conflict: when Stanley neared Livingstone, he involved himself in a battle in which he and his Arab allies mustered 1500 guns. Thereafter, the more guns Europeans took, the more belligerent they became, increasingly refusing to pay *hongo* and seizing rather than trading for food. It was not technology alone that caused the change, but European technology gave expression to European psyche: by century's end, the machine gun and the high-powered magazine rifle were loud where, two generations before, the flintlock had been seldom heard.

But no amount of gear and guns was going to grow legs and walk its own way across East Africa. Essential to every journey, and part of the maddening experience of Zanzibar, was the hiring of Africans. Several specialities were needed – interpreters, guides, gunbearers, porters, askaris, personal servants, cooks – but above all what was looked for was the trustworthy headman. Experience was essential, verified by the Sultan or the British Consul if possible, and inescapably that experience had been gained in the early days with the Arab caravans. Thus, continuity with the Arab trading safaris was maintained and then extended.

Sidi Bombay – 'one of Speke's "Faithfuls"' – served as a gunbearer with Burton and Speke, then again with Speke on his second trip, and then with Stanley in 1871. Chuma, liberated from slavers by Livingstone, was with him on his last long journey and was one of those who carried his body the 1000 miles to Zanzibar; then he was with Thomson in 1879, 'none to equal him as a caravan leader'; he spoke English and 'about a dozen active native dialects', although 'lies came natural to him'. Livingstone's Susi, however (the other who accompanied his body to the coast), was not hired by Thomson because of 'bad drinking habits' and status problems with Chuma. Muinyi Sera 'or Mauna Sera, the head-man of Stanley in his journey across the continent', was with Thomson and later was the 'celebrated Muhina Sara' who served Frederick Jackson as headman. Mhogo, a cook, had been with Speke and then with Cameron, and he was still at his craft when Teleki hired him, 'not a first-rate caterer for the table, but . . . unrivalled in knowing how to manage in the wilds'. Mabruki was with Thomson on his second journey, with Johnston to Kilimanjaro, and with Jackson.

Competition for such men became keen. Quite simply, no safari could get on without them: they mediated between the leaders' language and the half-dozen African ones spoken by the 100 or more people of the safari, and they had important personal qualities of leadership. (Neumann's Mnyamiri was a Swahili 'proficient . . . in many African languages and dialects and thoroughly at home in Masai'.)

Nor were headmen the only ones competed for. Porters, the absolute essential of safari travel, were almost always in short supply. Burton in the 1850s found Arab traders beating him to the best; 30 years later, Teleki hurried to hire his porters because Stanley wanted 500 for his third expedition. Speke watched the price of the best porters climb to almost double as other caravans began to form. 'A good headman was essential here, too, getting many of the porters, undertaking the tasks of going to the bazaar and the porter communities to find them, interviewing them, spreading the word that a wealthy safari led by a notable *mzungu* (European) was going to the lakes for two years. How was a European to do this? How was a man with experience only in India or England to seek out porters in Zanzibar, to communicate with these young men, to overcome European aversion to body smells and physical closeness, to find out the truth of 150 men's experience and trustworthiness, when the men spoke three languages of which he had not a word?

Until the 1880s, many porters were slaves whose wages went to their owners. Professional porters were found, however, among the Zanzibari, the coastal Swahili, and the Wanyamwezi, 'practically a race of professional porters, than whom there are no better in Africa . . . willing, cheerful, and never idle'. One hundred and thirteen of them went with Speke and Grant, who found them 'frank and amiable' until they deserted with their loads, perhaps because they were in their own territory. Porters often took a safari one way, stayed for some time, and then took another back, signing on not for the round trip but one-way, at least in their own minds. The practice led to the institution of 'safari wives' at the long stop away from the real home.

Competition was not the only problem. Thomson said that European expeditions had such a bad reputation by the 1880s that many men would not go with them. 'After the terrible loss of life in connection with Stanley's expedition and others, it seemed to be something of a forlorn hope to join a European caravan.' Sometimes, as a result of this fear, of seasonal changes, or of depletion of the labour stock, porters were simply unavailable; then the risky step was taken of starting anyway, with the intent of picking them up later. Speke got only 100 porters at Zanzibar and hoped to hire more inland; other Europeans left Zanzibar hoping to find men in the coast towns of Pagani or Bagamayo.

Askaris, personal servants, gunbearers, and the rest were often easier to find than porters, often showing up, 'chit' (recommendation) in hand, at the

Europeans' lodging. Askaris, whether provided by the Sultan or brought from Aden, Somaliland, or even India, were an expense best put down under necessary evils. Livingstone on his last journey had a miserable escort of armed sepoys; they abused his animals and caused him endless trouble with their laziness and cruelty. Old Africa hands continued to urge their employment into the twentieth century, however, Jackson advising hiring one per ten porters – with an additional porter to carry the askaris' gear! They expressed the abiding European unease, the suspicion of Africa itself.

Among the remaining personnel, gunbearers were perhaps the most important. Whatever hunting was done – and hunting for meat was essential to every expedition – the European needed the gunbearer. The relationship was a peculiar one, partaking of both service and shared affinity. Especially when guns were heavy, as the double rifles of this period were, *carrying* the things was mere service. On the other hand, when European and African confronted a dangerous animal together, both carrying guns – hunter a rifle, gunbearer a 'bone-smasher' – their very lives depended on each other. The hunter protected the gunbearer from a charging animal; the gunbearer, by handing the heavy gun over at the precise moment in precisely the right way, made the life-saving shot possible. Some men spoke with enormous affection of their gunbearers, and understandably so: here were the men who had shared the ultimate moments – the great shot and the missed one, the good kill and the bad.

The relationship was close. In theory (and later by law) gunbearers did not shoot, but Neumann gave his gunbearer an old Snider single-shot 'as a weapon of defence.' His 'trusty Juma . . . [crawled] at my heels' as they got into range of an elephant; he had the 'unconquerable habit' of handing up the gun '[wrong-end-to] or left-handed . . . but never lagged behind'. Delamere's gunbearer, Abdullah Ashur, saved Delamere's life by grabbing a wounded lion by the mane, then by the tongue, until Delamere was able to break free and shoot it. Such men were worth searching for.

Like other safari workers, however, they were not very highly paid. Stanley paid Bombay £16 a year; like Speke, he probably paid a year in advance. Porters fared less well: Thomson paid his about £1 a month, Jackson about 16 shillings at the end of the century, half in advance.

For this, they worked long hours, no days off until a permanent camp was reached, with the only perks a cooking pot per five or six men, a blanket, and meat. Meat, Europeans contended, was the great lure, and account after account tells of porters devouring fresh-killed game half-broiled on a crude kebab at an open fire. Ten pounds of meat per man at a sitting was common, they say, and such a thing is easily possible in a culture where meat was a rarity. The porters paid for it with terrible indigestion, inevitably cured by the whites with a cathartic. The Europeans paid for it with constant hunting at a level of poundage so high that all but the most enthusiastic hunters could grow weary. A hundred and fifty men could easily eat a ton of meat a week, would eat much more if supplied. An antelope might provide 150 lb, a big eland

700 lb, and even in the great days of huge game herds, such animals were not simply knocked over from a position at the head of march. They had to be hunted for, then skinned, butchered, and carried in – extra work for half a dozen men or more.

And safari work was hard. The 60 lb load was already standard by the 1880s, although with gun and personal gear Thomson thought each man was carrying 80 lb. Much later, A. Blayney Percival said of these early days that there were one-, two-, three-, and four-load men; the last carried a double load and made two trips a day. The one-load men had the other duties of cutting grass in the camp, collecting wood, and building grass huts for themselves and the others, who rested after their double and triple loads. This seems to have been a rare arrangement, however; most porters carried the standard load, with all taking part in the camp chores.

When the gear was assembled in Zanzibar and the loads counted out, the prized headman found, the gunbearers and cooks and askaris and porters hired, the travellers were at last ready to leave Zanzibar. They had been there for a couple of months or more; they had come to loathe the place, if only because it had kept them from the real Africa (though they might long for it before too many weeks). Now they could set out – they and their little army.

Speke and Grant had the English leaders, 9 other whites (including their valets), a 'native commandant', a 'factotum and interpreter', a 'commander of Zanzibar men', 3 private servants, 1 groom, 179 porters, 11 mules, 5 donkeys, and 25 'Belooch soldiers'.

Stanley started with 3 whites, 23 askaris, 4 'supernumeraries', 4 'chiefs', 153 porters, and 27 donkeys.

Teleki and von Hohnel had, besides themselves, 9 askaris, 9 guides, 200 Zanzibari porters, and 450 other porters. Willoughby took 3 other whites, one of them a headman-guide; 6 headmen, 16 askaris, 130 'mixed Zanzibaris' (armed), and 120 'mixed mission men', i.e. Christianized porters.

For 3 whites in Somaliland, on the other hand, Wolverton had only 88 men, but he took 66 camels, 7 donkeys, 8 ponies, sheep, and oxen.

Camels, donkeys, and ponies could replace porters where it was feasible, as in Somaliland, but the tsetse-fly and other scourges made them useless in most areas. On the other hand, a European could simply go light, as Neumann did. 'I have heard even two hundred [porters] spoken of as insuffcent to ensure safety', he said, but he thought 30 to 40 enough for a year.

The safari might get a few women, as well. Accounts are unclear, but it seems that Europeans ended the practice of having women along, certainly ended that of having women as porters. Stanley's distrust of sex (it delayed more important matters) may represent the cause. Europeans saw exploration, and then hunting under the rough conditions of the early days, as a male activity. Nevertheless, women accompanied some European safaris. Speke and Grant had a number, 'quiet, decent, well-conducted, tidy creatures', some with babies on their backs. They cooked for 'their men' and lived in 'bell-shaped' huts built at each stop. Teleki in the later 1880s had local women offer to work as porters when his men deserted, the women even starting 'to bargain with us about taking them'. By the 1890s, however, women were not welcome.

The gear and porters and their women were at last packed into whatever local boats were available, and the Europeans found something better, even a ketch they had brought along for the purpose, and they got everybody somehow across the 20 miles of water to the coast, and made their way to Bagamayo – and dug in for more delays. Some Europeans even rented themselves a stone house there. Delay was again inevitable: a boat had run aground with half the porters; or all the trade cloth had got wet and had to be unpacked and washed and dried in long strips in the African sun and repacked. Or men began to desert. Or to get sick. Or to cause trouble.

Bagamayo had prostitutes and alcohol. The day the leaders finally fixed for setting out, the men were sometimes too drunk to walk. Next day, they were too hung over. Then they needed the solace of the Swahili whores and the 'trashy bazaar'.

Yet it came, at last, to an end. Suddenly there was a day of trying out the loads, 'a ludicrous scene of confusion and squabbling'. Men who yesterday had seemed satisfied and ready, today seemed uncertain and finicky. 'None were satisfied with [any load] allotted . . . All wanted the lightest; none wanted rigid boxes.' But a good headman showed his stuff. '[He seized] this man by the ear and that by the throat . . . in an hour . . . the noise and confusion died away. Each man knew his load.'

And they wrapped their cheap blankets around their heads for a turbanlike pad, and hoisted the load up, and stepped out, each subgroup led by 'their captain, distinguished by a high head-dress of ostrich-plumes stuck through a strip of scarlet flannel'. Somebody had a drum or a box and a stick or a gourd full of grain to give the beat. The white hearts lifted; it was said the black ones did, too; it was said the porters really did it all for the thrill of travel.

And then, drumming, chanting, singing, they started. The snake formed itself: first the flags, the Europeans on foot or briefly on horseback (until the horses died), then headman and porters, porters stretching back for a mile. And the askaris last, to stop the deserters, except for a tail of wives and a few Bagamayo women who would walk along for a few days and then drift back to the coast, and the *totos*, the children too young to be porters but old enough to carry the gear of several porters and to help cook their food and build their huts, the apprentice bearers of bearers. (No evidence exists of any sexual element in this relationship. African taboos on homosexual acts are still strong.)

And they all sang:

Back to the brown mounds [dirt-covered elephants]
The sun making our backs black and hard

Dust, soft, making our footprints clear
Return to our homesteads to feed
Brown mounds, there before [us]
Wearing our caps of [cloth and feathers].

A starting-out was an occasion. The headman's status depended on having strong porters, a look of organization and preparation. Thomson's safari was mustered by drums and led by a 'vanguard with tents and collapsible boat'; the 'main body' was accompanied by a drummer 'fantastically dressed', and the lead porters wore 'feather head dresses and crimson robes', one man carrying the British flag. Porters and onlookers fired off their muskets as the safari pranced out of sight.

After which the first march was an anticlimax, for it was always short, sometimes only a mile. The idea was to prove the snake before help was too far away. The rest of this shortened day could be used to teach the men to use the obsolete guns they had now been issued. The catch was that sometimes men walked back to Bagamayo for the night, again to get drunk, lose themselves with the whores, and all of it all over again. Again they had to be assembled in the morning (some hung over) and the snake got moving, but each morning thereafter became easier. At best, a 12-mile march made up a day's travel; some Europeans, probably on the advice of their headmen, took it easy on the first marches to condition the porters. But even a shortened march was enough, with 60 lb on your head.

Some porters thought better of it and deserted. Desertion was a constant problem, in fact, unusual with the Wanyamwezi but common with the 'riff-raff of the bazaars of . . . Zanzibar and Bagamayo'. Jackson called it 'a loss to be counted on in every safari', but no less expensive for being predictable. Teleki had so many desertions in the first few days – when most took place – that he sent his companion, von Hohnel, back to the coast, which he 'blockaded' until he had captured seven deserters. He then took them to the Sultan in Zanzibar, got his permission to deal with them, and took them back to the coast 'in chains', where he had them and other renegades 'publicly flogged' and chained together by fours to return to the caravan. The Sultan was still nominally the ultimate authority, at least near the coast; a hint of the future came when, farther inland, von Hohnel appealed to an official of the infant German East Africa Company to deal with three more deserters.

Now at the nightly stops the organization – or lack of it – showed. The well-run safaris had their men divided into nearly self-sufficient 'messes' of five or six, who cooked, ate, slept, and marched together; they now set about gathering firewood for the cook, picking a latrine area, building themselves little grass huts to sleep in. The Europeans rested by or in their tents – their tents were erected first thing by the askaris and tended by special tent-servants. The whites sat on the folding chairs bought in London or Port Said or Zanzibar, only occasionally in this period sipping alcohol. They wrote in their diaries or brought the map up to date or planned furiously for the next day (Stanley's way).

The cook spread his pots by a huge fire. Now he showed his worth: after the difficulties of the day, good food was respite. The tinned delicacies from home were husbanded for special occasions. Locally shot game was the regular fare, and welcome were the days when trade produced vegetables or a melon. The cook who could bake good bread was treasured.

At their own little fires, the porters prepared 'posho', any of several grains boiled, but usually the maize meal now called *ugali*. They ate it day after day after day, varied with meat or greens when they could be traded or foraged for. Posho had to be carried; a pound and a half per day per man became standard. As W. S. Rainsford was to point out in 1910, this portion meant that for a month's safari, one man in effect carried 45 lb of posho just for himself, making him the bearer of only 15 lb of gear or goods. Therefore, the sooner an area could be reached where cloth and beads and wire could be traded for grain, the better.

Night came suddenly, and the whites rarely lingered. Physical fatigue marked every day now, however exhilarating Africa. A good tent was pure gold. The tent was home, all of Europe that there was; having a good one made the difference between sleep and misery. Most Europeans preferred the heavy canvas ones with 'a bathroom attached to the fly on the Indian principle'; several men were needed to carry one. Thomson made the mistake of taking small tents that had no room for chair and table, one so small he had to enter on hands and knees, and so thin it leaked.

Around their own fires, the Africans joked, told stories, shared confidences, entertained themselves with 'obscene or topical improvised songs in a monotonous scale to the accompaniment of beaten tins, sticks, and boards'. Grant thought the sounds 'jolly' and said that sometimes the Europeans could not hear each other talk for the noise. Then the velvety night closed in and everything was silent, except for the snores, moans, and flatulence of 200 men.

Next day, they moved on. The land lifted as they walked inland, becoming drier and finally cooler. Along the well-trodden routes the people anticipated the comings of the safaris, and there was trading at many stops. Local bigwigs got presents and sometimes demanded *hongo*. The porters and askaris traded for eggs and milk and vegetables, although presents were sometimes made to the Europeans of sheep, milk, or oxen (for which presents in return were in order).

This was the order of their days, then: a 'cheery salutation . . . at four [a.m.] . . . leaving the camp about 4:45', eat little, walk. Rest in the middle of the day, walk again and make camp by 3 p.m. or thereabouts; hunt, write, or talk until darkness, which fell very early. Sleep and rise again and set off with 'the cry of "Haya safari!"'. Walk. Hunt. Sleep. Walk. Sleep. Walk, arriving at the next camp 'more weary and worn than I had ever been in my life'.

They camped where there was water. Water was the great essential. Nobody could carry enough water to go very far, so every waterhole and puddle took on the value of a diamond claim. Europeans were disappointed, sometimes disgusted, at the condition of the camping-places, which were often filthy with litter and improvised latrines. Several hundred people made much waste, and the same places were used over and over because of the water.

The water itself lay in anything from hollow rocks to muddy depressions pocked with animal tracks. The water came in many colours and densities. 'What we assuaged our thirst with was yellow, like weak tea, with a strong flavour of vegetables', but that was an emergency draught from the stomach of a zebra. Where one end of the waterhole seemed clearer, the Europeans posted an armed guard, so that the porters would draw water and wash at the other end. Bilharzia, the African schistosomiasis that can enter even through the skin, had not yet been identified. Many Europeans walked, then tottered, then had themselves carried, suffering from vaguely diagnosed dysentery, diarrhoea, 'indigestion', the all-purpose 'fever'. Little wonder. It was not until well into the twentieth century that most travellers insisted on boiling all water.

Yet, most of the early travellers (with the exception of those who had the ill fortune to go with Stanley) survived, and despite bad water and litter and travellers' malaise, the camps became sources of pleasure. '[A] picturesque and pleasing sight to view the men . . . encamped in the wilderness round their many fires, with the various groups feasting, singing, and narrating adventures'. As they pushed far inland, base camps were set up and longer halts were made. Now, loads shuttled back and forth between camps, trophies moving toward the coast, food and trade goods moving inland. At their base camp at Taveta, Teleki and von Hohnel 'overhauled . . . every bale', and the 1000 needles they had brought were put to work stringing the hundredweights of beads.

Far from the Sultan, the safari leader was like the captain of a ship. He became physician, judge, governor. Leadership – as distinct from management, which was the business of the headman – came to the fore. Men like Thomson and Lugard had it, toughness and will crossed with intelligence and compassion. Livingstone, all compassion, lacked it, although he had the will to drive himself unmercifully. Stanley and Peters had toughness and intelligence and will, but they lacked the other essential and drove men unmercifully and punished vengefully. Neumann, who lived closest of any European to his men, may have been best of all, though in England he was an antisocial loner. Coming back once after a gruelling day's hunt, the rain pelting down, he found no fire and no dry wood gathered, and the maize meal left in the wet. Calmly, he sent some men off for wood while he split the dry heart out of a log and then built a fire that was 'the comfort of the whole camp'. Then he divided the meat he had brought, cleaned his guns, and only then had 'my hot sponge-down, so that it was eleven o'clock before I got any dinner'.

Neumann rarely punished. Unlike many Europeans, he did not resort to flogging, 'except in the most extreme cases, such as looting ... or grossly insulting one's headman, proved by ample evidence.' Others were not so restrained. Peters had two deserters followed and shot and their 'corpses ... thrown into the river', another 'laid in chains and flogged before all the people. I now announced ... a scale of punishments ... This ... produced a decided impression.'

Stanley was a great user of the whip, in a more general sense a great user of force. 'The only possible way of inducing [my men] to move was by an overpowering force, and exercise of my power and will'. When his demands caused a near-mutiny, he armed himself with a buckshot-loaded double gun and held it to a mutinous head. 'If I did not succeed in cowing this ruffian, authority was at an end.' His terrible pace and his ruthlessness were rooted in an idea: 'A white man never breaks his word, and my reputation as a white man would have been ruined had I stayed behind or postponed the march'.

In contemporary illustrations, Stanley was often shown in some confrontational pose, weapon in hand. His costume was paramilitary; his placement within the frame was focal, heroic, and he was usually shown hectoring mutinous porters or dominating a black 'king' or shooting at hostile black men. The visual image of the engravings was of a violent but heroic Stanley in a dangerous and 'savage' Africa that must be dominated by force. That image would persist, although its visual expressions – engravings and woodcuts – were created not by Stanley but by illustrators who had never seen him or Africa.

Stanley 'lived by the will'; ego – expressed as pursuit of a self-defined goal – dominated his African existence. He was a driver of men, himself as well as others; his constitution stood the strain, but others' did not. Eighteen men died on the mission to 'find' Livingstone, along with 29 pack animals that were driven too hard by the men Stanley drove. Yet the mission itself was 'completely devoid of all serious motive'; it was 'primarily for "news"' and it made news, made Stanley a 'star' of nineteenth-century print media, star of those illustrations that were reproduced again and again with the image-making power of today's television.

Stanley brought one other attribute to safari leadership: unlimited means. Others had been 'hampered at every turn by lack of adequate funds. Stanley had *carte blanche*'. Each of his safaris was big, dwarfing Livingstone's last little expedition, which Livingstone thought lavish. Stanley did not stint. To meet the doctor, he trotted out a new suit and new helmet, and he entertained Livingstone on a Persian carpet and a bearskin, and showed off 'my knives and forks, and plates, and cups, saucers, silver spoons, and silver tea-pot ... shining and bright', and 'my great bath-tub', all of which had come 1000 miles on men's heads.

Such lavish scale created a new problem. More gear demanded more porters; more porters demanded more food. The need for locally supplied food caused more and more trouble as the European safaris multiplied. The earlier increase in Arab traffic had inspired an agricultural production system among some peoples, and 'Masai agricultural groups . . . in the nineteenth century special-ised in supplying long-distance caravans'. The Kikuyu 'produced food far in excess of their daily needs in order to . . . trade with their neighbours, as well as the European and Swahili caravans', but that trade depended on limited numbers of caravans and on mutual goodwill. When excessive demand or seasonal and annual variations in supply caused shortage, caravans 'took to raiding the countryside . . . This led to a period of unprecedented violence in the [Kikuyu Kenyan] highlands . . . [and] to counter raids from the local populace. Such violence continued into the 1890s and the IBEA (Imperial British East Africa Company] caravans were forced to prey on the countryside.'

Already by the 1870s, caravans were having difficulty in East Africa; 10 years later, 'fighting between the Kikuyu and the foreigners had become common'. Peters thus felt justified in 'falling back upon the right of self-preservation and the right of arms' and took what he needed. Teleki and von Hohnel more or less fought their way across the Kikuyu highlands for the same reason; von Hohnel further justified force as 'the only means of producing the necessary impression' and stated baldly that he 'would far rather follow in the footsteps of a European who has known how to make himself feared than in those of some roving philanthropist'. (E. N. Buxton would later find him 'rather unpleasant as he was not very scrupulous with natives'.)

Thus, the localized African system of growing excess crops for trade was destroyed, and hostility towards Europeans was enhanced. European self-interest sometimes took a still more violent form – outright theft of food, raiding, 'punitive expeditions' like Stanley's at the Bumbrie Islands, where he left 47 dead and twice that many wounded, leading even Burton to say that 'Stanley . . . shoots negroes as if they were monkeys'. Yet, European might made European right in the European mind.

A few whites became disgusted. Rainsford would write in 1910 of 'men [who] fell under [Africa's] evil spell of prevalent lawlessness . . . If the truth were known about the many expeditions undertaken for sport or even for exploration . . . it would make gruesome reading.' Delamere 'believed strongly that no compulsion should be used to make the native part with his surplus grain', and his 1896 expedition used 200 camels, many of them loaded with food so he would not have to trade.

For most travellers before the late 1880s, however, violence was not thought necessary. The safari went its way, fell into its routine, achieved its end. Rich in experience, these men at last turned for home. The days went on as before – rise, walk, hunt, sleep – but the safari was homeward bound, eventually retracing part of the outward path, and the whites came back to the coast and headed for Europe after the greatest adventure of their lives. Some were broken in health; a number died young because of Africa. But most wanted to go back. And some did – Speke once, Thomson once, Stanley twice, Delamere for good.

The safari's end, where it was not desperate, was as colourful as the beginning. Speke and Grant, to be sure, walked north to Sudan rather than back to the coast, and they met Samuel Baker with hardly more than the rags on their backs, their men in bark-cloth tatters, sick with tapeworm, malaria, and 'fever'. But they were 'home' (in Gondokoro, deep in Sudan) and delighted with the long-missed 'tea, sugar, coffee, bread, wine &c'. More prosperous returns were made to Bagamayo or Mombasa, and when Neumann came back with his tons of ivory carried by a long line of porters, people lined the streets to see the 'picturesque sight [of] men jumping up and dancing about with their hundred-weight tusks'. The headman would stop in the street and refuse to move until a fee was paid (a kind of *hongo* in reverse) and then he would move on to another spot and stop again, building a final fund of *baksheesh*.

And then the men dispersed, the relationships of a year or more dissipated. Europeans said that the men spent their earnings overnight, but they meant that they saw a few of them next day gaudily dressed, in the arms of a woman, perhaps. And why should it not have gone quickly – a few pounds, a year away from pleasure, two households to maintain? And these were mostly young men.

The whites kept their trophies and their mementoes and their guns, but the gear was given away or sold up, and it became possible to buy used equipment cheaply toward the end of the century. The coastal stores always had room for a new line.

And then they took ship for home, to write the book, to tell the stories, to remember.

But not all safaris ended so. When Delamere came down from Somalia in 1898 after two years' marching via Marsabit, Lake Turkana, and Eldama Ravine, he arrived, long-haired and threadbare, at a place called Machako's in what is now southeastern Kenya. There, in the 'dry, scrub-covered plains', he met the future: a gang of Indian labourers building a railway. The railhead had advanced as far as Tsavo, where, shortly, several man-eating lions were to stage a famous disaster and make themselves and an engineer named Patterson famous. Then the railway would push on into the future, giving the safari the two things it needed to complete its transformation into the greatest rich man's recreation in the world: a quick way in from the coast, and a centre where other people would relieve whites of all the trouble of hiring porters, of dealing with Indians and Arabs and blacks, of learning Swahili, and of waiting and waiting and waiting.

The year 1900 was the end and the beginning. Stanley would die in 1904; Neumann would kill himself in 1906, and Stigand would say that his time had passed even before then. Stigand may have been thinking of any number of changes – the coming of game laws, the coming of government, the coming of settlers – but he could have taken for his benchmark the driving of the final spike in the railway that joined Mombasa to Lake Victoria.

East Africa had become safariland.

SAFARILAND
Landscapes and people

THE landscape of the safari after 1900 was limited by geography and by the accidents of colonialism to the once and former 'British East' – modern Kenya, Tanzania, and Uganda, with some extensions into Rwanda, Burundi, and Sudan. This highly varied country lies below the Horn of Africa, which pokes into the Indian Ocean like a rhino's nose; East Africa is a little like the rhino's throat.

For part of the safari period, Tanganyika (Tanzania minus Zanzibar) was a German colony, a fact that made a great difference in a land that until then had never heard of red tape. After the First World War, Tanganyika became a British protectorate and the border effectively disappeared. None the less, the German presence created a different colonial culture, one that did not greatly affect the safari because the safari's centre was in Kenya. The great proportion of safari-goers after 1900 were British or American, and the values and the culture of the safari became distinctly Anglo–Indian, not German.

European politics also defined the boundaries of what one travel book has called 'safariland'. South of Tanganyika lay Portuguese Mozambique, an unsympathetic place for reasons of both politics and culture: the Portuguese spoke a language even odder than French – to the English, at least – and their presence in Africa was very different from Great Britain's, as subsequent events have shown. To the west lay what was then the Belgian Congo, now Zaïre, running from the western border of northern Uganda all the way to the central western limit of Tanganyika. Again, the difference of language marked an important African dividing line. To the north lay Sudan – British in influence, but distant and difficult of access, and often dangerous and even fatal; Ethiopia, a sovereign nation with its own languages and cultures; and Somalia, which the European powers chopped up so that the British portion bordered Kenya. It was not of great safari potential, however, because of its rather forbidding climate.

The geographic world of the safari, then, was an area of close on a million square miles bounded on the east by the Indian Ocean and on the west by the Congo watershed. Within that vast area, the actual venues of the safari were defined by the comfort needs of two kinds of animal: Northern European human, and all the others the human animal wanted to shoot, photograph, or look at. Different wild animals existed in different habitats, to be sure, but, whether the object was hunting, photography or observation, certain kinds of habitat were always preferred because in those the desirable animals were to be found and the human animal was comfortable: not too wet, nor too hot, nor too arid.

Quite simply, the recreational safari was not a venture into the steamy botanical nightmare that books and films, calling up unconscious memories of Stanley, make it seem. East Africa was not central Africa; despite straddling the equator, it was not hot except along its coastal lowlands, which were for that reason mostly avoided. The principal areas visited lay inland and were as much as a mile and a quarter high, and therefore cool.

To be sure, habitats varied. The gorilla country above Lake Kivu – actually on the fringe of the Belgian Congo – was high, cold, and rainy; the deserts of eastern and northern Kenya and northern Tanganyika were dry in season and very rocky. Elephants were often to be found in rain forest in Uganda and western Kenya, in swamp in eastern Kenya around the Tana River; the rare sitatunga in swampland; lions in the rolling savannahs of Tanganyika and southwestern Kenya. In general, however, the climate of the safari was a temperate one, chosen to match the tolerances of the traveller within the limits of the available game. The only inescapable factor was the sun, which beat down on all but rain forest with a fierceness that inspired superstition.

Below this variety of habitat lay a tormented geology. The area as a whole is roughly crescent-shaped, although it is a very fat crescent, really more like most of a pie with an enormous bite taken out where the Indian Ocean curves into the Kenyan–Tanzanian coast. This curve is the current result of the breakup of the primordial mega-continent Gondwana, product of geological activity whose other effects still characterize the region. The Gondwana breakup some 180 million years ago was accompanied by cataclysmic volcanic activity, whose continuation at places across the continent has left characteristic cones, lava rock cover, and what is called rift faulting – all to be found in East Africa. Although much of the region shows an undramatic sedimentary rock cover, tectonic and volcanic activity have created some of its most spectacular landscape, of which the outstanding feature is the Rift Valley.

A rift is a split or cleavage that in East Africa has become monumental. The Great Rift Valley, a broad depression between two uplifted, partly parallel fault lines, is a colossal Y whose base rests in Tanzania and whose slightly canted arms form the Red Sea and the Gulf of Aden. The Rift runs north-northeasterly the length of Kenya and is as much as 60 miles across; it is fairly flat-floored, between, in some regions, towering escarpments whose ascent or descent provides some of the most exciting and dangerous driving in the world.

Like the Rift, lava rock and volcanic cones are evidence of upheaval, of which the most famous is Kilimanjaro on the Kenya–Tanzania border. Towering above 19,000 feet, the snow-capped mountain is the inescapable backdrop for the European idea of East Africa, and the emotionally logical place to begin or end a safari. Often cloud-hidden during the day, it becomes visible at evening and early morning, a broad-based cone less perfect than Fuji but breathtaking for its size and its solitude, dominating the landscape up to 50 miles away.

Three hundred miles north, the twin peaks of Mount Kenya are hardly less significant – the peak of Mbatian, named after a Masai spiritual leader, tops 17,000 feet – although they are visually less impressive because the surrounding country is much higher and they do not dominate their surroundings as Kilimanjaro does. Two other dormant volcanoes are major game areas: Ngorongoro far to the south in Tanzania, and Marsabit to the north in Kenya. The first offers a broad crater floor crowded with game, the second a mountain peak with its own rain forest and ecology, and a noted elephant and kudu herd. Elsewhere, from western Uganda to northern Kenya, ancient craters have filled and provide lakes of stunning beauty.

Two other major land forms dominate safariland: plains and steep-sided mountains. The plains are the home of the grassy savannahs, scene of animal migrations; they are bounded by distant hills or escarpments that seem to contain them as a river's banks contain water. The mountains, especially in Uganda and Rwanda–Burundi, are young and therefore steep, rising into cloud that makes them cool and wet in contrast to the dryness of the plains and the Rift floor.

The visual impact of this varied topography is astounding. The air is usually clear in the dry seasons; hills or mountains 50 miles away are a blue like faded denim behind the close-in vistas of the grasslands. From the volcanic cones, even such tiny ones as Lookout Hill in the shadow of Kilimanjaro, mile after mile of the land is rolled out for the eye like carpet. The escarpments provide sudden, breathtaking views seemingly straight down: that from Marsabit into the Dida Gilgalu desert gives the same sense of diminished size and vertigo as looking down from Anacapri's cliffs into the blue-green of the Mediterranean. From the northern desert floor, inselbergs of rounded, almost naked, rock rise from the flatness as if they floated on it, each inviting exploration, each seeming a world to itself, a thousand or so feet high, a few miles long.

This complex landscape is marked and divided by water: lakes in and near the Great Rift Valley, several important rivers and their intermittent swamps elsewhere. Two freshwater seas – Lakes Victoria and Turkana – now show on maps of any scale, Victoria at 27,000 square miles as a filled-in letter Q, Turkana at 2500 as a lower-case l. In addition, enormous lakes mark the entire western limit of safariland, and they were in fact the sign, on a geological scale, of an embracing land-form change: Lakes Nyasa, Tanganyika, Kivu, Ritunzige, Mobutu Sese Seku. Smaller lakes mark the course of the Great Rift Valley: Eyasi, Natron, and Manyara in Tanganyika; Naivasha, Nakuru,

Baringo, and three smaller ones in Kenya. Most important to safari travel was Victoria, so huge that it channelled travel around it or turned the traveller back.

Of rivers, the Nile was important for beginning its own journey here, flowing north through Uganda to Sudan and into Egypt, creating in Sudan the Sudd, the often impassable mass of vegetation that held Samuel Baker for months. In Kenya and Tanzania a major river system dominates each country. The Tana flows from the northern slope of Mount Kenya in a huge curve east, then south, to split the Kenyan coast so effectively that until very recently land travel along the coast from north and south ended at its banks. In Tanzania, the Great Ruaha Rufiji flows two-thirds of the way across the country from east to west, its sources along the divide that separates the Indian Ocean from the Lake Tanganyika drainages. Other rivers of less importance vein the region, most cutting it along east-west lines.

In the dry areas, intermittent rivers appear only in the rains, when they may create temporary and impassable lakes; in places they form year-round swamps, like Kenya's Lorian. Still smaller watercourses erode the sides of mountains and escarpments and cut tree-lined *dongas* through the grasslands; waterless in the dry months, they remain a tedious obstacle to travel with their steep banks and sometimes soft bottoms. In the rainy months – the 'long rains' of Europe's spring months and the 'short rains' of autumn – they carry impassable torrents.

There was, of course, a causal link between these kinds of landscapes and the habitats they supported – a connection that became vital to the safari. In part, habitat was important because it determined what animals were to be found; in part, it was important because of the kind of travel it would allow; and in part it was important because of diseases.

Tropical rain forest hardly existed within safariland, but a more temperate rain forest did, mostly on the mountains, as in the gorilla country of Rwanda; it typified parts of Uganda, as well, and the upper Uganda–Kenya border. Rain forest was a habitat for big elephant, and so it became a venue for one kind of safari.

Riverine swamps offered habitat to a different variety of game animals, from buffalo to sitatunga, but swamps were unattractive because they were hard travelling, and they gained a reputation for disease. Coastal mangrove swamp was even worse, and it had discouraged European penetration of the interior. The railway solved that problem, although the first miles of track were among the most difficult because of the very swamps they were meant to jump.

The elevated areas of hills, plateaux, and low mountains had game, but much of the high country was precisely the land sought by settlers, particularly as coffee and tea became important crops. Thus, the interior highlands of Kenya – the officially designated 'White Highlands' – were quite early taken over for agriculture and grazing; they became correspondingly unattractive to safaris as farming increased. The mountains of northern Kenya and southern Tanganyika, steep-sided, wooded, deeply cut by ravines, were not usually attractive for farming, but they proved hard travelling.

What was left to make up the principal habitat of safariland, then, were the plains. Here, in a dry but not arid climate (varying from sub-humid to semi-arid, as meteorologists rank such things), with a mean annual temperature in the 80s (Fahrenheit) as compared to New York's 60 and London's 50 – but with the temperature lowered for most of the area by altitude – with bountiful sunshine, an almost perfect habitat for outdoor human activity had been created. In northern Tanganyika and southern Kenya, the plains were savannahs, rolling grasslands with occasional trees and thornbush, and denser vegetation along rivers and watercourses. Except for animal holes, travel by foot or horse was feasible; even before 1910, the Athi Plains were travelled in light buggies and buckboards.

The grassland watercourses presented surmountable obstacles in the dry seasons; in the rains, safari travel was unattractive, anyway – not least because the 'black cotton' soil turned to a grease-like mire, sucking at boots and hooves and wheels, and even trapping elephants if enough water fell.

Some of the plains were drier, verging on deserts; to a degree, the farther north you went in safariland, the drier it got. A coarse, reddish, sometimes lavender, sand often lay underfoot; rocks from egg- to head-size were everywhere. Inselbergs rose abruptly; volcanic cones dotted the northern semidesert. The grass here, unlike that in the savannahs, was sparse. Candelabra succulents grew huge. Acacias offered lacy, much-needed shade. Termite mounds rose like petrified morels six feet above the ground. The air was cooler, especially at night.

Such landscapes seemed, and indeed could be, hostile; as travellers pushed north into the deserts around Lake Turkana and north and west of Marsabit, survival could be threatened. For the indigenous people who lived here, the camel and the goat were the preferred domestic animals, not the horse and the cow. The elephant-hunter Arthur Neumann came here, probably anticipating Teleki at Lake Turkana; Donaldson Smith and Delamere pushed through the same country in the 1890s, but they had set out from Somalia to explore the contested northern boundary between Britain's new colony and the bumptious Ethiopia.

Two diseases of these varied habitats affected safari travel: malaria and sleeping sickness. By the 1890s, these illnesses had been observed; notions existed, but disease vectors were not well understood. Malaria was certainly the more familiar, having found its way into popular literature as a sign of service in the tropics – 'fever and chills', 'my old malaria again'. That a connection existed between malaria and certain sorts of terrain was without doubt; the Roman campagna, for example, and even the Colosseum after dark, were associated with malaria before mosquitoes were identified as the vector. That connection was finally made in the late 1890s by an Italian physician. It was enough for Europeans in Africa to suspect a connection with certain kinds of habitat, however – swamp, 'miasma', lowland – to steer at least some away from the lakes and swamps. Until modern prophylaxis, however, the disease seems to have been treated more casually than it deserved, many Europeans tolerating it until it turned to 'blackwater fever', a condition so severe that the urine turned dark.

Sleeping sickness was a major illness of the southern shore of Lake Victoria and adjacent areas of Tanzania and Kenya, and to some degree it still is. Like the dengue fever of West Africa, its localization was easily identifiable. Connection with the bite of the tsetse fly came later, but popular wisdom recognized that certain areas were dangerous because of the disease – and avoided them. Actually, the lethal effect of tsetse on cattle and horses was more important to most Europeans but had the same effect of keeping them out of 'fly country'.

Geography, then, with its product, habitat, and habitat's effects – animal life and disease – reduced the square mileage of safariland. Nineteenth-century explorers might go anywhere, travelling with different goals and taking risks as they came, but people bent on recreation had a much narrower idea of acceptable risk.

Safari travel was restricted by one other factor: local inhabitants. The indigenous peoples varied greatly in their attitudes toward interlopers, but, after 1900, Europeans were dominant and were able to move fairly confidently, although small wars recurred and the far north was never considered safe. In 1906, for example, a District Commissioner's wife wrote that they were 'making war' on the Embu, a typical localized punitive raid; as late as the 1950s, the Mau Mau 'uprising' showed how extremely fragile the white notion of security was. Looking at the whole experience of European travel in East Africa, however, you have to conclude that safariland was turned into a white pleasure ground with remarkably little trouble. This is not to say either that the indigenous peoples welcomed the Europeans or that they refused utterly to resist them, but there were none of the pitched battles that marked South Africa or Sudan.

Human occupation in East Africa goes back as far as humanity can be traced anywhere on the globe. The Leakey family's discoveries in Tanzania and northern Kenya gave evidence of *Australopithecus* occupation and tool use more than 1½ million years ago; their and others' research shows *Homo erectus* here, as well as elsewhere in Africa, within a million years. In the last Stone Age, climatic conditions quite different from those we now know (a considerably higher water level, for example, with Kenya's Lake Turkana – now a salty sea isolated in a desert – flowing fresh to the Nile) created prime living conditions in what are now inhospitable areas. The residents were hunter-gatherers, not farmers, and so they remained long after farming had been developed in West Africa and Egypt. By the time the Egyptian civilizations were rising along the northern Nile, some of the people of East Africa had begun to domesticate cattle. It appears that they were supplanted by, or merged into, the Iron Age people who moved into the region from the west and the north – so-called Bantu and Nilotic people who were the ancestors of modern tribes and who spoke the languages that were the roots of the modern East African languages (including Swahili).

When Europeans first looked with interest at East Africa, they found a variety of indigenous people with widely differing cultures. What they did not see was the integrity of those cultures or their interconnectedness. 'Everything was localized', as one historian has said, and the lack of central authority, except in Uganda, led most Europeans to insist – mistakenly – that East Africans had no culture at all.

Uganda – coveted by Britain for its supposedly strategic location – was a comparatively rich area with a highly developed agrarian economy. It was judged 'more civilized' than neighbouring cultures, but was also thought more bloodthirsty and unpredictable, the more so when Christianity and Islam became rivals there.

To possess Uganda, however, Britain had to approach through either Sudan or Kenya, and the Sudanese route was closed for crucial decades by armed resistance. A way in from the Kenyan coast was thus created – the Uganda Railway.

The best-known peoples in 1900 Kenya – in fact in East Africa – were the Masai. When Joseph Thomson published *Through Masai Land* in 1885, he engraved the name of a single East African group on the popular European consciousness. Rider Haggard made them the villains of part of *Allan Quatermain*. No one ever wrote a *Through Kikuyu Land*, and so the Masai emerged as the archetypal East Africans, although the Kikuyu have been more important to the region's modern history. The Masai presence dominated British colonial thinking well into the twentieth century. Whether their warlike reputation was deserved or not (Arabs and Swahili may have exaggerated their importance to keep rivals away), they became established in the British mind as the ideal of East African tribalism – courageous, xenophobic, warlike, colourful, 'natural'. They were first the bogeymen of safaris, then the object of them. Nowadays, knowing their reputation, they sell their images to travellers by posing for *piksha* – Swahili for photos.

The Masai appear to have entered East Africa from the north in the eighteenth century. By Thomson's time, they lived in small, semi-permanent groups of tiny houses surrounded by thorn fence. They were pre-eminently cattle herders, and they lived by and for their cows, following the grass for the sake of their cows, taking their cows into their villages at night, literally sleeping with their cows. They claimed huge areas of land as occasional pasturage for these herds, for, although their population density at any one time was small, they needed far more pasture than their human numbers suggested. At one time, they occupied or claimed much of northern Tanganyika west of Mt Kilimanjaro, southwestern and western Kenya to the west wall of the Rift, and northern Kenya above the Aberdares and Mt Kenya. They may have had even broader lands earlier.

In the north, as well, the Samburu, a people related to the Masai by language and tradition, occupied and claimed country from the Tana north toward Marsabit. Other peoples (the Nandi of western Kenya, for example) have aspects of Masai culture that suggest an earlier connection.

The Masai, then, represented a psychological limit on the early expansion of safariland. Had they defended the territory they claimed, safaris would have been limited to a small region. In 1904, however, the Kenya Masai *laibon* (religious leader) Olenana agreed to put his people into two reserves; these two were reduced to one in 1911 – roughly that area between the Mara River and Oloitokitok on the Tanganyika border – into which the Kenyan Masai for the most part peaceably withdrew. Olenana had predicted the coming of the British and the railway. (So did a number of other African leaders. Considering the intricate webs of trade and communications with the coast, these predictions were probably more like news reports.) Perhaps he understood British power; certainly, he spared the Kenyan Masai a war they must have lost, and, for better or worse, preserved them to this day in somewhat the culture that Olenana knew.

The Kikuyu were old rivals of the Masai. Agriculturalists, they occupied much of the very highlands wanted by European farmers. Von Hohnel correctly predicted they were 'destined to play an important part in the future of East Africa'. Patterson had been told they were 'cowardly and treacherous', but he found them 'well-behaved and intelligent'. The American Stewart Edward White called them 'the unambitious, weak and despised Kikuyus', one of the grosser misjudgements ever made of them.

It was their fate to accept Christianity and schooling, and to be ejected from much of the highlands, which thereafter became white until *uhuru* – independence – in 1963. The Kikuyu provided much of the labouring and servant class of colonial Kenya – and much of the Mau Mau. For the safari, they were often the higher-level workers – translators, cooks, headmen. Now a dominant Kenyan group, they again occupy the centre of the country as farmers and much of the centre of the society as technicians, teachers, and officials. They have gone on a quite different, perhaps opposite, tack from the Masai: their old culture is mostly gone, and they are modern Kenya.

Also, a group of often hostile northern peoples were scattered in the Kenyan deserts. The Somalis were prized as household servants by the British; they were also enviable riders and fighters, and Europeans came to respect them and romanticize them – not least for their physical beauty. Another group used by hunting safaris was the Okiek, usually then called Ndorobo or Wanderobo. These secretive hunter-gatherers were probably remnants of pre-Bantu days, self-sufficient and usually invisible, although they had a special trading relationship with the Masai. Safaris hired them as local guides and trackers.

The British government – represented first by the Foreign Office and then by the Colonial Office – saw the indigenous people as troublesome wards and was highly paternalistic to them, alternately protecting and punishing them. British settlers saw them as an annoyance, or worse, but desperately needed them as cheap labour. Neither government nor settlers saw the people as themselves. It seems not to have occurred to them (and the perception would have been an obstacle if it had) that these scattered and seemingly disorganized people had both culture and intercultural connections.

An extensive infrastructure and a technology adequate to the environment existed: when Petherick came to Sudan in 1854, he found the Djour smelting iron and making 'lances, hoes, hatchets, &c', as the Turkana, Masai, and others were also doing. An extensive trade had grown up: Petherick found Venetian beads from West Africa at Bor in Sudan; Neumann found in the 1890s 'crowds of Embe women' harvesting soda from a lake for trade to the Kamba 200 miles south. In fact, it was the Kamba who had, from their homeland northeast of Kilimanjaro, dominated East African trade since the eighteenth century, creating a caravan tradition quite distinct from that of the Arabs but with a continuity that was also useful to the British, 'from men like Kivui, Kithusi and Mbuu to individuals like Nthiwa wa Tama, one of the earliest appointed headmen under colonial authority'.

After the first third of the nineteenth century, some of this extensive Kamba trade was grabbed by Swahili caravans that started north of Mombasa. (Paradoxically, Swahili wealth was increased by the European pressure to end slavery: blockading of slave ships made cheap slaves available along the Kenya coast, allowing cheaper agriculture and excess for trading.) Like the Arabs to the south, the Swahili 'established a number of camping places . . . Caravans of 1,200–1,500 were not uncommon'. They went as far north as the Ewaso Nyiro river, making a major stopping-place at Ngong (near what would be Karen Blixen's African farm.) These routes were still in use in 1899, J. H. Patterson finding such a 'caravan road . . . for smuggling slaves and ivory', although 'trading' would have been a better word than smuggling. And such trade was considerable, Mombasa's exports (mostly grain and ivory) averaging better than £500,000 annually, those of the rest of the coast £1.3 million. Somali export from Kismayu, much of it ivory and rhino horn traded in from northern Kenya, totalled £15,000 in 30 months in the early 1890s. Although such figures showed vigorous indigenous trade, the end result of that trade – because Europe and India were at the other ends of the export line – was 'an unequal exchange . . . subordinating the East African economy . . . and preventing its development'. In fact, that development would be pushed aggressively by Anglo-Indians and Europeans as soon as the trade's products were shown to be profitable in India and Europe.

By and large, then, despite their interconnected cultures, indigenous people could not (and often did not try to) stand in the way of British expansion. Indigenous trade was co-opted as the travel routes had been. Few barriers to safari travel (which can be looked at as a kind of trade) were put up, therefore, after the beginning of the twentieth century (although conflicts like Tanganyika's Maji Maji rebellion of 1907, the Nandi wars of 1904–6, and various Masai unrest through the 1920s caused temporary interruptions). Until the end of the nineteenth century and even after, some indigenous people – especially the Masai – made safari travel more exciting than it has been since; thereafter, they mostly affected the safari by providing an exotic colour that became one of the safari industry's prime assets. They were, after all, one of the proofs that the traveller was in Africa. Their artefacts – shields, spears, knives – became desirable souvenirs.

'At one and the same moment there could be seen rhinoceros, giraffe, zebra, eland, wildebeeste, Grant's antelope, hartebeeste, pallah, ostriches, and hyenas, while buffaloes were also in great numbers hidden in the dense bush', Thomson wrote in 1885. He 'followed a herd of nearly sixty giraffes'. 'Game is to be seen in marvellous abundance. The giraffe ... appears against the horizon like some unearthly monster.... The wildebeeste, imp-like and fierce in appearance, frisks with uncouth movements, or speeds with stiff, ungainly gallops.... Zebras in long lines pace leisurely along.... Hyenas slink home.... Lions satisfied with the night's venture express their sense of repletion with reverberating roars.'

Again and again, newcomers used two images to describe the spectacle: Eden, and the zoo. They called it 'the paradise of Big Game'. They tried to count and lost count. They made estimates – five, ten, twenty millions.

It was the earth before the coming of man.

It was the world of the Pleistocene.

No one had seen such herds of game since the very early days in South Africa, those herds now vanished. No European had anything with which to compare them at home. And the clear African air and the blazing light allowed the newcomers to see hundreds of thousands of them, miles of them, generations of them. It was wonderful and unbelievable – and, as they all knew, it was the last experience of its kind on earth. Viewing it from the unfinished railway, however, was inadequate. A destination was needed – a centre, a town, an organizing hub.

In late 1899, the railhead of the infant Uganda Railway pushed beyond the old caravan stop at Ngong and came to a resting place a mile above sea level. It was not an inspiring spot. 'A black, swampy stretch of soppy landscape, wind-swept, devoid of human habitation of any sort.... The only evidence of the occasional presence of human kind was the old caravan track skirting the bog-like plain.' The insect-ridden swamp was fed by a little river that had a name that meant, in Masai, cold water. The railway engineers, deciding to put their repair yard there, called it by the Masai name: Nairobi.

Nobody foresaw the place's future in 1900. It was only 'a dreary windswept plain' still, its few citizens living mostly in tents, 'a brand-new town of corrugated iron and green canvas'. But it lay in a unique position, which other factors had dictated were perfect to give it its new importance. Without the railway, it would have been only a swamp; because of it, it was the ideal centre of a web of routes to the most wonderful game lands in the world.

To the south and southeast were the Athi and the Kapiti Plains, abounding in every sort of animal. Beyond them and to the east were the rich country around Machakos and the Athi River. Beyond the Athi was a vast area of dense thorn scrub and hard travelling, thick with rhino, in what is now Tsavo East National Park. Still farther south and then west was Kilimanjaro and its southern slopes and the beautiful region near Arusha.

To the west lay a route into the Great Rift Valley and its grasslands, and, when such a thing became possible, southwest into the Sotik and the Masai country of the Mara. Another route would go east of Kilimanjaro into Tanganyika, pushing eventually into what is now the Serengeti. Determined travellers going west across the Kenya Rift with plenty of time could continue into Uganda and even down the Nile, which had a steamboat service after the British Army's victory at Omdurman in 1898.

North lay the highlands and the Kikuyu Reserve, the wooded slopes of Mount Kenya and the Aberdares range, and beyond that the Ewaso Nyiro, boundary of the northern desert and its mountains – mostly *terra incognita* until after the First World War. But the Ewaso Nyiro ran east into the elephant-rich Lorian Swamp; south of that lay the Tana River country and more elephant. South again and west, past the unique mountain Ol Doinyo Sabuk, and you came full circle, back to the place called Cold Water.

Safariland had a capital.

BIG MEN, IRRESISTIBLE MAGIC
The golden age, 1900–1920

THE reasons for going on safari were many. One man wanted 'to get back into a state of life more simple and more natural'. Another had wanted to see Mt Kenya ever since reading Rider Haggard as a boy. For another, the lure was 'the splendid ferocity of the African sunrise'; a woman sought Africa's 'blaze of amazing light'. Vivienne de Watteville sought a heightened reality in details 'like having breakfast under the tree with cicadas shrilling through the stillness, and how good porridge tasted out of doors; and never having to go indoors again . . ., and in bed I could put out my hand and feel the earth warm and somehow inexplicably friendly'. Carl Schillings summed it up: 'The thousand dangers and hardships draw us . . . with an irresistible magic'.

And so they came to British East Africa – BEA as it was quickly known – to see and touch and shoot. These 'first-comers . . . literally had both railway and country all to themselves'. Most were not familiar with the word 'safari' at first; it still had to be defined as a 'shooting expedition' in 1906, and Theodore Roosevelt felt he had to explain the word in 1910 ('both the caravan with which one makes an expedition and the expedition itself'). The redoubtable W. S. Rainsford, an accurate reporter but a dreadful speller, called it a 'sefari' in 1908. The word probably came into popular use through officialdom – 'safari reports' were a regular part of a young Assistant District Commissioner's paperwork – so that by 1905 or so, it was colloquial in tiny Nairobi but unknown in London. The American Warren Page gave it a unique turn when he coined 'safarist' in the 1960s – not a usage that caught on.

The first years of the twentieth century were wild and woolly ones in BEA. The first settlers were filtering in, making little Nairobi a frontier village. The American West was conjured up with big hats and prominently worn guns; Boer War veterans rubbed elbows with Lord Delamere, one of the first to arrive. Mombasa was the port of entry, two weeks and £50 out from Europe, 30 days and £100 from New York. The first sportsmen put together their safaris in the wet heat of Mombasa the way that Thomson, Speke, and Stanley had in Zanzibar, but the hunting country was inland and the coastal swamps were awful. Getting up-country by train became too attractive to forgo; the only catch was that the fare up for porters was a pound a man – £100 for a safari of any size – and, wealthy though some of the visitors were, most of them complained of the high cost of everything and were therefore probably money-minded folk. They decided there had to be a way to find porters at Nairobi, even though the experienced Swahilis and Wanyamwezi were all on the coast.

Mombasa had a special flavour. It was in BEA but not of it, ancient and Arab, with burgeoning suggestions of Britain in 'a very nice English club . . . where ladies may go in the evening, after they have taken their exercise at the Sports Club in the form of tennis, badminton or other games'. But it was *hot*. After a quick peek at its rickshaw tramcars and Fort Jesus, many people got to the station for the first end-of-day 'up-mixed' (Nairobi-bound mixed freight and passenger train). Several ran each week, although in the early days the schedule was relaxed, allowing for stops to shoot at game or to wait for elephants on the track.

Doors banged, voices called in three languages – five or six if somebody had paid to take his porters up – and the tough little engine tooted. It was not the Orient Express. 'I had to take my own bedding, and sleep on the seat . . . there are no wagons-lits or restaurant cars'. Some people were not pleased. 'Perfection is said to be impossible of attainment, but anyone wishing to experience how nearly the acme of discomfort can be attained while travelling might try a journey on the Uganda Railway'.

The rolling stock was simple and the sleepers were 'embedded in red clay, which later sends up a fine, penetrating dust' that got into everything and made passengers look like the last road company of *Metamora*. None the less, it was for many 'the most wonderful and interesting railway journey in the world'. Not the steamy early miles across the swamps, or the miles through the darkness, trying to sleep on a bouncing seat with somebody else's feet in your hair; but when the sun rose, the now brick-red passengers turned their swollen eyes to a spectacle that still gives the heart a bound: the animals of the Kapiti plains. There they were in their thousands, a great zoo through which the little trains ran as if on an excursion.

Sam Pike, an early engineer, would stop his train if a passenger saw a particularly good shot, 'wait patiently until the deed was accomplished, the beast skinned and cut up . . . accepting a choice joint of venison' for his trouble. For most passengers, the stop would be part of the novelty. They would stop a couple more times at 'dak' bungalows (Indian words and customs belonged to the railway, which was 'after all an Indian show') to eat surprisingly good food, most thought. When they arrived at Nairobi late that day, bone-rattled and red with dust, they would believe they had had their money's worth.

Nairobi was a greedy, bawling, ill-mannered infant. Its mother's milk was the railway, but its heart was the bazaar and the cluster of Indian merchants there. More than 30,000 Indians had been brought in to build the railway; close to 7,000 of these stayed, but already in place on the coast had been traders and merchants whose predecessors went back to the European Middle

Ages. A man named Kirparam kept pace with the railway, setting up at Simba in 1898 and Nairobi in 1899; Shankar Dassji was in Mombasa, Nairobi, and Kampala in 1900; Karman Jetha was in Nairobi in 1901. The first mosque was built in 1902, 'modest in style and not very large in dimension'. By that same year, 11 Indian traders were 'settled in the [Fort Hall] district' north of Nairobi. By 1907, A. A. Visram was advertising 'solid safari goods' in the *East African Standard*; by 1910, Meghi Amad and Company and Suliman Virgee were sources of camping gear.

The Indian role in British expansion was essential; the British attitude, however, was ambivalent. The Indian traders were a mercantile advance guard for tax-collectors and policemen, their *dukas* (stores) preceding Her Majesty's benefits by several years. Many of the British admitted 'the indispensability of Asian traders and artisans in the opening up and development of the interior', and so essential were Indians to the police that records were kept in Urdu and were unreadable by most British officers. Indian philanthropy helped to mitigate Nairobi's 'dismal swamp', the first park – with statue of Queen Victoria – being built by S. A. M. Jeevanjee, who had made the money (not so philanthropically) providing food for the Indian railway gangs and contracting many of the workers in from India. When push came to shove, however, Indians were neither white nor equal, and they were denied admission to the prime farming land in what became the White Highlands. (They were not alone. Africans were simply *hors concours*; Jews were barely tolerable in groups of one. When it appeared that the government might open Uganda to Zionists, locals referred to it as 'Jewganda', and an English outfit in Mombasa advertised in the *East African Standard* that 'East Africa may be Jewed but you won't be at our stores'.)

For the earliest 'safarists', however, the Indians were the indispensable link between them and the bush. The Indians *spoke English*. They sold gear, stores, food. They may have been able to put whole safaris together, although there is little evidence of that; most English visitors in the early days left such organization to British 'agents' like Scott, McKenzie, and Company of Mombasa, who had come to East Africa in 1877. When, in about 1905, the focus turned fully to Nairobi, the stout of heart tackled the Nairobi bazaar themselves after a bracing stop at one of the hotel bars (there were at least two) for information and advice.

The medium of exchange was the Indian rupee, one rupee equalling about one and a third English shillings. Americans must have been driven mad, converting first into pounds and then into dollars. Costs were highly variable – bargaining was essential – but they were inevitably high because everything was hauled up from Mombasa. Many a would-be safarist must have wished for a helping hand, even one that had first to be crossed with rupees.

Nairobi in those early days was changing so rapidly that somebody who had been away for a year was like a novice. In 1903, there were only about 30 settler families; by 1907 there were 600 'Europeans and Eurasians' and another 7500 Indians and Africans; the 1909 census found 799 Europeans, 76

Eurasians, 591 Goanese [Christian Indians from Portuguese Goa], 3171 Indians, and 9524 Africans. The majority of Europeans were British South Africans, who brought with them ideas of race and class, and words like *kraal* [cattle enclosure], *veldt* [plain], and *kopje* [rock hill] that would become part of the colonial language. The great proportion were men, especially among the Europeans; children were scarce.

'The only shop' in 1902 was 'a small tin hut', the only hotel 'a wood and tin shanty known as Wood's Hotel and sometimes as the Victoria'. An elephant ruined somebody's garden and a rhino broke up a horse-race that year. Everybody commented on the quantity of corrugated iron used in construction, nobody flatteringly. It was a town with 'many undesirable European characters ... from South Africa, and drunken orgies frequently ended up in a fracas'. Knowledgeable travellers arrived with their kits already put together elsewhere: tents from Edgington of London; food from the Army and Navy Stores; varied gear from Shaw and Hunter's catalogue or from the Citadel Stores of Cairo. Everybody arrived wearing a hat or helmet from Simon Artz of Port Said.

By 1904, it was still being called 'Tinville' but had six nominal hotels offering minimal comfort and little privacy. It now looked to some like an Indian hill-station, however, asserting itself with rows of blue gum trees and a circle of barbed wire to keep animals out. (It didn't. It was doubled, to little avail.) By 1908 there was a rifle range south of town, and the station had roses growing at each end of the platform and 'beds of violets round each lamppost', and half an hour in the bar of one of its 'several good hotels' would give 'sufficient advice to carry one through the rest of his life'. W. S. Rainsford thought it was a bad place for Africans but 'beautiful and most interesting'. Like many, he praised the handsome mile-long road that ran from the railway station's roses to the door of what had become the Shepheard's, the Brown's Palace, the Ritz of Nairobi – the Norfolk Hotel.

Opened in 1904, re-opened under new management in 1909, the Norfolk was to become the standard of East African hotels. It still is. It offered comfort (for a price) and, rather quickly, tradition as well. But Babault found it '*ne rappelle en rien, si c'est le prix, nos palaces Européens*', ('but resembles in nothing, unless it is price, our European palaces'). You can't please everybody. Its bar was the place to see local notables like Delamere and fashionable visitors come for their safari.

By the end of its first decade, then, Nairobi was a vigorous little place of considerable character, but it inspired varying reactions: 'new and unattractive', 'a curious mixture of an African dorp and an Indian hill station', 'a very attractive town', 'the town *par excellence* of British East Africa', 'this horrible place'.

Some Europeans were put off because the white enclave was cheek by jowl with 'its large native quarter and its Indian colony'. In fact, although the physical spread of the European colony was large, the numbers were small; the reverse was true for the Africans and Indians. The bazaar was a horror to some Europeans; burning it down was a ready response to disease. The 'native quarter' – more like a cross between a slum and several separate villages – was inescapable and indigestible in its strangeness, its nakedness, its impaction. As late as 1910, hyenas and panicked zebras continued to appear in the little city, although lions and leopards were becoming rare there.

Changes in Nairobi and BEA after 1900 did not alone cause the changes in the safari; rather, they took a parallel course: from individualism and confusion, through entrepreneurship, to establishment of an industry. Or, to put it differently, from the bazaar to the office, from the Indian trader to the British businessman.

Denis Holman asserted that 'almost with the first Indian shops in [Nairobi], there were Indian safari agents', but I have seen no evidence to support this idea, although it is a sensible and attractive one. Rather, a 1900 handbook listed Messrs Boustead, Ridley & Co, of Mombasa, who could 'supply you with porters, head men, trade goods of iron and brass wire, beads of the requisite colour, cloth, etc.' This was an offshoot of Boustead, Ridley's real business and never came to much, largely, perhaps, because they did not move it to Nairobi. (Nor did they do it particularly well, having been unable to find porters for May French Sheldon in 1891.)

In 1902, the Aga Khan started his 'shooting party' at Mombasa. That same year, E. N. Buxton was also putting his 'caravan' together at Mombasa and sending it ahead on foot to Voi, where he joined it by train to head for Taveta and Tanganyika. Buxton, like Boustead and Ridley, was still in the shadow of the nineteenth century – loads of trade goods and, for Buxton, eight askaris with 'old-fashioned rifles'. In the same year Powell-Cotton tried to get official help in Nairobi to put a safari together but gave up and went back to Mombasa to do it there like everybody else.

In 1903, Heubner and Co of Nairobi, Merchant Bankers and Transport Agents, advertised a 'speciality' of 'Fitting Out of Shooting Parties'. They would have been a treat to watch, running a bank with one hand, organizing safaris with the other, but they seem not to have stuck with it, unless they were the 'agents' whose 'energy' got an otherwise baffled Briton's expedition under way 'in three or four days' in 1904.

It was at about this time that the letters column of the *Field*, Britain's leading field-sports weekly, became the place for sportsmen to exchange information about BEA. The exchange itself was a sign of BEA's emergence as a hunting venue; the substance was the pace of change. Scott, McKenzie, Boustead Brothers, and the Grand Hotel (all of Mombasa) were now able to 'engage gun-bearers and porters'. Mombasa had 'several agents' who could find porters, cooks, gunbearers, and others. But beware! not only were commissions 'enormous', but the firms were 'extremely casual about forwarding goods'. The letters to the *Field* were symptomatic of another change too – one in the would-be safarist. Sportsmen like Buxton, Willoughby, and Powell-Cotton had been self-sufficient. They had had hunting experience in India or South Africa and they knew how to organize a hunting expedition and how to deal with non-English people. But what they lacked in expertise they could make up in money.

In Nairobi in 1905, three new arrivals from South Africa had an idea. After one false start in their new land, they had formed a business, or a combination of businesses (doing one thing with one hand and something else with the other was common in the new society) that promised to do well: auction and estate agency. This combination seemed to offer alpha and omega opportunity, selling newcomers land when they arrived and selling them up when they failed. To this diptych they then added a third panel almost by accident: safari organizing.

'The preliminary arrangements were prepared for us by that young and enterprising firm Newland & Tarlton.'

V. M. Newland and Henry and Leslie Tarlton had founded an industry. Carl Akeley said he was their first customer, in 1905, and that they 'fell' into the business when he wandered into their office and asked for help. From their plain, tin-roofed building in Nairobi, with its noisy and cluttered yard, would go most of the important safaris of the next 10 years. Leslie Tarlton would become a friend of Theodore Roosevelt, a correspondent of the rich and the famous, and a professional hunter noted for his skill with the rifle. The real golden age of the recreational safari had begun.

Leslie Tarlton was an Anglo-Australian with an easy, 'gentlemanly' manner and quiet but very real authority. He stayed out of the more passionate disputes of early Nairobi, yet became highly respected by other settlers. The most visible member of the firm in the safari end, he was the ideal man to forward it, able to meet the President of the United States on terms neither superior nor servile, at home in the bush or the Muthaiga Club, comfortable with hunters as well as their wives and their sons. By 1907, Newland & Tarlton, under Leslie Tarlton's leadership, were organizing simultaneous safaris for 'Lord and Lady Cranworth, Mervyn Ridley, Maitland Wilson, Percy Madeira, Lord Wodehouse, W. Flower, H. G. Watson, N. C. Cockburn, G. G. Longden, C. K. Corn, C. Bower Ismay, and W. A. L. Fletcher', these only some of the many done that year.

Unqestionably, Newland & Tarlton were the first successful non-Indian safari firm in Nairobi – the first to advertise in London, the first to grasp that complete safari outfitting was what the new breed of customers wanted. Other firms continued to advertise and continued to offer partial services – safari gear, forwarding, commission work – but Newland & Tarlton did it all.

Others tried to move into the field – the Norfolk Stores of Nairobi (a company formed by a number of settlers, including Delamere); someone named Seymour in Naivasha; a Captain Riddell, who, like Newland & Tarlton, advertised in the columns of the *Field*. Newland & Tarlton seemed to be the only ones with both stamina and enterprise, however, until Riddell formed a raffish outfit with two other men for the risky but profitable business of running ponies down from Abyssinia. '1908 witnessed the arrival, at Diredawa Railhead of three accredited representatives of the Boma Trading Company, Major H. F. Ward, Mr W. Sewall, and [Jack Riddell]'.

Boma turned Riddell's individual management of safaris into part of a larger business. 'Captain Riddell, MVO, an experienced sportsman . . . has charge of [this line of the business]'. Boma could supply gear, provisions, 'a large staff of servants . . . including porters and carriers (Swahilis), shikaris [Urdu for hunters or trackers] and gunbearers (Somalis), native guides, runners (Masai) . . . a good cook, and a staff of domestic servants'. For much of Boma's short life, however, Riddell preferred running ponies while Sewall and Ward set up outposts at Moyale, Marsabit, and Dolo, which became government stations when, in 1910, Geoffrey Archer (after whom the present Archer's Post was named) was sent 'to take over from the Company their camps, military equipment, and rifles'. Riddell said much later that this takeover ended his connection with the company, but a 1913 advertisement still connected his name with it. That year saw about the end, however, of Boma Trading; its 'buccaneering flavour' may have been too gamey for the new safari clientele.

While they lasted, however, Boma Trading Company had their successes. In 1908, the *East African Standard* reported on several of their shooting parties, including the Count of Turin's (managed by Boma, outfitted by London's Army and Navy Stores). In early 1910 they captured the plum of the Duke of Connaught's safari (Riddell had helped with the Duke's four-day visit in 1906), but in fact this was to be their peak: in 1908 they advertised themselves as 'curio dealers' and 'sole agents for the Gramophone Coy.', among other things; and in 1909 they were selling mules that Riddell had brought down from Addis Ababa; and their little Beau-Geste forts at Moyale and Marsabit had been fun to build. But they were sprinters; Newland & Tarlton were in for the long run.

There was other competition: Lawn & Alder in London; Konrad Schauer in Mombasa, who successfully set himself up to book 'hunting and Scientific Expeditions' in both British and German East Africa; Charles Heyer & Co; and provision merchants like Nazareth Brothers and Valibhai, Hasham & Co, who advertised themselves as 'safari outfitters' but really sold safari gear.

Newland & Tarlton brought out its first advertising catalogue in 1908. It was a sophisticated, well-illustrated piece of work. They set up a London office next door to the famous taxidermist's, Rowland Ward, whose big-game record book one American hunter called 'Valhalla'. Newland & Tarlton was already the name most often mentioned in the *Field*, and now they began to use the expression that Leslie Tarlton almost certainly coined and that was to become the key to the organized safari experience – 'white hunter'.

'White hunter' meant professional hunter, but it also meant exactly what it said – *white* hunter. There can be no doubt that this usage was deliberate. The Newland & Tarlton catalogue defined the term as 'a white man who knows the ropes and speaks the language . . . Where a lady accompanies the party, it is often found to be advantageous'. *Professional* hunters had in fact been used earlier, and a number of 'professional hunters' had advertised themselves in the months before Newland & Tarlton's brochure. These professionals were men of great experience, many of them ivory hunters, most of them the very men whom Tarlton would employ. But somebody, probably Tarlton, saw to the heart of the new safari clientele and saw that heart's desire: a calm, assured, cool, *white* face. Within three years, at least eight white hunters were working in Nairobi, although Stewart Edward White still put 'white hunter' in quotation marks for his American readers in 1913.

The undocumented tale that Delamere coined the term to distinguish Alan Black from an African black is kind to white sensibilities but illogical. I don't doubt that Delamere was witty enough to say, 'My white hunter is Black', or something of the sort, but such a joke depends on the expression 'white hunter' being already current. (Indeed, if the quip was ever made, it was more likely made by Tarlton, who was Black's employer when the term 'white hunter' was coined in 1907.) Black was referred to as a 'guide' for a Lady Hamilton's rhino hunt in late 1908, and some weeks later as having 'charge of the outfitting and preparation of the parties' for Newland & Tarlton, so there is no doubt that he was in the safari business early. That connection explains nothing about the coining of 'white hunter', however.

'When you arrive in British East Africa . . . you will hear of Newland & Tarlton so often that you will think they own the country.' They certainly did seem to own the safari business – one director said they had more than 300 clients in their best year before 1914, although the figure seems too high. There were several reasons for this pre-eminence – Tarlton's genius; timing; stamina – but if a simple exemplary cause could be found, it would be their handling in 1909–10 of the safari of Theodore Roosevelt. The irony of that event was that they almost did not get it, and when they did it was only through the back door.

In 1908, Teddy Roosevelt was nearing the self-imposed end of his presidency. President through accession, then elected in his own right, he could almost certainly have been elected again but chose to pass the office on to his Vice-President, William Howard Taft. (He would shortly regret doing so.) In his 50s, overweight but still vigorous, he wanted to go straight from the White House to an experience that would compensate with its excitement for the surrender of power. He decided to have an East African hunt.

He was not disappointed.

And, through the enormous publicity that his presence generated – countless newspaper articles, a feature film, magazines, his own books – he shared the experience with the world. Thereafter, 'safari' was an institution, very shortly a fashion.

Roosevelt was to learn quickly that planning for a safari is almost as much fun – and work – as the safari itself. It is not quite clear when he decided to go, but the *East African Standard* said as early as 1906 that 'persistent rumours' were saying that he would go. In fact, he does not seem to have decided until late 1907. He then did what most of us would do – looked about for advice. As President, he could look almost anywhere, and he began to fire off letters to the great names of African hunting – 33 in 18 months to Frederick Courtney Selous, 40 to Edward North Buxton. By the end of 1908, he was in the midst of a vigorous correspondence with Selous, Buxton, W. S. Rainsford, J. H. Patterson, and Sir Alfred Pease, all of them sending lists, ideas, samples of this and that – and far too much advice for any one man to take.

Selous was the South African hunter *par excellence*, said by some to be the living embodiment of Haggard's Allan Quatermain, but he had virtually no experience of BEA; Buxton had, and had written a book about it; so had the strong-minded Rainsford, who was in fact still there. Patterson was the East African Protectorate's Game Ranger (head of the game department), but, during the correspondence, he involved himself (unknown to Roosevelt) in the scandal that ended his East African career. (Roosevelt either did not learn of the scandal in East Africa or refused to credit what he had heard, for he entertained Patterson both before and after the safari.) Pease was an amateur hunter who had written about BEA and owned property there.

'I was rather afraid that Buxton, Selous and I all writing to you about arrangements you might exclaim "Save me from my friends"', Pease wrote on 13 September. If he did, Roosevelt never said so; he was a politician, after all, used to listening to every point of view.

Yet Roosevelt was to go as a private individual, and, as the advice mounted, so did the safari's complexity, from a simple two-man trip of the sort he had known in the American West (he was taking his 19-year-old son, Kermit) to a complex scientific and hunting expedition that would use 500 porters, 3 scientists, several professional hunters, and in all the biggest safari Nairobi had ever put together.

In fact, Roosevelt could have gone much lighter and cheaper, but his well-to-do advisers had him taking (and so buying) every gadget and bit of gear each of them had ever found useful in Africa, as well as three kinds of hat, spine and cholera pads, coloured glasses for the sun, specially tinned prepared lunches, enough jam for the whole of the Rough Riders, and a tent that took three porters to carry. Roosevelt proposed a light tent of waterproof silk (21 July 1908). Selous didn't like that idea at all; it wasn't the way he did it. A green canvas that would take three porters to carry, with another to carry the poles, was ordered in London (Selous, 8 August 1908). Roosevelt was philosophical; he supposed 'we can get plenty of porters' (22 August 1908). David Abercrombie of the great New York outfitting firm of Abercrombie & Fitch was not at all pleased. They had been going to make the silk tent (25 August 1908). And they did so, anyway: on 21 November, Ezra Fitch, president of Abercrombie & Fitch, wrote to Roosevelt's secretary in answer to his letter

of the day before: 'We shall immediately make up a khaki waterproof silk tent
. . . with seamless telescopic steel poles'. There would be no charge for the
tent. They would 'esteem it a favor' if they could market the new tent as the
'Roosevelt tent'.

So, Roosevelt, after getting all that advice and agreeing to the British canvas
dreadnought, went ahead anyway and got the American lightweight. That is
what he got his Nobel Prize for – tactful manipulation.

Nor was the tent all!

Take lots of jam and 'a good deal of lard or beef marrow fat to cook the
meat of lean African antelopes' (Selous, 24 May 1908).

Lawn and Alder are sending out 36 boxes, contents made up into pleasingly
varied food for two people for four months (Selous, 8 August 1908).

'[Mister Roosevelt] should take all his liquor from England. The stuff bought
in Nairobi is mostly poison' (Charles Bulpett, quoted in Selous, 6 August 1908).

'I advise three ordinary felt hats . . . one double terai hat, and a pith or cork
helmet' (Selous, 30 August 1908).

'I loathe a helmet' (Roosevelt, 12 October 1908).

'I have ordered you a splendid pith hat . . . This hat you will soon find gets
shabby; you ought to have another in a tin case for ceremonial occasions . . .
I have ordered you a smart white military helmet for this purpose' (Buxton, 9
February 1909).

Surely a frock coat and top hat are unnecessary, but 'ordinary evening dress
and its equivalent in white linen would do' (Roosevelt to Sir Frederick Jackson,
3 November 1908).

The presidency had its perks, of course: the Fox shotgun company built a
complimentary 12-gauge (12-bore) for him and sent it along; Buxton and his
English friends gave him a custom double .500/.450 rifle. Pease built a
bungalow for his use on the plains, and a new Arabian horse was provided for
him, one not yet infected by tsetse. (No matter; of eight horses, only three
lasted until the safari's end, four dying of tsetse bite.)

Yet foremost on Roosevelt's mind were not perks, but game. He had two
concerns: he wanted to shoot it, and he wanted to be thought well of for doing
so. He listed 16 varieties, of which he and Kermit might shoot two each – 64
animals in all. Then again, 'a dozen trophies between us . . . you can with a
clear conscience tell the Colonial Secretary that I am not in the least a game
butcher' (21 July 1908). 'I am no game butcher, but I desire greatly to shoot
specimens, male and female, of each of the big game animals' (25 September
1908). 'I particularly want to avoid anything that will savor of butchery'
(26 November 1908). 'I am no butcher, but I would like to *see* plenty of game'
(? 1908). He thought they might shoot two rhino each – one to hang on the
wall and one for a museum.

This concern also raised an issue that was to prove far-reaching: should
Roosevelt have a professional hunter? Pease, via Buxton, suggested Riddell

(27 May 1908). Selous suggested a man named Will Judd, who had been going out with visiting sportsmen since at least 1906. 'It would save a great deal of worry and trouble if you had a first rate white man who knows the country and the natives well and speaks their language' (5 August 1908). Lawn and Alder of London recommended him, Selous said. 'If the addition of another £200 . . . is not a serious consideration to you, you ought to have a reliable white man with you to relieve you from all the small worries' (8 August 1908).

But Roosevelt reacted surprisingly. He had heard from an Anglo-Irish sportsman of a Goanese hunter, M. A. DaSilva, 'as to whose social position there would be no doubt' and preferred him 'to a white guide' for that reason.

But Selous, and then Pease, pressed for Judd ('a better man . . . than Riddell . . . & more likely to defend you from unnecessary expense', 13 September 1908). But Roosevelt seemed firm: DaSilva would hunt with Kermit, and Roosevelt would hunt only with 'native Shikaris'. Any Englishman hired to run the safari 'would not hunt at all' (10 September 1908). By early October, Roosevelt had 'engaged' DaSilva for three months 'to accompany my son Kermit most of the time' (5 October 1908). At the same time, he was writing to Selous about hiring the 'white head man', who would do no shooting. By that time, however, the name of R. J. Cuninghame had been added to the mix, and Roosevelt shortly received from Buxton a copy of a friend's letter evaluating the two British candidates:

> *Cunningham.* [*sic*] One of the old S. African big game hunters, has a good knowledge of the game, a dead shot, very quiet, very capable caravan manager, has a very good knowledge of Kenia Province from Kenia to Guaso Nyiro, and also the Athi plains.
> *Judd.* Good shot, keen hunter, good knowledge of game, and game districts. Of the two I think I would recommend Cunningham the more highly.

While Roosevelt was pondering this, the Acting Governor (Jackson) advised him to use Newland & Tarlton as 'agents'; he did so, but a month later instructed Boma Trading Company to get in touch with Pease about horses. Thus, by December he had three professional hunters, two safari companies, and four advisers on the string. Yet, the day after Christmas, he wrote to Newland & Tarlton to say that 'Cuninghame will have charge of my safari'.

The difference was Rainsford. A clergyman and outdoorsman, Rainsford was opinionated and eloquent, and he made two passionate pleas to Roosevelt: *no* Somalis (one of Boma's specialities), and *no* Will Judd. Cuninghame seems to have sought out Rainsford in Nairobi, not to argue against Judd but to argue for a white *hunter* in addition to himself as safari manager. Rainsford hectored Roosevelt on the subject: he needed somebody to back him up in dangerous situations, and that person should not be Judd because Rainsford had seen Judd let somebody down and get a gunbearer badly injured. (Later in a book he would mean Judd when he wrote about the white hunter 'who afterward proved to be a very nervous shot himself [and] failed his man badly, [missing his first shot on a lion and then shooting the lion in the wrong spot]'.

Rainsford was persuasive. Judd was out. (The tradition that Judd lost out on the flip of a coin has no basis in fact.)

The arguments for a hunter – at this point, Cuninghame was hired as a 'manager' – proved too powerful. On 31 January, Roosevelt wrote to Cuninghame to 'engage any man you think best; but be sure he understands that *I* am to do the shooting!' He had heard well of A. C. Hoey, but 'I don't suppose Mr Tarleton [sic] would come'.

In fact, Leslie Tarlton would come. On 8 February, Cuninghame cabled, 'Tarlton accepts appointment with thanks'.

The shape of the safari was now set: Cuninghame was in overall charge, with Newland & Tarlton acting as Nairobi agents for Roosevelt. Tarlton himself would back up Roosevelt in the field. Boma would handle some minor matters, but Newland & Tarlton in fact had the commission. Somewhere between the end of January and the actual beginning of the safari, the Goan DaSilva was dropped without a trace. The correspondence releasing him has not survived.

Roosevelt thus made firm a relationship that had until that time been a little muddy because new: that between the white hunter and the client. Now matters were clear: the trophy was the client's, and the client shot first. The white hunter protected the client in dangerous situations but, ideally, put no bullets into the trophy. (This last clause was to be more honoured in the breach in later years.) In fact, it can be said that the correspondence setting up Roosevelt's safari is a gloss on the early definition of the white hunter, his duties, and what Roosevelt called his 'social position'. After Roosevelt, the role was defined and the tasks clear, where before him they had been rather variable. And Tarlton, by serving as Roosevelt's hunter, fixed the type: gentlemanly, skilled, socially equal.

Roosevelt and Kermit sailed from New York on 23 March 1909. With them were Edmund Heller, J. Alden Loring, and Edgar A. Mearns, the scientists. The party met Selous on the ship to Mombasa, then took a special train as far as Kapiti station, not going first to Nairobi as most newcomers did. Roosevelt, after all, was the greatest celebrity ever to visit BEA (Winston Churchill and even the Duke of Connaught could not compete). His safari would come to him – and there it was near the tiny Kapiti station, 'the army of porters and tents . . . as if some small military expedition was about to start'.

By the time Roosevelt and his son left Africa 11 months later, he had endeared himself to the settlers of BEA. If there had been an election, he could have been Governor. He had been in and out of Nairobi several times, had been fêted with dinners and with Masai 'dances'. He had had several occasions to wear his formal clothes and his white helmet. And he said and wrote things that sounded to the settler-listeners like the music of the spheres.

'The English rule in Africa has been of incalculable benefit to Africans themselves'. Here were places 'where the English flag stands for all that makes life worth living'. 'Over this [barbaric] people – for its good fortune – Great Britain established a protectorate.'

And, best of all, he praised the type and actions of the settlers themselves, in whom he saw the reincarnation of his own beloved American West, 'the spirit of daring adventure . . . the hope and the heart-breaking disappointment'. It was a love feast.

The speeches and parties were not the wilderness experience he had originally envisaged, but the truth was he remained a politician and a self-defined 'great man' who needed the oxygen of applause. He had demanded that the press let him alone, had wondered in a letter if he could ask the Governor to keep the press out, but he worried about what they might say about him all the time. 'I had never been with a man before who evidently considered every day what the world would think, say or write about his success or failure', Pease said. '[He] enjoyed being "important" [he told me] and added, ". . . Of course, I like to be a big man, *everyone* likes to be important and to have power and influence."'

No better experience existed than the safari for feeling 'a big man'. And Roosevelt played the role. He rode at the head, horns tooting and drums thumping behind him. His tent was erected in the central position. His massive expedition split into several branches, Roosevelt going off to his beloved hunting with Tarlton, Kermit with Cuninghame, the scientists for months to remote spots with their own support. Then they would convene somewhere again under Roosevelt's aegis, then split again. (Selous had gone off on his own small safari – with the rejected Judd as his hunter.) When the American cartoonist John T. McCutcheon caught up with Roosevelt late in the year, he, Tarlton, Heller, and Kermit were together; Mearns and Loring were studying fauna on Mt Kenya; Cuninghame was scouting for Roosevelt in Uganda.

The safari on the march, even a part of it, moved with a military flavour that recalled Stanley and Peters. Roosevelt rode first, followed by a man with a huge American flag. When camp was set up, the tents went in crisp rows, Roosevelt's and the other whites' in front, the flag by Roosevelt's like a fleet admiral's. The porters' little pup tents went behind.

Yet he was capable of simplicity. Once, he went off with Kermit and the naturalist Carl Akeley with nothing but his bedding and personal gear. Another time, seeing no point in waiting while an elephant was skinned, he struck off for the base camp with a gunbearer and a guide. At least once, he camped apart from the main party to savour isolation.

Always, the magnificent hunting kept him on the move. Roosevelt couldn't leave the game alone. He was not a particularly good shot because of his eyesight and used up a great many cartridges, but he had 'perseverance and common sense' and he was a keen hunter. A Winchester .405 was his usual lion gun, along with the gift .500/.450. An 'army Springfield, 30 calibre, stocked and sighted to suit myself' was also used. (This was a customized Model 1903 with the cartridge of 1906 – the justly famous .30·06 – but not the post-First-World-War 'Springfield Sporter'.) He slimmed down somewhat, although the Africans, who usually gave sportsmen nicknames, dubbed him 'Bwana Tumbo' (Mister Belly). Hunting was male self-definition to Roosevelt, 'a craft, a pursuit of value in exercising and developing hardihood of body and the virile courage and resolution which necessarily lie at the base of every strong and manly character'.

It was like his youth in the West. 'There was much to remind one of conditions in Montana and Wyoming thirty years ago . . . the plains still teeming with game.' He had said again and again that he could not believe there were as many animals in BEA as his correspondents said; now he saw they had not exaggerated, and he rode and stalked and looked and shot like a man on the hunt of a lifetime.

His days were rigorous (and, therefore, so were everybody's). Buxton had recommended 'early to bed . . . 8 p.m.' (15 January 1909), and fatigue saw to that. The days started early. 'We might be off by dawn [on horseback], and see the tropic sun flame splendid over the brink of the world; strange creatures rustled through the bush or fled dimly through the long grass, before the light grew bright; and the air was fresh and sweet as it blew in our faces.' They often hunted all day, throwing themselves down in the shade during the midday heat, then going off again. 'As the shadows lengthened I would again mount, and finally ride homeward as the red sunset paled to amber and opal, and all the vast mysterious African landscape grew to wonderful beauty in the dying twilight.'

Years later, Tarlton asked him if he remembered a particular hunt. Roosevelt replied, with the passion of a man who remembered it all, 'Our night ride with the lioness, which we finally skinned outside the Masai Kraal, at midnight . . . all that day's hunt with you – the long ride in the day time, the fight with the lioness at dusk and the ride home through the darkness – made an impression upon me which I shall never forget'. He was 51, just on the edge of age; he was teaching his son a 'pursuit of value'. It was an intense, a great, experience.

When it was over, and the trophies were packed and sent home and the kills were totalled, his 'dozen trophies between us' had turned into 512 animals, of which 9 were the rare white rhino, 7 were cheetahs shot by Kermit, 17 were lions, and 11 were elephant. Many of these had been shot for supposedly scientific purposes (and many of the 512 were meat animals). No matter; the uproar that followed publication of the Roosevelt kill was as bad as he had feared in the beginning. Cranworth remarked on 'the devastation that is done in the name of or on behalf of museums. Do these nine white rhinoceroses ever cause ex-President Roosevelt a pang of conscience or a restless night? I for one venture to hope so.'

Attacks came from everywhere. 'Every Briton must be delighted that the ex-President had a real good time . . . but it must be fairly questioned whether he did not take a somewhat too severe toll of a wild fauna, which, although still remarkable in number and species, is, as we all know, steadily being reduced.' 'One must . . . regret the fact that Mr Roosevelt and his son thought it necessary and were permitted to shoot so many as nine of the rare white rhinoceros.'

Jackson, perhaps feeling betrayed because he had been one of those who helped Roosevelt, later wrote, 'It was . . . a matter of great regret . . . that he was so utterly reckless in the expenditure of ammunition, and what it entailed in the matter of disturbing the country; and that he so unduly exceeded reasonable limits in certain species, and particularly the white rhinoceros'. He especially found Roosevelt's account of a buffalo shoot 'most unpleasant reading'.

One criticism led to another: Roosevelt was found not only greedy, but also vain; he had 'an abominable habit of being photographed with every zebra and kongoni he shoots for the pot as if it were some great feat'. So it was to be a great man – greatly loved when found right, greatly despised when thought wrong.

Roosevelt had another problem – the safari's cost. In the end, it came to a stunning £15,000, a colossal sum for the day. He paid his legitimate expenses out of the £10,000 he got from *Scribner's Magazine* for his articles on the trip (after turning down £20,000 from *Collier's* because *Scribner's* was more dignified). The rest was scientific and altruistic and was subsidized by Andrew Carnegie.

The safari had been big in every way – big man, big kill, big cost. And it had a big effect. Every American hunter, and many Britons, walked in Roosevelt's shoes thereafter. Roosevelt became to later safaris what Stanley had been to earlier ones. He was the archetype of the new safari client – a newcomer to Africa, able to command big money, eager to gulp down everything at a big swallow, hungry for trophies.

'Big.' 'Manly.'

Roosevelt brought his bigness and his manliness with him. Those who followed would seek those qualities in his shadow.

Others of the period discovered what Roosevelt had discovered about expense: unless you knew the ropes and did it all yourself, a safari became very costly, quickly. A rueful R. Gorrell Barnes cited the two ways to outfit. 'One is to do it yourself, and the other, and the usual, to sit down and let an agent do it for you, and then pay the bill, if possible.' Barnes preferred the first way, but he was able to outfit himself in the bazaar with a 'smattering of Hindustani', and his room at the Norfolk 'began to look like the nucleus of a jumble sale'. None the less, he got away for £30 a month.

Rainsford advised using the outfitting companies but being prepared to do much oneself: write months ahead of time, be clear about what you can afford, where you want to shoot, how much time you have. He knew what he was saying; his first safari (before the founding of Newland & Tarlton) had been disastrous because he had lacked such good advice.

Yet if one of the companies was used, expense would mount. Newland & Tarlton took a commission of one rupee per head for each man it supplied, plus five per cent of the client's total bill, plus extras for services like packing and shipping trophies. McCutcheon estimated that total costs mounted to £100 per month 'for each white man', where in 1906 – just before the advent of the white hunter – English hunters' costs had been just half that for somebody willing to bring his own tent, guns, and ammunition.

Thus, there was a new way and an old way to go, just as there was a new and an old kind of client. The old way was unquestionably cheaper; the new way was unquestionably easier. Selous – advocate of the old way, a man who could have set up an expedition anywhere on earth – had told Roosevelt he could make the trip for £700, of which £200 would be licences and fares (3 April 1908). Patterson, just returned from BEA, estimated £80–100 'per "white" head per month, *everything* included' (23 June 1908). In the event, these estimates were ludicrous in Roosevelt's case, but they would have been practical for a different man going in the old way.

Costs to the newcomer appear to have risen as soon as the British firms took command of the industry. Their commissions represented only part of the increase; the rest was in the added services they supplied, most of all the white hunter. You could organize a trip for yourself on the cheap if you wanted, but you couldn't do that when talking to Leslie Tarlton or Riddell. They did not sell privation.

Using Riddell's services (pre-Boma), one visitor spent £475 for three months, of which £60 was for ponies (which were rented at a high rate or bought outright because they sickened so quickly), £16 was an extra elephant licence, and £80 was guns and ammunition. Edgar Bronson estimated £70–100 a month, not including £100 sea transportation and £30 for a horse. By 1909, however, the *Field* was getting letters objecting to the expense of BEA and preferring North East Rhodesia, where things were not 'cut and dried for [the hunter]'. What the old-timers were watching – unhappily – was the rapid growth of a new industry with a new kind of consumer. Arthur Colville saw 'very rich men of every nationality that visit the country in search of sport regardless of expense' as the cause, along with unnamed parties who would give 'every assistance' in spending money.

Certain costs, however, were unavoidable. The visitor's licence, introduced in 1905, cost £50, no small sum. Horses or mules cost at least another £10 a month. A white hunter cost £1 a day. Transportation from Europe was £40, from America £100. Salting, curing, treating, and shipping skins 'runs up into surprisingly large figures'.

Porterage continued to be the most common means of moving the safari, with numbers varying from 30 to 100 for most safaris. Some added Boer ox-drawn wagons where the terrain allowed their use, but they were slow and were used mostly to move supplies and trophies between Nairobi and base camps, as on Roosevelt's safari. Porters continued to be paid about 15 rupees (£1) a month. (For comparison, the Governor got £250 pounds a month, the Senior Game Warden £32, a Goan clerk £14, and a female English postal clerk £9.) Askaris – a disappearing species at last – got a bit more than porters; gunbearers, cooks, and personal servants earned two to three times a porter's wages and headmen five times as much.

Thus, a one-person safari using 30 porters, 1 white hunter, 1 headman, 1 cook, 4 servants and 2 gunbearers would have a monthly labour cost of at least £80. It is obvious where this could be drastically reduced – the white hunter and his gunbearer – but few newcomers after Roosevelt dared to take this step.

Boma Trading Company and Riddell had advertised Somali gunbearers and Swahili porters. These, too, were part of a way already old – the neo-feudal system that treasured the Somalis, particularly, for their aristocratic ways. Newland & Tarlton, too, would provide Somalis – but at £5 a month each, double what other skilled safari workers got. Handsome and dashing as they might be, therefore, and no matter how well they rode or how much they preserved their own dignity, Somalis were an unnecessary expense. They gradually disappeared, along with coastal Swahili porters, replaced by once-despised Kikuyus.

The Kikuyu were the closest people in large numbers to Nairobi and the European highlands. They were, therefore, in great demand as labourers; however, it took them some years to see any reason to labour for somebody else. Money was unimportant to them until the British instituted a tax on each hut in the Protectorate, after which the logic of going to work to prevent the burning down of one's home became clear. As porters, they got only seasonal work (the European autumn and winter); as agricultural workers, they earned less but had a longer season. Early on, they had a bad reputation as porters – lazy, savage, and, worst of all, *vegetarian.* (Vegetarians ate expensive maize; meat-eaters ate free venison.) In fact, they were not vegetarians, but they were accustomed to their own goats and sheep and their own plentiful maize and beans; so game, posho, and 'herbs' (as the British called wild edible greens) did not seem worth leaving home for.

Finding enough porters in Nairobi, therefore, continued to be a problem, even as it had been in Zanzibar in the 1860s. Matters were even worse in the bush. One couple who organized their own safari (pre-Newland & Tarlton) hired local people at Naivasha; these then deserted. More were hired, but refused to climb the escarpment; then they made camp but would not set up the whites' tents. More deserted. The whites responded by 'capturing' and 'waylaying' other locals and roping them together. Even then, the press crew refused to do anything but take a straight route back to Naivasha.

Nor was portering entirely safe. Stewart Edward White accidentally hit one of his porters with a ricochet bullet; the man died. Another safari client had to amputate a porter's arm after it was mangled by a crocodile. Safaris were still being regularly scattered by rhinos, which blundered into the line of porters, sending loads in every direction.

Nor was it easy. The 60-lb load was still standard and 12-mile marches normal. When porters were shipped somewhere by train, 'according to the benighted custom of the country [they were] locked into iron trucks assigned them.' Rainsford's were locked in for two days without food, 'yet cheerfully they shouldered their unusually heavy burdens, and marched more than five hours'.

No wonder that porters became scarce despite 'large wages'. Out of season, Barnes was able in 1910 to telegraph to Nairobi for 'professional porters', but when plague quarantined the Nairobi bazaar in 1912, White and two companions had to seek porters in the 'villages' at the edge of Nairobi. White's account gives an unusual insight into the profession. He estimated that 10,000 Africans lived there for the safari trade, from among whom he hired 29 Wanyamwezi, Swahili, Kavirondo (from Lake Victoria), and Kikuyu. His estimate seems very high, even including families; however, it is interesting that so many – including the old Wanyamwezi and Swahili professionals – had been drawn to Nairobi and lived detribalized lives there. The account says something for the impact and speed of European influence.

The safari companies outfitted their porters in coloured jerseys (the blue with 'N & T' on it became a familiar sight to Newland & Tarlton customers). The government mandated that porters must be issued shoes; many still marched barefoot, the shoes saved for more important times and worn around the neck by the strings. They rarely cut grass for little huts any more; after 1900, they had little tents, in which they slept in very tight quarters, five or six getting what would now be called a two-person tent. These added to the visitor's costs – 5 or 6 rupees (7 or 8 shillings) each for a tent 3 feet high. (The white client's tent cost £15.)

Yet the life of a porter, the optimistic Roosevelt concluded, 'is attractive to them. They are fed well; the government requires that they be fitted with suitable clothes and given small tents, so that they are better clad and sheltered than they would be otherwise; and their wages represent money which they could get in no other way.'

The high season, when porters were most competed for, began at the end of September. Safaris were shorter than those of the nineteenth century but still too long for Europeans to undertake as a working-man's holiday. Hepburn spent 38 days in the field, 17 of them moving from place to place and 21 hunting. Barnes argued for unlimited time; a trophy buffalo, for example, could take weeks to find. Roosevelt's safari was unusual for its length, but two months in BEA may be taken as typical.

Old and new ways contested. Cranworth, his safari organized by Newland & Tarlton, was amused by a headman 'struggling against the advent of new ideas and new methods ... He insisted on the march discipline of the old days ... Tents came down on a bugle note and loads were laid out in exact order. At another blast they were raised and the march started.' A less

Stanley-like way was coming in, however. With so many safaris leaving Nairobi in the season, the colour and flash were going out of them; they were no longer an event, but a business.

Yet much did not change. The day still began at dawn. 'Rising before daylight, we took our coffee.' 'Up at 4 a.m. for a cold dip and a light breakfast; off as soon as you can see your rifle sights.' 'The whole joy and glory of the tropical day are confined to its earliest hours.'

Marches were five or six hours. This was a good ride on a narrow horse, a good walk if you footed it. As always, big safaris would string out for a mile or more; sometimes porters got lost and straggled in late at night, even the next day. But practised porters and good management made for order, jobs done quickly and without seeming confusion. 'I counted fourteen tents and our three big ones, pitched perfectly and trenched complete . . . in eight minutes from the time the first bundle was thrown down'. Once the tents were up, 'the pile of camp baggage, jars, hides, provisions, boxes, potio [sic – Rainsford never could spell], saddles, ammunition, etc, is laid on brushwood or logs, a trench dug around it, and the whole covered with a waterproof ground sheet'.

Not all camps had Roosevelt's military crispness, but the theory behind the layout was the same – separation of the whites' and the porters' tents, protection of the mound of camp goods (from theft and animals) by rows or circles of tents and fires.

The Europeans' days ended pleasurably. Servants waited 'with a long drink . . . [One] removes your boots and generally acts as valet, while his mate has a bath and dry clothes all ready. Another "boy" stands by with sponge and towel.' Europeans debated the comparative debilitating effects of hot versus cold baths, but most of the new clientele chose 'screeching-hot', after which they dressed in pyjamas and soft, high footgear called 'mosquito boots'. They then dined, and, growing sleepy, listened to the sounds that Stanley, Peters and Thomson had known: the night music of the porters. Muslims chanted and prayed. Kikuyu sang, sometimes danced. The talk hummed in languages the Europeans did not understand. The fires crackled with dry wood, the air aromatic with the smell of burning cedar in the hills, pungent with burning thorn on the plains. The sparks floated up and mingled with the million unfamiliar stars of the African sky. And next day it began all over again.

Some Americans accustomed to roughing it would always find the baths and the servants unsettling, even embarrassing. But the British insisted that comfort was essential in Africa. And, after all, they argued, it was nothing to what you found in India.

By 1910, the Uganda Railway was advertising BEA as a 'veritable mecca for sportsmen'. Perhaps ominously, they directed their readers to 'follow in the Footsteps of Fashion'. Lord Hindlip had estimated 30 safaris a year in 1905; in 1908, Bronson could find no porters because of 30 safaris in the month of

"LOOK OUT, YOU DROP THAT BOX—I'LL SHOOT YOU."

The seminal image of safari: H.M. Stanley in a typical pose

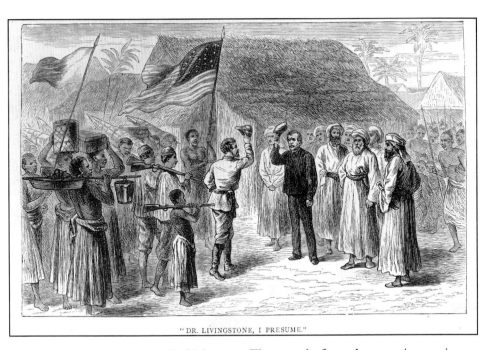

"DR. LIVINGSTONE, I PRESUME."

Stanley says the magic words to Dr Livingstone. The guns, the flag and a new suit were vintage Stanley

Like a snake, the safari wound its way over the land, with porters sometimes
stringing back for a mile (c. 1890)

A small part of Theodore Roosevelt's safari of 1909. Until the motor car,
whites often rode horses – at least until the horses collapsed from tsetse

For Africans, safaris were often hard work

The pay was about 3 pence a day

In the days when rhino were abundant, they regularly broke up the line of march
with their near-sighted charges

Not all safaris travelled on foot. The Boer ox-wagon was slow
but sure (c. 1920)

'On the Athi Plains', south of Nairobi, in a rig that anticipated the shooting-car (c. 1910)

The motor car changed the safari forever. Gone were the porters, and the whites' chance to make contact with them

Motor safaris were not all beer and skittles. In the rains, cars might make only a few miles in an hour

Safari created its own costume. This is the bush outfit in embryo, about 1895. The potables, carried on black men's heads, were typical aspects of 'home' taken into the wilds

Burberry had called this the 'veldt coat' during the Boer War. By 1910, it was a prototypical bush jacket, but without pockets

The early bush outfit in full flower – epaulettes, cartridge loops, puttees and topi (c. 1910). The subject wrote his own caption – 'Dressed to Kill'

London tailors created fashionable safari clothes – complete with button-on spine pads to protect against the fatal 'actinic rays' of the African sun

Clothes make the sportsman (1910)

Berkeley Cole and Tich Miles of Cole's Scouts. White colonials created their own units in the first months of World War One. Perhaps in the belief that the war would be an extended shooting safari, they costumed themselves in a kind of safari outfit

Two hats were better than one: the double terai at work and play. The horns belong to a greater kudu

Where the safari industry began – Newland and Tarlton's yard and shed, Nairobi (c. 1910)

'White hunter' was a hegemonistic term, and its bearers were culture heroes. Here, the great R.J. Cuninghame, former ivory hunter, manager of the Roosevelt safari

Denys Finch Hatton: 'My wife's lover and my best friend,' said Bror Blixen

By 1950, the white hunter was a threatened species. Hollywood, however, was turning him into a sex object

Camp was a few square feet of Europe in the bush, limited in its luxury by the number of men you could afford to carry it there (c. 1890)

'What a storm . . . can do to a strong tent' (c. 1905)

A tent for all seasons, 1912 – no floor, no bug-proof door

By the twenties, many tents had floors and bug-proof doors, but they still took three men to carry them

All the comforts of home in the bush (c. 1930)

November alone. The Athi Plains were said to have so many visiting sportsmen that you were more likely to be hurt by a bullet than a lion. By 1910, McCutcheon noted 30 safaris already in September (although a summary of the Governor's report for that year noted a falling-off from the year before). In 1911, Tarlton told Roosevelt he had 43 parties out at one time.

It was almost too much for Newland & Tarlton. Boma were fading from the business. Both Leslie Tarlton and Newland were ill. At the end of 1911, Tarlton confessed to Roosevelt he was thinking of giving it up; what did Roosevelt think of his coming to America?

In fact, the increased safari business was not the only stress. BEA and Nairobi were changing. Nairobi particularly had reached a turning-point that marked the end of the little frontier village.

In 1912, an editorial in the *Leader* noted the changes, marking particularly the 'almost eclipse of the early leading Goan firms by the more enterprising and smarter European trader'. Nairobi had a Ford agency ('sole agent for BEA and Uganda') offering a four-cylinder for £225 FOB Nairobi. Garvie's Bioscope was showing films, and the lack of a theatre was partly filled by the Gaiety, where Miss Marie Wadia 'of the Royal Opera Covent Garden, Albert Hall and Queen's Hall Concerts' was to sing. The Norfolk advertised itself as 'The Fashionable Rendezvous of the Big Game Shooter and Tourist'.

The 'almost eclipse' of non-European firms (an overstatement, but with some truth in it) extended into the bush, the pioneering Indian dukas joined or replaced by stores run by Europeans: Will Judd had a 'trading store' on the Mara River in 1913, a man named Vandermeyer another on the Narosara, and the hunter Boyce Aggett another down toward the border.

The place that only a dozen years before had appealed to people of frontier spirit was becoming tame.

The signs could have been read all along. Porters were colourful, but other kinds of transport were on the way. As early as 1902, Buxton and his daughter travelled the Kilimanjaro area by bicycle, once encountering a lion that simply stared at the novelty. In 1906, the *Globetrotter* opined that 'the only motor car in the country at present is the property of the Sultan of Zanzibar', but a 'steam motor wagon transport' was running between Voi and Taveta that same year. Roosevelt noted people arriving in automobiles for a Nairobi race meet in 1909, and in 1910 a short-lived lorry service was running between Nairobi and Fort Hall. In 1912, Berkeley Cole made an 'epochal' car journey to the Uasin Gishu plateau in western Kenya; that same year, motor laws were being considered for the Protectorate.

In 1913, Rainsford completed his last safari. He left many friends behind. The *Leader* noted more than the end of a hunting career. 'It is to some of us a sad reflection that the advance of civilization, naturally followed by the thinning of the royal game, must inevitably lose us such good men as the worthy Doctor.'

The next August saw the advance of civilization begin to take many more good men than Rainsford. The First World War began.

It started slowly in East Africa; there was briefly even talk of honouring an old agreement to keep German and British Africa neutral. But wars at their beginnings inspire enthusiasm, and volunteers poured into Nairobi from the farms, ready to beat the Hun on African soil. Leslie Tarlton and Newland had both got their health back, but the pressure of business was relieved, anyway; safaris fell off to almost zero (two, in fact, in 1915). 'The Coy's business has suffered severely through the war', Tarlton wrote to Roosevelt. The Game Department 'virtually ceased to exist', and the five wardens were taken for intelligence work. Men went off and did not come back: 85 per cent of eligible whites volunteered; 200,000 black Kenyans were conscripted.

The effects of the war would be profound in BEA, and the safari industry would not recover easily. When it did, it would be different.

4

NO TRIP FOR A WOMAN
Women and safari

T HE war decimated the white and black male populations of East Africa, both English and German. To a considerable extent, this enforced male absence made visible a segment of the East African population usually forgotten: its women. Mostly, the European women took over the running of the farms, managing well enough to bring the region through the war in as good (some historians say better) condition as they found it. Fears of theft, rape, and even uprising by black Africans were groundless: not one instance of black violence to these women or their farms occurred. Black women remained less visible – the bearers of huge loads in rural backwaters, the occasional half-nude subject of a white man's photograph.

Although the safari industry was comatose, this emergence of women serves to remind us of their usually neglected roles as safari leaders. The Arab–African beginnings and the European heritage of the safari were conspicuously male, but a number of women, forgotten now except by specialists, made themselves quite at home in this masculine institution.

She was rather tall for a woman, but what people noticed first about her were her luminous eyes. Enlarged now by anger and tension, they burned in her oval face. The African rain pelted down, soaking her grey travelling dress, whose skirts were already heavy with the mud of walking. She held a pistol in each hand.

She was 50 miles out from Mombasa, and she was facing a rebellion of her Zanzibari porters.

The leaders wheeled around, halted the line of porters following, pitched their loads in wild disorder upon the ground, saying I did not know the road, and refused to budge, and as the porters in the rear kept coming up they were inclined to manifest the same spirit. The minor headmen made futile attempts to rally the men . . . all to no effect. Hamidi, my factotum, was in the rear far away; and Josefe, my interpreter, was simply guyed and scoffed at for every order he issued from me.

She did one of those things, irrational and wild, that save or lose the moment. A vulture started from a tree. She raised one pistol, fired – and the vulture fell to the ground.

> I started through the centre of the rebellious throng, pointing first one, then the other pistol in quick succession at the heads of the men, threatening, and fully prepared, determined, and justified to shoot the first dissenter.
>
> As with unflinching, angry eyes fixed upon them, I exclaimed, 'Get up! take your load! one! two! th---!' and before the three was pronounced the man addressed was on his feet, grasping his discarded load. After half a dozen men were thus warned, and the entire throng revealed uneasiness and were stirring, I turned upon them and said, 'Every man who is not on his feet with his load on his head, when I count three, I will shoot!' They knew I would.

Her name was May (Mary) French Sheldon. The year was 1891. Fear of the Masai still dominated British thinking; despite the establishment at Mombasa of 'IBEA' – the Imperial British East African Company – the country 10 miles inland was still unknown and believed dangerous. And coastal porters still tested the authority of the leader before they were cut off from the coast: H. H. Johnston's men had tossed down their loads only 20 miles out from Mombasa. Johnston had used a stick on them, not a gun – but Johnston was a man.

Born in Pittsburgh in 1848, married to a wealthy expatriate, May French Sheldon had trained as a doctor but had never practised; one of her sisters, however, was a well-known woman physician of whom she was very proud. Perhaps it was a sense of unused potential that urged her to Africa; perhaps it was her friendship with Stanley and his protégé of the Emin Pasha expedition, the dashing Herbert Ward.

A brief biography said that she undertook the safari 'to study [African] women and children in their primitive state', but the reason she gave in London in 1890 was that she wanted to gather background for a novel. No doubt that seemed a more believable goal for a woman. Stanley – famous, lionized, his African reputation achieved – was a good friend of her husband's, and he wrote to Francis de Winton at Mombasa that she was 'an American lady litterateur' who wanted 'to obtain some local colouring for an African romance'. In a letter to George S. Mackenzie, head of IBEA, Stanley called her 'an accomplished writer' who wanted to 'study native customs etc etc', his condescension perhaps justified, at least in his own mind, because he was after all the *man* who had made three dangerous and extended African journeys, none of them with a hint of 'etc etc' about them. He asked Mackenzie to help in any way he could 'to gratify her penchant for African matters to the full'.

James E. Blaine – 'Blaine of Maine', two-time American presidential candidate, then Secretary of State – wrote formally to his diplomatic officers that she wanted to visit coastal East Africa 'for historical purposes'. The notion that she would *stop* at the coast was one favoured by her male friends. The message inside their messages was clear enough: East Africa was no place for a woman.

What men believed she had told them she was going to do and what she believed she was going to do were rather different things, however. No doubt she was accustomed to having her ideas manipulated – and to manipulating – in this way. She was, after all, a Victorian woman, moneyed and privileged. Nothing in her expedition planning, however, or in her behaviour once she reached East Africa, suggests that she had any goal less demanding than to reach Kilimanjaro, and nothing suggests that writing a romantic novel was her real motivation. Later, she would be praised for her ethnological findings; she would be admitted to the Royal Geographical Society; and much would be made of the ability of a woman to elicit information that men could not – once she had done so; but before the event, she faced male disbelief, scorn, and strong opposition.

'[T]he English Parliament sat in judgment upon her apparently impracticable scheme, and did all in their power to prevent "that crazy woman" from starting out', a journalist wrote some years later. Sheldon herself said that 'at Zanzibar I found that my world-renowned reputation of mad woman had preceded me, to my prejudice. In America, England, Aden, and Mombasa, and now here, I had to listen to and confront as best I could public censure.'

She knew perfectly well what the *spoken* male objections to her expedition were: 'The fact was, it was feared that the consequences of a woman's leading a caravan might throw the natives into a frenzy, bring difficulties about which would involve the IBEA Co in trouble and expense to come to my rescue'. The unspoken objection – that success would take some of the lustre from masculine accomplishment – she left for men to deal with, if in fact she understood it.

She was amused by this male reluctance. 'Had I visited East Africa to study the anthropology and ethnology of the white man, instead of the native races, I have no doubt the research would have afforded novel results', she said. She planned, however, to study tribal women, and she would have preferred to do without men on the safari altogether.

Stanley and others in London provided lots of advice, and she arrived at Mombasa with her outfit complete and planned to the smallest detail. (Her expedition cost £4000 – of her own money. She had none of the institutional and governmental support that helped men like Stanley and Roosevelt.) Personnel, beads, and cloth remained to be got in Mombasa, but the rest had come with her by ship:

> tents and poles, chairs, folding tables, large waterproof canvases enveloping cork ground beds; large pieces of waterproof cloth, the ground cloth with which the tent is carpeted to keep the damp from rising from the earth; boxes of candles, soap, cartridges in boxes, matches, flints and steel, cotton

waste to clean the guns [70 of her men were to be armed with rifles she supplied], cocoanut oil, kerosene in large square tin cans, when emptied used for water cans, or bartered to the natives; coffee in sacks; lanterns, by night swung on poles, carried by a porter, with a light load; water bottles; photographic apparatus and instruments for observation; tools; medicine cases; large tin buckets for water; bath tub, hammock for the sick, and all manner of trifling accessories, and luxuries, and endless etceteras.

At the heart of her physical preparations was a custom-made 'palanquin' that she had designed herself. Made of aluminium, bamboo, and rattan, it was light (70 lb) and self-contained, designed to serve as sedan chair, bed, and boudoir. It had 'linings and fittings [of] yellow Indian silk, the cushions of down, and the awnings green canvas'. A huge engraved certificate from the Chicago Columbian Exhibition, where it was later exhibited, explained that it was 'fitted with lockers for wardrobe, toilet articles, and medicines, also having an adjustable table which is used for eating, reading, and writing . . . It is the most complete article of its kind possible to make, combining comfort, privacy, and luxury.'

In fact, she travelled only some of the time in the palanquin, often walking at the head of her column, but she slept in it frequently at night (inside a tent), and it was while in the palanquin that she had the accident that ended the expedition. That misfortune, however, still lay ahead in February of 1891.

In London she had envisaged a caravan of female porters and guides. This idea evaporated, however, in the heat of the realities of Mombasa and Zanzibar. Planning to hire female interpreters so she could 'mingle with the native women and children', she was frustrated by the unwillingness of multi-lingual, mission-trained women 'to go on *safari*'. Mostly what the missions had brought the women of the coast was Victorian propriety and a loathing for the bush.

She did not hesitate, however. Frustrated by women, she would use men. She was a pragmatist.

There were no porters – male or female – at Mombasa. Stanley had warned her that IBEA would be using every available man and woman (construction of the Uganda Railway had begun), and Mackenzie, despite Stanley's letter asking for help, was quick to tell her that none were available and that none could be had at Zanzibar, either. Undaunted, she sailed to Zanzibar and there appealed directly to the Sultan, who, though now powerless on the African continent, was still master of his own island. What the Islamic ruler made of the 'renowned mad woman' is unknown. He was certainly polite, perhaps fascinated. He showed her his harem. And he saw that she got porters. She had a little revenge on the men in England and Mombasa who hoped for failure. 'I had the satisfaction of knowing that in six days the so-called impossible had been accomplished, and by a *woman*.'

Stanley warned her not to venture beyond Mombasa. Perhaps he believed she would take one look at the dry plain beyond the coastal belt and give up.

Let me tender you my honest advice which you may follow or not as you please. Having performed the part of a friend in giving advice – you may follow your own inclinations.

1st Don't try to go further than the Free Methodist Mission – nine miles beyond Mombasa – for your own sake. . . .

After seeing Mombasa & its neighbourhood I do not think you will care to see any more especially if you get a real fever. A long stay will only bring out any lurking malady that you may have and you will certainly lose your good looks . . . All that you may gather West of Mombasa will not be worth the expense, loss of time, and material comforts you have sacrificed.

Expense, loss of time, and material comforts – not to mention her good looks – had not the importance that Stanley thought. (Had anybody warned Stanley that finding Livingstone might ruin his good looks?) The moment she could get her 153 people together and pull out of Mombasa, she did so, and in three days she was standing in the rain with a gun in each hand, threatening to shoot the men she had had such trouble hiring.

Worse was to come. 'Difficulty in marching through heavy rains', she wrote in a set of notes scribbled some years later, perhaps for a lecture. She had chosen to go in the rainy season, when so much mud accumulated on the porters' feet and legs that they had to keep stopping to scrape it off; and she constantly fell in the slippery track, herself. 'Heavy winds swept my tent away. Fall from Native Bridge . . . Shooting lions. Attempted capture or kidnapping. Dropped in River – Thorn in eye – crushed knee – Sleeping sickness – Tsetse fly'. She did not mention the random musket ball that hit her in the leg (an accident, though none the less painful for that) or the accident to her spine that ended the expedition. She did not get sleeping sickness, but was threatened by it; the thorn in her eye – acutely painful and threatening blindness – came when the man walking ahead of her let the branch of a thorntree snap back, and an inch-long thorn lodged in her left eye. Another man carefully removed the thorn, and she doctored herself – there was nobody else – and recovered.

And throughout, like her male counterparts, she served as the commander of what was (thanks probably to Stanley) in effect a military organization. Her hope of having a less masculine, perhaps more benign caravan of women had been dashed in Mombasa. The few women who did go with her (including a few female porters) were 'a perpetual nuisance', although one, Suzani, gave her daily massages that she greatly enjoyed. William Stairs, a South African veteran, had advised her to take women to show 'peaceful intentions', but she found them 'a decided detriment, [the cause of] unceasing anxiety and chagrin'. Whether this would have been true if there had been few or no men is an open question, for the problem with her women apparently was that they were so few – and therefore so much sought after – among so many males. On the other hand, no male safari leader who had women along has left a record of such 'anxiety and chagrin'. Was this female triviality, or female perception of something men missed?

The demands of the safari in fact turned her toward an unexpected maleness of behaviour. She had thought she could run her expedition without physical punishment, but

> coaxing arguments and persuasive talks were disregarded and sneeringly laughed at, probably the more so because *I, their leader*, was a woman . . . I do not think I could have [maintained command] if I had not most unwillingly changed my lifelong ideas about whipping. An appeal to physical force has always seemed to me to be brutal, and degrading alike to victim and administrator.

To be the first white woman in East Africa, therefore, she believed she was forced by circumstance to become in part a man – a grim satisfaction, perhaps, to the men who had opposed her. But she had been cast in a role whose only models were male, and she had even dressed herself as half a one – her travelling dresses had military jackets and caps; she was a man, as it were, from the waist up.

She followed more or less the same route as H. H. Johnston's Kilimanjaro expedition from the coast to Taveta, stopping at the places established by caravan use. Her picture of some of these is not of an untouched Africa; one campsite was 'as filthy and disgusting as can be imagined . . . used before and cluttered with junk and rubbish'. She demanded cleanliness around her and had her clothes washed daily, bathing each evening in a separate bathing tent, using the palanquin as an island of purity. All her water was boiled.

The pattern of her days was the pattern of Roosevelt's and all the others': up with the dawn, under way in the cool of the morning, a site chosen and camp set up again some 12–20 miles along. When the area was right for contacts, she stayed for some days, following Stairs's guidelines for a camp on a military model: at the centre of a thorn fence were the myriad belongings of the safari, under waterproof covers if rain threatened. To one side was her tent, with palanquin, table, and chair. The porters' fires and beds were laid out in a large circle just inside the fence.

She would send out messengers to bring local people, especially women, into her camp. There, seated in her palanquin or standing on a rock or a box (she came to prefer the elevated position, especially among the taller Masai), she received. Her normal costume was one of the walking outfits she had had made in London, one with gold braid on the front and a little peaked cap. For eminent visitors or difficult moments, she wore the gown in which she had appeared at Victoria's court, studded all over with imitation jewels. By the time her expedition was done, most of the jewels were gone, given away as gifts.

She had a great sense of style. She was also something of a performer. Knowing she was an oddity – there was no question that a white woman was remarkable – she encouraged the idea that she was a visiting ruler. The European press later turned this into a lot of 'white queen of Africa' journalism (the spirit of Rider Haggard still reigned), but it is certain that the white self-image of superiority had hardened, and she took advantage of it. Male Africans were impressed. Here was a woman for whom 150 black men worked.

She gathered ethnological materials, and she gathered people. Especially women. She lured them with a combination of glamour, gifts, and genuine sympathy. With one – 'The Woman of Taveta', as Sheldon called her – she spied on an all-male celebration and on a funeral. She did some doctoring, that inevitable emanation of power that would be expected of all safaris. She exchanged visits with local power figures (a wily old *hongo*-extorter, Mandara, was still soliciting gifts on the slopes of Kilimanjaro) and collected data on activities as diverse as Chaga metal-smithing and the making of honey beer. And when she was done, she had accomplished what men had not – she had looked into the lives of East African people.

In part, this achievement was the result of sympathy – not a racial sympathy (tribal people were 'primitives', to her, not 'savages') but a psychological one. But, partly, it was the result of process: setting a different goal for her safari. She was not there to hunt; she hunted only as much as was necessary to shoot meat for some of the men. She was not there to rescue somebody. She was not there to 'discover' some geographical first. (She did climb down into a volcanic crater and paddle about Lake Chaga, and this was an act of courage, but it was hardly an important accomplishment in geography.) She was not there to convert or to preach or to save from slavery. She would build no railway, survey no boundary, subjugate no tribe.

Ironically, she accomplished most by being denied accomplishment in those areas that men had defined as important. Instead, she established a new reason for going to East Africa: to meet the people. She was, in a sense, the first East African tourist. Put more accurately, she was the first real East African traveller.

Homeward bound in German Tanganyika, she suffered the accident that abruptly ended her observations. Halfway across a rope bridge in the palanquin, she was dropped into a river when her porters slipped; when they pulled her from the water and tried to carry her up the bank, they dropped her again, her spine landing on a rock. Half paralysed and often unconscious, she was returned to Mombasa and put on a ship for home. She brought with her her notes and the great collection of material culture she had gathered on and around Kilimanjaro. She proved that East Africa was a woman's country, too.

'A great deal depended, not on the fact as to whether women or men went among these people, but on the manner in which they went and how they conducted themselves', she said in a speech to the British Association. The remark was met by cheers, it was reported.

Yet some confusion persisted in her own mind. Two years later, she was quoted as saying that 'exploration is not the forte of woman, because it requires too much self-sacrifice and too great power of command'. And years later, after time spent in the Belgian Congo, she wrote, 'Africa reveals to everyone who sojourns there any length of time, *himself*... Africa is undoubtedly a most fascinating wild mistress. She gets a tenacious hold on most persons, bewitching, magnetic, that is almost irresistible and once experienced is never lulled into forgetfulness.'

The sexual metaphor and the reversal of genders were ironic, although not, probably, intentionally so.

Even at the time that May French Sheldon visited Kilimanjaro, some of Stanley's cautions (including its being unsafe to go with even 1000 rifles in Masai country) were out of date, if they had ever been justified. By the time of the next solo female traveller (1907), so quickly had change come that she was able to make part of the journey without any armed guard at all, and for most of her time in East Africa to make do with only two soldiers. None the less, hers was a remarkable undertaking – an adventure of more than a year that took her from the tip of South Africa to the mouth of the Nile. While she was not the first to have covered the entire continent from south to north (a male empire-builder named Ewart Grogan had done that in 1898–9 and had taken Rhodes's dream for the journey's name – Cape-to-Cairo), she was most certainly the first woman, probably one of the first handful of people, to do it at all. And yet, when she returned to London, the Royal Geographical Society had her make only one speech on her accomplishment – for an audience of children.

Neither geographer nor anthropologist, she was of that formidable sort of Englishwoman represented by Celia Fiennes, the tireless seventeenth-century traveller. Already in her late 40s by the time she started in 1907, she was strong-bodied, far from sylph-like, quite imperturbable. Having taken up travelling for her health years before, she had already ranged widely over the world, but this was her first – and only – trip in Africa. Her name was Mary Hall – always *Miss* Mary Hall.

Railways and inland steamers now carried passengers over much of Mary Hall's route, and she was able to use the chain of lakes that separate East and Central Africa as a highway. Yet formidable obstacles remained: disease, vicious local wars, unpredictable services, stretches of wilderness that took up to three months to cross on foot. Mary Hall was up to the challenge, bringing to Africa, besides a huge curiosity and a tolerance for solitude, the traveller's saving grace of humour. Facing a charge of hundreds of spear-carrying men who thought she had kidnapped a fellow tribesman, she compared her likely fate to that of St Sebastian, 'mentally substituting spears for arrows'. She waited for the attack, 'sitting on a box of food, which I hoped I might live to want, even although it was in tins'. The attack became a friendly embassy when she apologized, made reparations (in salt) for the man her askaris had 'borrowed' from his village, and chatted with the young leader of the avenging party.

She also had the sensible virtue of not crying over spilled milk, even less over milk that had almost spilled. Set down in German Tanganyika at a point where the German Commandant came within an eyelash of refusing to let her proceed, she said, 'I cannot imagine what would have happened. . . . But there is no need to reflect on what might have been.'

That hers was an essentially sunny cast of mind is clear from her habit of comparing even the wildest of places to familiar ones that could be considered only benign and safe. A pleasant morning in southern Tanganyika reminded her of Westmorland or Cumberland; grass fires burning at night on the Belgian Congo side of the border reminded her of 'the promenade at Hastings or Brighton with the piers illuminated'. Rwanda looked like the West Indies; the Great Rift Valley looked like the London Zoo. In a companion, this habit of comparing the exotic to the familiar quickly wears; to the lone traveller, it was undoubtedly at times a comfort.

And lone she was. She took no servant, no companion. From Rhodesia north, she had a small dog, which managed to live through the trip despite their being continually in leopard and hyena country. She kept it in her tent at night, perhaps not understanding that the little animal was the favourite food of leopards, which would not have balked at coming in to get it. Perhaps she was lucky, along with everything else.

She first touched East Africa in southern Tanganyika, when she left the Lake Nyasa steamer at Karonga. From there, she proceeded on foot to the southern end of Lake Tanganyika, then by another boat the length of that lake to Usumbura. A very long foot safari awaited her there, taking her across a good chunk of western Tanganyika to Bukoba on Lake Victoria, where another steamboat would take her across that largest of African lakes to Uganda, where, again, she would organize a new caravan and set out for Lake Albert and, after yet another foot journey, the navigable portion of the Nile. The ease of this lake travel should not be misunderstood: the boats were small and passenger accommodation was sometimes crude (leaving her once living on deck); the lakes themselves were small oceans, with sometimes deadly storms.

Land travel was not necessarily either easier or safer. Only 10 years had gone by since the battle of Omdurman had ended a violent anti-Western regime that had gripped all of southern Egypt, Sudan, and parts of Uganda. The Germans were fighting major actions in parts of Tanganyika (the Maji Maji rebellion), and the British had just 'punished' the Nandi of western Kenya for objecting to a great many things, not least among them being taxed for the privilege of being governed. Malaria and sleeping sickness were rampant along parts of the route, including the southern end of Lake Victoria. The overland parts of the journey would take her up to 5000 feet and down almost to sea level – into autumnal cold and sweltering heat. She would, for weeks at a time, be the only white in black territory, at a time when neither she nor blacks were able to think in any but racial terms. Her whiteness isolated – and marked – her. So did her gender.

Yet she never hesitated.

She took 2 askaris and about 35 porters. This was the sum and substance of her expedition – without institutional or governmental support, without scores of advisers. Some canned food (which she despised), the usual beads and cloth to trade for her porters' posho, and she was off – two or three months through the bush, then a dissolution of that little safari at a lake port, and then the formation of another at the end of that lake's steamer journey. You would think she had been 20 times in Africa – no headman, no white hunter, no Stanley advising and cautioning. 'A caravan of forty gives one woman rather more than she can do, especially if she is unacquainted with the vernacular', was all she said. She sounds just a little like that other loner, Neumann.

Her version of May French Sheldon's palanquin was the machila, a form of sedan-chair she had used in Mozambique. In English countries, she called it a hammock, but it was more elaborate than the word implies, with stout double poles for carrying, a canvas roof, and adjustable canvas sides. The men who carried this took turns during the four- to six-hour days, *running* with it for much of the day's journey. (In Uganda, so good were the roads that she used what she called a 'ricksha', a wheeled sulkey pulled by several men.) Mornings, she walked in good weather – often 8 or 10 miles – and then used the machila when the heat came on. She was no fading flower.

Starting out with this caravan for the first time, she found that 'nothing is done quickly in Central Africa'. She had to re-check all her supplies. Then 'my part was to concentrate my mind on the choice of a few of those delightful tinned delicacies to which I had the least objection'. She could never hide this distaste for canned foods, but she enjoyed 'soups, biscuits, California fruits, jams, cocoa, and condensed milk', as well as the dried foods, rice, flour, and so on that her men were able to carry.

Finding porters at the ends of the lake journeys was a hit-or-miss task. Unlike May French Sheldon, she had no mandate from the Sultan of Zanzibar, but only the help of harried local officials.

The askari brought round, and marshalled before me, the most bloodthirsty looking set of reprobates imaginable, accompanied by a note from the [German] Commandant, saying that these men did not wish to go to Victoria Nyanza . . . but that he would force them to go my way if I wished it.

I soon made up my mind that, as I wished to live to tell the story, I would much rather he forced them in any other direction than mine. So I sent back a note, saying that 'I was extremely obliged, but that if it came to force I would rather wait until I got to [my destination] to exert it'.

At another setting-out point, she was made to deposit £20 as a bond against her killing any of the porters.

There was a touch of humour about this arrangement which rather took my fancy. There was I, one poor, unprotected woman, without firearms of any description ... with forty savage-looking blacks, who were armed with spears and other warlike implements ... and I was asked to give my assurance that I would do them no harm.

Yet, she inevitably concluded that each set of porters were 'good fellows'.
Astonishingly, she had never slept in a tent before, never lived off the land.

It was my first experience of camping, and of being alone with so many natives. Lion and leopard stories, highly coloured by a vivid imagination, were very fresh in my memory; also, the recollection of the expostulations of nearly all my relations and friends, against the foolishness of such an undertaking. ... [Yet] I was relieved on waking [the first morning] to find all and everything intact.

Off early, she walked for several miles, then had herself carried. It rained a good deal, and much of her journey was in swamp, yet the porters were heroic in keeping her above the water, even in breast-deep rivers. At one particularly deep river, she confessed, she was rather looking forward to going behind a bush, stripping herself to the skin, and walking 'through the water in my mackintosh'. She was disappointed that this measure was not required. Perhaps that African imp of the perverse had bitten her, that desire to throw off Western clothes – even in the shelter of a raincoat.

When camp was made, her tent was put at the centre, and a circle of 'charming little circular huts of interlaced grasses and reeds, thickly thatched with banana leaves' went up around it. The two askaris, each of whom had his own porter, had their own small tent, as well as two canvas camp chairs, in which they lounged while the others worked. She took this to be normal military behaviour. None of the Stanley-inspired military organization of the Sheldon camps prevailed.

A hot bath was prepared for the Englishwoman, the water not always of the best, but she seems to have preferred even hot brown mud at the end of the day to nothing at all. 'There was only time in the morning for a "lick and a promise", the promise always being fulfilled by a hot bath half an hour before dinner.' The bath-tub itself – apparently a metal one, not folding canvas – was used also as a washtub; despite precautions, her clothes kept shrinking more each time they were washed, 'a serious matter when the nearest outfitter was 1,000 miles away'.

Her greatest fear was of a chill. The source of chill was damp; therefore, she put her clothes at night in a tin box and changed to dry ones each morning and after each wetting. Tents, not then having waterproof floors, easily became flooded, and damp 'mists' rose through the camp bed; the preventive for this was ditching, but in a downpour the rain came in, anyway. After the rain, therefore, came the drying-out.

As soon as the rain ceased all my things were removed . . . and the wet earth scraped away. Several small fires were then lighted inside [the tent], the warm ashes from which were afterwards spread about to dry the ground . . . the driest leaves that could be found were brought in and placed under the ground sheet, and the tent once more became habitable.

As she knew nothing of tents, this process must have been the initiative of her porters. Perhaps they were 'good fellows' because she treated them as such.

Toward the end of the overland portion of her Tanganyikan journey, her two askaris reached the limit of their territory and left her. 'The whole caravan was now without a firearm of any description, and still eight or nine days must elapse before I could expect to be under the protection of Europeans once more.' That night's camp was in wild bush; 'a more desolate spot it would be difficult to imagine'. She found comfort in her situation, none the less: without the askaris, 'we should get along better with the people *en route*', and the wilderness campsite 'had its own peculiar enchantment'.

Needless to say, she made it quite safely to the shore of Lake Victoria. How could it have been otherwise?

A lake steamer took her to Port Florence (so named after the wife of the engineer of the Uganda Railway, a name that lasted less than two years), from which she took a side-trip on the railway to Nairobi and back. Only nine unusable miles of the railway had existed when May French Sheldon left Mombasa, and Nairobi had been an unpeopled swamp. Now Masai warriors walked to the little stations to show themselves off, and the railway carriages provided folding berths for travellers (but bring your own bedding). Nairobi she found a bustling town: 'The private residences, the Barracks, and the Club with its beautiful tennis courts, are built on a hill overlooking the town'. The *Globetrotter* reported on her brief visit.

She returned to Port Florence by rail and crossed Victoria, this time to the northwest, and disembarked in Uganda. From there, her journey led her north – to Lake Albert by ricksha, then across the lake and along the Nile; and so down that river that so recently had seen so much European and African blood shed, so many ambitions and visions destroyed, and that had so quickly become a merely quaint and picturesque means to float the tourist's steamer.

So she spins away in her wheeled buggy, the ricksha-men's dark legs churning up the dust – to stop once, as a faster runner overtakes them, carrying in his cleft stick a letter for her, its envelope marked, as with the thumb-print of history, 'On His Britannic Majesty's Service'.

She died in 1919 of pneumonia. She was 62. The last view she had out her window was of Hampstead – which reminded her, perhaps, of the green fields of Africa.

These were not the only safari women. One can point to many more: Agnes Herbert; C. G. Buxton, who hunted from Gondokoro to Victoria in early 1910; Karen Blixen (Isak Dinesen), who led a train of ox-carts down to Lake Magadi at the beginning of the First World War; Mary Akeley, whose husband died in the gorilla country of Rwanda, leaving her to carry on their expedition on her first trip to Africa; Vivienne de Watteville, who did the same when her father, gathering specimens for a museum, was killed by a lion. By and large, however, we know little of the women who led safaris, probably because it has been men who have left most of the records. The suspicion that this is more than accidental must not be ignored: is there a vested interest of male-written history that supports the myth of the safari: Stanley's army of men with rifles, Thomson's glorification of the danger of the Masai?

In fact, the world of East African women is learned only with difficulty from safari accounts. Gonera, 'a wealthy Indian widow', was merely mentioned by Stanley as one who 'exports much cloth, beads, and wire into the far interior, and imports in return much ivory', but clearly she was a major trader. Much of what we learn of women we get by indirection (Peters's 'the houses in which the porters are lodged, in many cases with their young wives'), sometimes by implication and sometimes by what is not said rather than by what is. And what we learn is complicated by the fact that 'woman' is confused with 'sex' (in a way that women writers do not confuse 'man' and sex).

Indeed, the whole subject of sex and safari is complicated – and complicated even further by the ways in which white and black are seen. What should be remembered, however, is the relative lack of white women in East Africa before 1920, and the situation of black women. As we have already seen, women had had an established place in the Arab caravan trade. Safaris using female porters were rarely seen as late as 1913 (White encountered an all-female safari carrying goods for an Indian trader) but had earlier been common. 'Safari wives' and at least casual prostitution were common (although prostitution in the European sense – for money or keep – may in fact have been 'practically unknown' until 'civilization' came). Sex seems to have been a normal aspect of safari life until the Europeans showed up. Then a shift was made: women were eased out of their working role and were made furtive about their sexual role (into which they were now driven by lack of employment?).

It was against this background that white women entered the safari. If they entered it in defined sexual roles (Buxton's daughter, Petherick's wife) they were accepted but unnoticed. (Only bibliographers, for example, notice that Katherine Petherick wrote most of *Travels in Central Africa*.) If they tried to enter in any other role, they had difficulty. The nature of that difficulty changed from period to period.

Safari accounts are typically as sexless as Boy Scout handbooks, the matters at hand, it is implied, being carried forward without any interruption from the loins. On the other hand, it is a staple of Western imagery that the sort of man who goes on safari is also the sort of man whose libido brooks no obstacle. What, one dares to ask, did the men do all those weeks?

Until at least the 1930s, men who wrote about safaris frequently referred to black women – or included photographs of them – in vaguely voyeuristic sexual terms. Rainsford referred to 'smart black women, often with very fine figures', Edwardian code for bare-breasted. Photos of those breasts can be found in book after book, often with giggly titles like 'Masai belles'. Behind this rather adolescent peeping lay a sometimes cruel reality: white men's sexual use of black women.

'In a community dominated by males, [men] . . . were not so bigoted . . . where sex was concerned. . . . Concubinage was recognized (if unmentioned) as one of the perks.' As early as 1904, Nairobi had whorehouses stocked with 'Masai and other tribal women', at least some of whose clients were white. Richard Meinertzhagen noted a white named Smith who told young Kikuyu women that to be Christians they had to sleep with him, and 'he [slept] with one or two . . . a week'.

White officialdom was no different. 'Every [railway official] in Nairobi keeps a native girl, usually a Masai, and there is a regular trade in [them].' (Some Masai lived close to Nairobi, but so did many Kikuyu; a preference for Masai 'girls' may have come from an aspect of Masai culture that involved pre-circumcision women in permissible non-reproductive sex, which would have meshed nicely with the white males' demand for non-reproductive sex.) 'If a man tires of his girl he goes to the village . . . and gets a new one, or in several cases as many as three girls. And my brother [military] officers are no exceptions.' This matter of what officially became known as 'concubinage' reached parliamentary debate at least once in the decade, and by 1909 was the subject of a confidential enclosure in a Colonial Office circular that appealed for 'loyal co-operation in vigorously reprobating and officially condemning' it. Co-operation, like cold showers, was apparently not enough: as late as the 1950s, John Gunther was still reporting on 'white men' who were 'much more apt to have liaisons with black women than vice versa'.

Thus, white male permissiveness toward white male sex with black women existed before and during the safari period. At least one white hunter has left an account of being asked to pimp for his clients. Hemingway's protagonist in *The Green Hills of Africa* (autobiographical) asks his gunbearer to get him a young black woman, and Hemingway himself had a possibly non-sexual 'affair' with a young Kamba woman on his second safari. A number of men have written of being offered women by African 'chiefs', a situation that may rather murkily show either habitual practice, self-aggrandizement, or factual decoration.

There is no question, then, that black women were seen as permissible sex partners on safari. Even less, however, is there any question that white women were impermissible partners of any kind on safari. 'One woman in a party was always a devil of a nuisance.' 'They're best left at home . . . By and large they simply aren't tough enough, and when they are they're often inexplicable.' 'No trip for a woman.' And when women were grudgingly found acceptable, they were found so in terms that shifted credit to the other gender. 'She has the brains and knowledge of a man without the fine gossamer threads of a woman's feelings having been injured.' '[Hers] was the voice of a boy . . . She was all like a boy, straight, flexible, narrow in the hips . . . And that was no doubt why he had liked her; there was nothing consciously feminine about her, nothing that insisted on her sex.'

In other words, if you had to have a woman along, you wanted a woman like a man – or, better yet, like a boy.

In other words, the trouble with women was men.

Matters had not (and perhaps have not) changed much since Stanley's day. Stanley found women (that is, sex) always getting in the way. The first night out from Unyanyembe, he wrote petulantly, 'one-half the men had returned . . . to take one more embrace of their wives and concubines'. When he wanted Bombay, he was 'found weeping in the arms of his Delilah'. Shaw, another Englishman, 'was taken very ill last night . . . I suspect it is a fierce attack of venereal infection.' In other words, sex is the devil's work, and woman is the devil's tool.

Very late in the safari's life, when they had formed the East African Professional Hunters Association, the white hunters voted to ban women from membership.

I suspect that there were actually two reasons for men's distaste for women on safari. One was sexual (white women complicated things like sex with black women), and the other was political (if women can do what men can do, what is a man?). The second has probably been the more important.

Many women went to East Africa for different reasons from men. Some went to hunt, to be sure, but some went merely to see (Mary Hall, for example) and some to study the place from a new perspective (May French Sheldon). That they did not go to conquer or to kill allowed them to go in a different way – with many fewer guns and with much less complex organization. What such women suggest may be that the paramilitary organization handed down from the Arab slavers through Burton, Speke, Stanley, and Thomson to the hunting safaris was more myth-making than substance – necessary to male sense of self rather than necessary to the actual conduct and organization of a safari.

Yet the maleness of the safari dies hard, and the male idea of the rarity of his own accomplishment dies even harder. Most male safari accounts are still couched in terms of violence and danger, so it is worth remembering that, only six years after Ewart Grogan made his Cape-to-Cairo journey, that 'remarkable journey', as the *Oxford History of East Africa* has it, Mary Hall did the same thing. And within months of the young Astor Chanler's 'expedition of 180 men around the mountain of Kilima-Njaro and through the land of the Masai, where Henry Stanley has said it is not safe to go with even a thousand rifles', May French Sheldon did the same thing with fewer men and only 70 guns – which she did not really seem to need. And that despite Blaney Percival's contention that a safari to the wilds was 'no trip for a woman', many women did in fact thrive on it.

What the women who led safaris suggest is twofold: that women were as capable in the line as men; and that, going with different goals and different methods, they made many of men's endeavours seem over-wrought and, just possibly, self-serving.

5

LIONS AND CHAMPAGNE

1920–1940

THE effects of the First World War on East Africa were immense. The map changed: what had been German East Africa became a British colony, Tanganyika. Terminology changed: the East African Protectorate became Kenya Colony and Protectorate. The population changed: under a scheme to reward war veterans with land, a new influx of whites – the 'soldier settlers' – quickly took place, and the 3000 Europeans of 1911 became 9000 by 1921.

Wartime had been difficult. German East Africa was a battleground for years; its black residents were conscripted by first one side, then the other, as the British drove the Germans south. Kenya and Uganda gave up 390,000 African men between them; Kenya alone suffered 44,000 black casualties. Agricultural production, at first damaged, see-sawed; 1917 saw a famine 'during which it [is] estimated that 3000 [black] children died' in the Fort Hall District.

The immediate postwar period was even worse economically. A recession, coupled with an enforced devaluation of currency in 1920, left residents overnight with sharply increased debts and sharply decreased assets. Yet population continued to increase – 17,000 whites and 40,000 Indians by 1931. The European population began to change its social structure (and some of its values) during the 1920s, too, producing that 'Happy Valley' group who were its most extreme – and visible – form. The pioneers had been killed in the war or they were tired or they grew old, and in their place were a new, less adventurous group, very much of the period. These were the times of *The Vortex*, *The Green Hat*, and *The Waste Land*, of short skirts, Kraft-Ebbing, and potted Freud. People in England sniggered at the joke, 'Are you married or do you live in Kenya?' and Anthony Powell created a character who 'had never been the same after Kenya'. The period gave birth to a new kind of luxury in the bush – what Denis Holman has dubbed the 'champagne safari'.

The war had had another impact. Game herds were reduced. The Game Ranger estimated that 40,000 head had been killed for meat for the army; worse yet, much of the killing had been in the Southern Game Reserve, where he estimated 'far more' had been killed in two years than in ten on legal hunting lands.

Nor had all the killing been for food. British soldiers with military weapons had 'killed off most of the rhinos' in the Reserve for recreation. Some of the game would come back, but never to the old levels. And as they recovered, they would face a pressure far worse than machine guns: an expanding population and a growing agricultural economy.

'Nairobi was the heart of the big game country and nearly every sportsman who came to Africa to shoot big game outfitted in Nairobi.' That much had not changed. By the early 1920s, a new arrival found it 'a fine town, modern in its conveniences, its streets filled with motor-cars, with policemen on point duty'. Visitors still arrived by ship at Mombasa and took the overnight train up, but the trains were more comfortable and the ride less dusty.

By 1928, Nairobi had begun to fill up with people who imitated the pioneers – that is, the old days had so entered the consciousness (and, thus, were so completely over) that they were the subject of nostalgia. 'Ridiculous looking "dudes" roam up and down the streets, dressed in khaki and bulging with firearms.' 'Nairobi was largely.peopled with young men wearing corduroy plus-fours or shorts, lurid green, orange, blue and purple shirts, and Stetson hats. Some had revolvers in their belts. They imparted a certain Wild West atmosphere to the town.' Depending on the observer's temperament, the place was either 'one of the shabbiest and shoddiest towns I have seen' or 'the Paris of the East African coast'.

The well-to-do traveller's focal point was still the Norfolk, 'the old stone hostel ... the rendezvous of English officials, sportsmen, white hunters, travellers, and the more fortunate empire pioneers'. There was also the New Stanley, where you could stay for less than £1 a day, but one visitor found it 'dirty and inefficient and full of white tykes'.

As the safari industry rebuilt, the Tanganyikan town of Arusha developed as a secondary centre, made possible by the Englishing of the former German area. Located on the slopes of Kilimanjaro in an area of beauty close to good game areas, Arusha drew English settlers, as well, and some white hunters moved their businesses and their homes there in the 1930s. White settlement remained small, however, and the tone of Tanganyika was different from that of Kenya: few European farmers, no 'agonizing day-in day-out colour bar', no native reserves.

With Tanganyika a British mandate, the safari professionals discovered two new wonderlands: the Serengeti plains and Ngorongoro crater. Both were too far from Nairobi for most visitors, but the motor car would change that. The Serengeti, contiguous with the Kenyan Mara country, was a vast home to plains game and lions; Stewart Edward White had heard of it before the war – 'a grass plain many days' journey across, with a lake in the middle, swarming with game and lions ... some big volcanoes ... with forests and meadows and elephants in the craters'. Ngorongoro was a miniature jewel, a crater floor only 25 miles across but teeming with animals, an East Africa in miniature.

Although the Arabs had known of it and a German had visited it in the 1890s, it was still *terra nova* to the British in the early 1920s. J. A. Hunter, James Clark, and T. Alexander Barns all saw it shortly after the war and were dumbfounded, Clark calling it 'that most perfect of all animal Edens'. East African Germans had had a plan during the war to slaughter the game and build a meat-packing plant in the crater, but the war turned against them before the plan was carried out.

It became possible to sail to Tanga on the Tanganyikan coast and take the German-built railway inland to Arusha. However, once the motor car arrived in numbers, Nairobi's hold on the safari market was reaffirmed, for you could drive to the Serengeti in a day – at least if you were 'someone who has no pity for his own bones or for his car', and Arusha remained only a secondary centre.

Even before the cars and the roads, however, it was clear that 'the Africa that was' had gone. Some old names disappeared: Selous had been killed in combat in the war (at 64); Cuninghame had retired; Roosevelt had died. In 1923, Newland & Tarlton went under, replaced by the new firm of Safarilands, which was to become 'the Cook's of big game hunting'. Leslie Tarlton and Cuninghame had a piece of it, but their influence was greatly lessened. In time, other companies like African Guides and Gethin & Hewlett appeared to give Safarilands competition.

The safari itself was altered. By the late 1920s, cruise ships were sending passengers for an overnight 'safari' by rail to Nairobi and back, viewing game from the train. People complained of the 'commercialization of big-game hunting for American tourists', but safaris had been 'commercial' since 1906; what was new was the complaint, not the thing complained of. The anti-Americanism was another symptom of change, although it had been fore-shadowed in the criticisms of Roosevelt.

By 1932, the Kenya Game Warden was writing that 'transport over almost all the shooting country in Kenya is now mainly mechanical', and the foot safari was 'a thing of the past'. In this new, more mechanical and perhaps more impersonal atmosphere, some of the heart had gone out of it all. '[My] trophies . . . represent neither skill nor courage', one hunter confessed.

The complaints suggest that there were more safari clients than ever. Yet the increased numbers, if they existed, were not reflected in a proportional increase in full hunting licences, which hovered below 30 a year until 1930 (except for 1925, when the Game Warden suggested that the visit of the Duke and Duchess of York inspired the 56 sold); this number climbed to 36, then 43, then tumbled to only 9 in the first year of the Great Depression, after which it averaged 20 a year until the Second World War. These numbers seem very low – hardly more than pre-war – but it must be remembered that the cheaper Tanganyika licence was selling 40-odd a year in the same period and the Uganda another 5 to 10, and a new 14-day licence was popular for wives, children, or penny-pinchers. None the less, the licence figures suggest that 'sportsmen' and 'big game hunters' were far fewer than legend had made them.

(But unquestionably there was a lot of hunting: in 1926, for example, more than 3000 licences of all kinds were sold, almost 90 per cent of them for bird-shooting. The remainder were divided among residents – a large proportion – full and 14-day visitors', and elephant-only licences.)

In fact, the safari image had been created and was being embellished. That image included an East Africa swarming with wealthy hunters after lion and elephant. The facts of licence sales suggest, however, a very modest number of hunters after the Big Five (lion, elephant, leopard, rhino, buffalo) and more after plains game or not on safari to hunt, at all.

James Clark believed that in the 1920s the safari became a wealthy fad, a '"thing to do," for it brought more fame and prestige to the otherwise idle rich'. However, a great many of the pre-war visitors had been idle and rich, too, or they would not have had the time and money to be there. The real change appears to have been in the perception of the safari client and the safari, rather than in the things themselves. Before the war, they had been – except for Roosevelt – the subject mostly of books and articles for fairly specialized readers; after the war, they became increasingly the subject of films and of general-audience magazines. The 1920s were a period of self-advertised wealth and idleness, which lapped over into the Depression as counterpoint to widespread economic want.

By the mid-1930s, it was accepted wisdom that safari clients came from three sorts of people: American millionaires, maharajahs, and movie stars. The perception was common enough to warrant satire: a safari with 'Silas K. Vanderoil, the Hon. Timothy Monocle; Sadie Vanderoil, daughter of the magnate; the Ranee of Salt Lake City, and Miss Googooeye Hollywood, the famous film constellation'. The facts are otherwise; most clients continued to be well-to-do businessmen who were working rich rather than idle rich, but perception of them was highly coloured by the publicity surrounding a number of safaris of the period: those of the Duke and Duchess of York (1925); George Eastman (1926 and 1928); the Prince of Wales (1928 and 1930); and Ernest Hemingway (1934). These safaris and their wealthy clients had that attribute so loved of these two decades and the 1940s, 'glamour'.

Glamour somewhat replaced Roosevelt's 'manliness' as the prime attribute of the safari visitor. (Indeed, it appears that 'manliness' now attached to the white hunter, who did not have the attributes of glamour – money, fashionable clothes, 'sophistication' – but of virility – independence, functional clothes, skill.) The change may explain Gandar Dower's sense that his trophies were meaningless. It also explains the 'champagne safari', which fairly dripped with glamour (gussied up in conspicuous consumption, one of glamour's favourite costumes). Luxury had always been possible on safari – witness Stanley and Donaldson Smith – but earlier periods had not focused on it. The 1920s and 1930s did.

For the safari had got caught up in the modern rush toward worship of fame and money. With Cunard liners, the Orient Express, fast cars, and air travel, it became a stage-setting for newsreels and feature stories about the new culture heroes.

And the safari got shorter. Clark blamed the motor car, which allowed people to get around quickly and hurry away so as to boast of what they had done. But the safari had been getting shorter since Stanley. (Roosevelt's was in fact an anomaly.) The car contributed, but the fact was that the world was speeding up, and East Africa was rapidly becoming a known quantity, not a great mystery that required months to solve.

None the less, the motor car had an incontestable impact. It drove the porter from the field, utterly changing the experience for the visitor. No more line of tiny figures snaking through the high grass; no more sound of chanting and drumming on the march; no more bustle as 50 or 100 men built huts or put up tents, gathered wood, cooked their posho; no more songs and talk in the darkness. No more for the European the ego-inflating sense of being captain of a ship far out at sea, master and judge of a mass of men; no more the godly dispensing of medicine, justice, food. In a word, no more African earth.

For what was lost was the whites' best contact with Africa and her people. Nairobi was not Africa; it was a segregated colonial after-image of a European city. The white hunter was not Africa. The tent, the mosquito netting, the guns, these were not Africa; they were in it but not of it, European fences against it. The car denied Europeans what Elias Mandala has called in a different context 'meaningful contact with Africans living outside the society of the colonizers'. Porters were rarely outside that society, but they stood with at least one foot over its border; they gave the European a chance to watch, hear, smell, touch people who actually had been born, lived, would die in this magnificent strangeness. And the car ended that. The few safari African workers who were left – gunbearers, cooks, personal servants – were becoming professionals themselves, men with both feet firmly in the colonial culture.

Porters did not vanish all at once. Barns and Dugmore, heading for Ngorongoro just after the war, gave up on their cars early, Barns at Arusha and Dugmore a day's travel farther on. Roads did not exist, and cars were light, their tyres vulnerable. Yet Maxwell in 1921 drove from Nairobi to Nyeri for lunch, and went on to Nanyuki for the night. In the same year, a man named Engelbrecht had the dubious historical honour of running the first *mutatu* (jitney) service – Nairobi-Nanyuki by Hupmobile.

By 1923, Vivienne de Watteville found 100 miles of road between Meru and the Upper Tana, and Leslie Tarlton drove all the way to Marsabit.

An American named Sutton, arriving in Nairobi for his safari in 1924, did the new equivalent of visiting the Sultan and scouring the bazaar for porters: he bought a Ford. Already adapted for safari work with a wooden 'box body', it had been first bought (by another American) for £225, used on his safari, sold to Sutton for £125, and was used and sold by him for £100. Local *fundi* (craftsmen) were and are wonderfully adept, and they soon created an open,

high-sided car body style adapted to hunting. (But Daniel Streeter said
unkindly that what they called a 'safari car' in Nairobi was what they called a
delivery wagon back in Buffalo, New York.)

Porterage hung on for a few years. A bastard form evolved: train or car as
far as it would go, then porters. As late as 1928, a safari went out with 100
porters, 2 skinners, 2 mess boys, and a head man. In 1933, on the other hand,
a safari went out with only 10 Africans.

In part, it depended on the country you were going to: were there roads?
But, especially on the plains, a usable road was merely somebody else's tracks,
and so the driveable part of safariland pushed out and pushed out, and soon
there was no need for porters at all. Everything went by lorries, which neither
ate posho nor demanded fresh meat nor sang.

Kodak king George Eastman had three General Motors cars and a mechanic
shipped out from Detroit for his use, but most people made do with what they
found in Nairobi. The box-bodied Ford remained a favourite, but other makes
quickly appeared – a 'Packard with safari body', a Rolls; and, for the Prince
of Wales's safari, '4 Albion lorries . . . [a] "Hudson" car, [a] "Buick" [which]
HRH drove himself . . . [two] "Willys-Knight" box-cars, the "Rolls-
Royce"'. Cars were 'sybaritic', but 'HRH had a time limit'. He was a man of
his time: more and more people had time limits. 'But it is not quite the same
thing as . . . *King Solomon's Mines.*'

Tyres burst, hissed, collapsed, and disintegrated, but the cars rolled on.
Buxton made 125 miles *in mud* in a day in 1927; the Vanderbilts made 200 in
1934 'but it took us all day, because the roads are so awful'; Szechenyi was
three days getting from Nairobi to Mt Kenya, 'up to the axles . . . in black,
bottomless puddles'. But that was in the rains, and cars still have trouble in
the black mud in the rains. Most cars were making 10 times in a day what foot
safaris had.

The Serengeti was suddenly close. The American hunter Al Klein located
a spring, making a permanent camp possible; he tried to keep it secret, but
others simply followed his lorry tracks. Petrol was a bigger problem: 'sometimes
we had to send a truck one hundred miles back to Nairobi for supplies and
gas'.

The car's gains were obvious; so were its losses. 'You may scrape [Africa's]
acquaintance by automobile, but you never touch the heart of her.' Clark found
a car 'the best way to ruin the whole thing . . . One is seeing nothing along
the way.'

The car had a more severe effect on game. 'Sportsmen' were delighted to
find that they could drive a car within a few yards of a lion without scaring it
off. If they were willing to take the shot from the car, they had a safe, almost
sure kill. One group shot 19 lions in three days. 'They did not walk; they raced
over the veld in three motor-trucks, and what they caught up with they shot.'
'The old safari days are gone . . . Lions now are hunted in six-cylinder cars,
and very often run down in the open veld, and killed from the driver's seat.'

Tarlton, beginning to show the 'old-timer's' reverence for days long gone, declared in 1927 that 'the motor-car has destroyed hunting as we know it, and especially lion and other plains loving animals ... Quite recently my company looked after a man of many millions, over 70 years of age, a good fellow ... Bag 20 lions in three months.' This was almost certainly George Eastman's safari; the lion kill was not Eastman's alone, by far. But Tarlton was right: one of Eastman's companions left a manuscript account of shooting plains game from the cars.

The theme of the disappearance of game was taken up by many; the photographer Cherry Kearton, who had been coming to East Africa since 1909, blamed the motor car 'as an aid to the week-end sportsman'. Blayney Percival blamed 'not the vehicle itself, but the rifles it carries, and the use some men make of the car'. He may have been thinking of the American Leslie Simson, who scored enormous lion kills by driving within 25 yards of his quarry.

It took only a few years of this for a number of outraged hunters to start a campaign to ban shooting from cars; the final result was the group of laws making it illegal to shoot within less than 100 yards of a car. But shooters were far from the Game Ranger, and compliance depended mostly on the white hunter. Most were ethical men. A few were not. In the late 1930s, one visitor met a girl in a car who had already shot an eland, a roan, and a waterbuck that morning, but her shoes were spotless, and it was clear she had never stepped down from the vehicle. Her hunter smiled complacently.

Nowadays, game-viewing from Nissan vans, you forget that the van itself is what allows you to get within such intimate distance. But if you try it on foot, you find how, suddenly, the game will not let you within 200 yards. They simply move slowly along in front of you. And then there is the safety of the vehicle, too. To shoot a lion or buffalo is to risk having it charge you – a far less acceptable risk when you stand on your two feet in the wide open than when you sit with two tons of steel around you. You understand the temptation to cheat. But you understand, too, that it *is* cheating – that if 'hunting' means anything any more, it means taking a risk of some importance. And it means accepting the current rules of the sport.

In the mid-1930s, the East African Professional Hunters Association passed a resolution that 'the Southern Masai Reserve and certain other areas ... be closed absolutely to motorised safaris'.

In 1930, the Prince of Wales – the man with 'a time limit' (Mrs Simpson was waiting in the wings) – found a new time-beater. It came buzzing out of the fleecy clouds one bright day with Tom Campbell Black at its controls and HRH in the passenger seat, a little aeroplane in which he was able to hop from place to place while two white hunters with two sets of lorries went scurrying over the ground ahead of him. When not needed to provide him seven-league boots, the plane was used to spot elephants.

Old-timers said the car ruined the safari. Now a new generation said the aeroplane did. By 1933, Beryl Markham was spotting elephants for the white hunter Bror von Blixen; in the long run, an aeroplane was far faster and therefore cheaper than smashing about the hot bush looking for big tusks from the ground. It was only a step for the wealthy to sending an aeroplane from the Serengeti to Arusha each day to pick up the newspaper. And then to flying out of a base camp to prime hunting sites, 'much easier than driving back and moving camp again'.

By the mid-1930s, Imperial Airways had a weekly, then a bi-weekly, service to East Africa. Distance – and therefore time – had again been compressed, the ship journey to Mombasa now reduced to the aeroplane's several days (the planes did not fly at night). The effects on the safari were not immediately felt; the numbers of passengers were too small, and a new war was to intervene. But a new element of glamour had been introduced, and just over the horizon from the first airliners were the fleets of jets that were to come.

The safari was more than ever a recreation of the rich. By 1923, a run-of-the-mill white hunter was getting £50 a month, a star like Tarlton three times that; before the 1920s were out, this had climbed again by a third, not including their expenses. With the new Kenyan shilling roughly equivalent to the English, cooks, personal servants, and gunbearers were getting 50 to 70 shillings a month in the 1920s; porters, when used, were getting 15 (actually less than in 1900), with these figures falling somewhat in the Depression. (The increased difference between the white hunter's and the others' wages shows – among other things – the growing importance of the white hunter. In Roosevelt's time, he had made in a day what a porter did in a month; now he could command per day what it took a porter eight months to earn.)

So long as porterage lasted, some whites showed guilt about the low wages. Mary Jobe Akeley wondered at the five American cents earned for carrying 50 lb seven miles: 'I have never been able to reconcile the recompense received and the service rendered'. Others saw porterage as the solution to a supposed unemployment problem, with safaris 'taking care of a great many blacks who would otherwise have no means of support'. Africans now had to carry a registration card from the Bureau of Native Affairs; visiting whites thought well of the system.

Getting a safari together and under way was now magically easy if you used Safarilands. It did take money, but it was efficient and fast. A few people were less organized; Denys Finch Hatton ran into 'Old Kitchener [hero of Omdurman and the First World War]; he arrived at Rejaf with a bed, blankets, a shotgun, 2 tins of petit beurre, and a set of false teeth . . . It was just as well that I had a certain amount of stuff and a couple of chairs with me.'

Costs through the safari companies rose in the 1920s and could escalate to £1000 per client per month rather easily. Archie Ritchie wrote that a 'filter-and-water safari' was cheap but a 'champagne-and-ice safari may run into thousands'. George Easman wrote to a correspondent that a safari for $10,000 would be possible, but difficult. Yet Stoneham was still insisting in the mid-1930s that a safari need not cost more than £20 a month per person.

In fact, the car actually made it easier to put together a do-it-yourself safari on the cheap than it had been in Roosevelt's day. But such a safari had no glamour and utterly no cachet. It was the sort of safari that residents and a very few visitors made – trot up to Nairobi, hire a cook and a servant and a black guide who knew the animals – but it took a good bit of independence (and some Swahili).

Precisely why the company-organized safari was so very expensive is not entirely clear, although safari prices rose as prices did all over the West in the 1920s. Limited and partly captive clientele, relative lack of competition, and the nature of the luxury market probably allowed safari 'value' to be set far higher than cost-plus-markup alone would justify. And the traffic bore it. (To a degree, the division between overpriced upper bracket and bargain-basement self-service still typifies the industry.)

The only unavoidable cost was the hunting licence. One visitor spent £300 in 1928 for two before ever leaving Nairobi (two full licences at £100 each, plus two elephant licences). That figure alone, to be sure, was enough to define the safari clientele at a high level.

But with the safari industry now in full swing, the complete safari was a wonderful thing. Everything could be made just right. 'Each tent had its shade, its facement to catch some of the morning sun and its coolness for the afternoon snooze. The girl [client] had some privacy in her trips to and from her lavatory tent.' Tents were double-walled, lined with yellow as an attempt at sun-proofing. Mosquito netting hung from the ridgepole over each folding bed, on which an air mattress lay. Tents could be made to connect with tarpaulins and ground-sheets. By the mid-1930s, sewn-in floors and zippers made tents at last truly bug- and snake-proof. Separate tents or gauze houses made the whites' dining safe from mosquito and flies. (The black servants stood outside.) Portable privies, chemical toilets, separate little lavatory tents made it necessary to walk only a few steps, hardly more than to one's bathroom at home, with the same privacy and sanitation. (But plainer safaris dug a trench and put a cloth around three sides of it, leaving the shovel so that after use the visitor could, with the same earth, extend the trench and cover his or her spoor.)

The safari day was still the same. 'Called at half-past four . . . [under way] at quarter of six – the sun rose at about quarter after.' Hunt or game-watch until mid-morning (coming to BEA merely to look was becoming acceptable), lunch and sleep, go out again until dark. Then cocktails – the safari became more alcoholic in the 1920s, as did everything, it seemed – and the hot bath, dinner in pyjamas and mosquito boots, often in front of a blazing pile of logs because the night air was cold.

If you made a big kill – lion, especially – the Africans lifted you to their shoulders and paraded you and the trophy around the camp. You distributed appropriate numbers of shillings for this bit of theatre. This became a custom of the country, as did the morning cup of tea before dawn.

Some things were not customary but were greatly welcomed. Somebody – probably Blixen – laid on an innovation called a 'safari hostess' for HRH; she was a hit, but did not become part of the Safarilands package. The Vanderbilts got hot-water bottles and a tin of coals to heat the tent on cold nights, perhaps as a substitute.

In fact, on a champagne safari you could have anything you wanted and would pay for. Champagne itself was old hat: Teleki and von Hohnel had toasted Willoughby with it at Kilimanjaro in the 1880s; Donaldson Smith had had to abandon some because his porters were too thirsty (for water) to carry it. But now you could have *iced* champagne – with the help of a 'patented ice machine'. Or ice cream, flown in from Nairobi. Or 'scores of servants, cases of rich food and wines, comfortable transport'. Or '38 boys altogether to wait on your every wish'.

Super-wealthy safari clients were willing to pay for large numbers of guests, as well as themselves. Their safaris ran into the hundreds. The Johnsons met 'the largest safari we had ever seen, that of the Duke of Orleans', who had brought a valet and a doctor from France; later they ran into an Egyptian prince who had 'other Egyptian noblemen ... a French cook, an English doctor ... and about fifty Egyptian servants, to say nothing of private secretaries, valets, etc.' J. A. Hunter tells of 'one of the most spectacular safaris ever to glamorize the bush', which had a private armoured car, a mobile movie theatre, motorcycle messengers, generating plant, medical lorry with X-ray unit, and a mobile drawing-room with grand piano.

The champagne safari thus invited satire, even when it had become its own parody. In a spoof of safari books, two colonists took on the persona of a dissatisfied visitor for whom 60 porters weren't enough 'to keep the safari in asparagus', whose marble bath 'had a crack in it', whose hot and cold water system didn't work properly, and whose bed was 'an old-fashioned Elizabethan fourposter with eiderdown quilt'.

It just barely managed to exceed the actuality.

In 1926, George Eastman came by special train to Nairobi with his personal physician, his three cars, his mechanic, and wealthy acquaintance Daniel Pomeroy. Eastman's first safari has no great significance, although it did have the distinction of gathering specimens and artists' backgrounds for the American Museum of Natural History's African Hall. (But the scientific justification was wearing thin. A few years later, it would be mocked by a fictional safari on behalf of the 'Chicago Tinned Can Museum'.)

Eastman himself was not unique among safari clients, although he was richer than most, and probably older (72), as well. His would have been just one more champagne safari, except for one fact: he made photography one of the two overlapping centres of his trip.

Photographers had been coming to BEA since the nineteenth century – Grant took photos, for example – and Carl Schillings had made an important photographic expedition at the turn of the century, but the idea of a photographic safari was still new. Professionals like Cherry Kearton and Arthur Dugmore had been drawn by Roosevelt's fame, Kearton staying to make some of the earliest motion pictures of the area. It was not until the 1920s, however, that photography began to catch on as a respectable safari activity, and it did so in good part because of Eastman's 'Kodak' products and the work of two Midwesterners whose lives became intertwined with his.

Martin and Osa Johnson were at once explorers, hustlers, film-makers, and self-promoters with the souls of carney barkers. They were of the first generation of media-created stars, and they scented stardom in East Africa.

Osa met Martin Johnson when she was 16. He was nine years older, rootless; he had already sailed the Pacific with Jack London, and now he was showing primitive South Seas movies in fly-by-night Midwestern storefront theatres. She saw him as a visionary, but her father saw him as a man who couldn't make a living. Time would prove that she was right – he was a pioneer wildlife photographer, explorer, flier – and that she, with the face of Mary Pickford and the short, plump body of an *Our Gang* tomboy, was the pragmatist who could bring his visions to reality. He cranked the camera; she carried the gun. He almost killed himself with exploding photo chemicals; she nursed him, 300 miles from the nearest doctor, ran a village of 150 men, and processed the photographs that he, half-blinded by the explosion, could not work on.

The Johnsons first saw East Africa in 1921. They had survived difficult times in Polynesia and Micronesia and knew a good deal now about non-Western people, about photography, and about living rough. The Johnsons were not really famous yet – Africa would do that for them – and they lived in part on their future, capitalizing film ventures in a day when documentary film was a real financial risk.

Eighty-five boxes arrived with them at Mombasa. The fledgeling railway on which Mary Hall and Roosevelt had ridden had grown up: refrigerator cars now carried the fragile photographic film. It had also become, they found, one of the most expensive railways in the world.

They were not really ready for East Africa. When they were about to set out from the Northern Frontier District, Blayney Percival discouraged her going, gun-woman or no gun-woman.

'"I wouldn't set my heart on going. It will be no trip for a woman."'

'"Oh!" It seemed to me I must explode. "No trip for a woman! *That* again!"' (She even wrote dialogue as if she were putting together silent film titles.)

Percival was wrong about her, but he was right about something else: they had not anticipated the responsibilities of a safari. And, given their circumstances, hiring a white hunter was out of the question. They would have to run their own safari, shoot their own meat. Osa – proving Percival wrong – became the major-domo, hunter, and trouble-shooter. Under her were the two gun-bearers *cum* straw-bosses, Jerramani – who had travelled with Roosevelt – and Ferraragi. Next came the cook, whom she had 'taught our way of cooking', which means she had taught a good English cook how to please Americans.

They reached the vast mountain called Marsabit. Marsabit spoke to something in both of them. A crater lake on the mountain, which is still a pristine and beautiful haunt of elephants, now in one of Kenya's game parks, looked like 'The Peaceable Kingdom'. Elephant and buffalo ambled out of the rain forest to wade in the weedy shallows and to drink. Baboons swarmed over the rocky shores. Waterbirds sailed across the lightly rippled water and stalked at its edge. Enormous greater kudu, the most gorgeously horned of the African antelopes, picked their way along the forest trails. There were no people. The crater lake was the world as God had made it – the world that a Midwestern American, the knowledge of the slaughter of the buffalo still fresh in his mind, believed guiltily he could not recapture. It was Paradise Regained.

They would later write and speak a great deal of nonsense about this lake – that it was not on any map, that it had been discovered by an old explorer and lost, and so on. In fact, Delamere and Donaldson Smith had both been to Marsabit in the 1890s and hunted it extensively, and J. H. Patterson had been there in 1908, camping on the lake. Boma Trading Company had put up its post there the same year, which became the ADC's boma in 1910 and was still in use when the Johnsons arrived. So it was hardly an unknown spot. But the boma – which would become the present town of Marsabit – was six miles from the crater lake, far enough to give isolation and solitude and to justify the name they gave it: Lake Paradise.

They stayed three months, and when the three months were done and they were running low on supplies and had to leave, they had resolved to come back to stay. Martin, the visionary, had made a leap of dazzling ambition: he would do nothing less than film the life cycles of the great East African animals, exposing – and developing on the spot – 60,000 feet of film a year for five years.

With the support of George Eastman and others, they arrived back in Nairobi in 1924 with one of the most ambitious expeditions ever assembled: 'Eighteen guns, twenty-one cameras, six Willys-Knight cars with *safari* bodies – water tanks, hardware, staple food stuffs, clothing, ammunition, photographic supplies'.

With 235 Africans in support, they pushed north as fast as the increasing rains would allow. Arrived on the mountain, they drove their men to erect the village that was to be home for three years: generator building, photographic laboratory, house, a village of huts for their men (and women, although they have gone mostly unrecorded). Martin plunged into the work of photography while Osa organized this town in the wilderness, directing the laying out of paths, the planting of gardens that were to provide them with fresh vegetables the year round. (Four years later, photographing lions in the Tanganyikan Serengeti, he was astonished to see her beginning a garden there.) Her chickens multiplied. Wild fruits came from the forest. Almost certainly – although neither of them ever admitted that other humans were so close – they traded with the people in what would become the town of Marsabit, six miles away. In the dry season, they made long safaris together across the desert, going for as long as three months into the N'Doto Range or down to the Ewaso Nyiro. Martin's whole life was now in wildlife photography, his days filled with scouting locations, building hides, shooting film, developing it.

When, then, Eastman came to BEA in 1926, he came to their paradise – the boss coming to dinner, in a sense – and found a unique conflation of the champagne safari and settler feudalism. Their men had built an 'elephant-proof' house for him. The Johnsons entertained him as a distinguished guest, then accompanied him for most of the rest of his tour, Martin taking hundreds of photographs.

Eastman and his 'pleasure fleet of motor cars and lorries' at last departed. The Johnsons returned to the States in 1927, bringing with them films, photographs, and writings that would make them the most famous adventurers (along with 'Bring 'Em Back Alive' Frank Buck) in the world of pop Africana. By that time Eastman, like so many before and after him, had decided he had to go back. He had wanted an elephant and hadn't got one, and he was a man accustomed to getting what he wanted. And now he wanted a white rhino – hadn't Roosevelt and his son got nine? Time was short: he was 73.

This time, Eastman decided to do in reverse what Roosevelt had done at the end of his safari – go to northern Uganda by way of the Nile. Such a journey was not a safari in the traditional sense, for most of it was made by a steamer specially outfitted for him by Thomas Cook's, but at the end of the Nile trip lay a true safari by car, truck, and then foot.

He gave himself two weeks of hunting to bag an elephant and a white rhino. Again, he took a doctor along, and, when two other guests had to back out, he persuaded the Johnsons to go.

Osa was now a crack shot and had a .30-06 star-marked Springfield Sporter ('national match' quality) with one of the earlier telescopic sights seen in Africa. Eastman shot a crocodile with it from the deck of his steamer, became so enamoured of it that he borrowed it at the end of the trip (and may not have returned it; a star-marked Springfield was among his effects when he died). He and Osa spent a lot of time together, some of it coaching the *Dal*'s cook in the use of an electric refrigerator and of Eastman's 'wheat gems' – biscuit mixes he had concocted himself and had had sterilized at the Eastman Kodak factory.

They were met by Nairobi's premier white hunter (Phil Percival, brother of Blayney) at the head of Nile navigation, with another fleet of cars and a ton of Nairobi rice for posho. They pushed through a corner of the Belgian Congo into prime elephant and rhino country, where Eastman – now 74 – got a week of classic foot safari and bagged a big one-tusked elephant and a dozing white rhino. Just like that.

They had pulled up one day at a Shillock town called Kodok in Sudan. Eastman couldn't resist the similarity to his brand name, Kodak. He made a big 'Kodok' sign out of a piece of cardboard and put it up on a grass house. Martin Johnson photographed him in front of it, Kodak camera in hand. The Kodak King at Kodok.

Amateur photography had come to safariland.

Nobody in Marsabit remembers the Johnsons now, although many of the local people are displaced Merus, perhaps descendants of their porters. Their crater lake is called Lake Paradise on the maps – but nobody remembers why. Kodok is still called Kodok.

Less than two years after the second Eastman–Johnson safari, the Great Depression began. Its effects on the agrarian economy of East Africa were severe: in 1930, coffee lost almost half its value; maize dropped to less than half its 1920 price, then to barely half that. By year's end, 'the prices of all Kenya's principal exports [dropped] below the cost of production'.

The safari industry was hit from two sides. Visitors, their own incomes reduced, stayed away; people who filled out their five months of safari work with another occupation, usually farming, saw that second occupation shrink. Some Europeans gave up and left East Africa. 'Liquidations, even bankruptcies' were seen, along with the 'axing of labour'.

It was the beginning of a bad period that would not really see relief until after the next big war, and then the relief would be temporary; in fact, it was the beginning of the long disruption in colonial life that would end with *uhuru* at the start of the 1960s. The Depression was first, driving down the number of visitors until at least the mid-1930s. In 1935, Italy's adventure into Ethiopia further depressed the safari industry, with local newspapers trumpeting 'Cancellation of Safaris Reported', and business 'distinctly quiet'. In 1938, the threat of European war again caused a drop in the number of visitors, and, from 1939 until 1945, the safari industry was moribund.

Hunting licence figures bear out the change. Uganda's 'Visitor's Full' licences fell from 14 in 1928 to 4 in 1929 – an 'unexpected decrease' – and to none in 1934, rising to the 1929 level in 1938 and then dropping to 1 in 1939. Full Tanganyikan licences fell from 44 to 34 between 1929 and 1930 and to 19 in 1934, dropping to 11 – 25 per cent of the 1928 number – in 1938. Kenya's Visitor's Full licences actually rose between 1928 and 1931 (27 to 43) but crashed to 9 the next year, rising to 27 in 1937, then falling to 20 in the year of Munich. Fourteen-day licences, however, rose through the period, suggesting a lowering of visitors' expectations – and their expenditures. The economic impact on the local economy cannot really be estimated, but Kenya Game Department income from licences, which was £13,285 in 1929 – down from the estimate because of 'fewer visitors and unfavourable climatic conditions' – was only £6703 in 1934, again an underestimate because of 'fewer visitors than anticipated', but also because the cost had been dropped from 2000 to 1500 Kenyan shillings for a Visitor's Full licence, a change that itself showed how severe the situation was.

Yet some people – Ernest Hemingway among them – continued to have the money for a safari. Hemingway's came from an uncle, who did not balk at an estimate of £4400 in the deep Depression year of 1932. In fact, Hemingway did not get to East Africa until late 1933, and then he spent more than three months in Kenya and Tanganyika with his wife, several companions, and Phil Percival as his white hunter. At 34, Hemingway was famous and widely respected, although cursed with a personality now too well known to need discussing here. The safari affected him as East Africa had affected Roosevelt; both saw similarities to their loved American West, and both had ideas of 'manliness' that were rooted in hunting and guns.

Yet the most important products of the Hemingway safari were not his trophies or his personal memories, but two short stories that created for their readers an indelible image of safari. 'The Short Happy Life of Francis Macomber' and 'The Snows of Kilimanjaro' were to prove two of the most famous stories of the period, widely anthologized, endlessly analysed, universally included in academic courses. Many people first heard of Kilimanjaro through Hemingway; many formed their entire idea of safari life and East Africa through his two stories.

Ironically, the stories are very dark. Both protagonists die. The women in both stories are 'bitches', both bound to money and success. Both safaris go bad, one when the protagonist suffers an injury, the other when he is shot dead by his wife (an incident told to Hemingway by Phil Percival and based on a scandalous event involving the J. H. Patterson of 'man-eaters of Tsavo' fame). They are among the best writing Hemingway ever did, but they use East Africa and the safari as a setting for decay and death, and a reader who knew nothing else of the subject would be forgiven for coming away from them with the conviction that safaris were inevitably dangerous and unpleasant.

The real picture of Hemingway's safari life was contained in a book that relatively few people have read, *The Green Hills of Africa*. It is a positive book, its picture of the land and the safari wonderfully vivid and pleasing. It has detail, honesty, and art, and to know what a hunting safari was like in 1934, there is no better source.

Hemingway's considerable influence (expanded through films of the two stories) helped to fix the mythos that went back to Stanley: Africa was a place of dangerous encounters, a place of infection, a place of betrayal. Men who went on safari were made virile by killing, but they were unmanned and even murdered by the women they had mistakenly taken along. The animal world was hostile and it pressed in like the dreadful hyena unless the man kept up eternal vigilance. Black Africans were peripheral, powerless figures. Art had no place in East Africa.

The Green Hills told another tale but had little influence: hunting was a joyful skill; black Africans were individuals with wonderful individual talents; women were peripheral but harmless; animals were beautiful, but the best of them – the biggest males – were to be killed. Africa was beautiful and challenging. Africa could be art's subject.

Like Roosevelt, Hemingway defined East Africa and the safari for a generation. Unlike Roosevelt's, however, his definition was vulgarized and simplified by a new force, one that Eastman and the Johnsons had pioneered: motion pictures. In the thick-fingered hands of Hollywood, the two Hemingway stories would reach millions, their artistry lost, their ideas reduced to bumper-sticker obviousness. Conclusion: safaris are hell, man.

But the Hollywood reduction of the myth of the safari would wait for a more important event: the Second World War. After mid-1938, Europe had little attention for recreation, and safaris were 'practically non-existent'. In 1939, the real shooting began, and Phoney War, Blitz, and Occupation wiped the safari off the world's consciousness.

In 1940, Armand Denis ran into the ageing American white hunter Al Klein in Mombasa. Klein summed it up brutally. 'Because of the goddamn war every client I had is back in the States by now'.

LASSO, TRAP, AND BALLOON
The stunt safaris

EW things in the twentieth century have proved resistant to the human ego. Rocks have acquired initials in spray paint. Mountain-sides have acquired sculptures. Outer space has acquired junk.

The safari has been no exception. It needed only to acquire enough notoriety to prompt someone to make his or her personal mark on it. You could argue that almost everybody went on safari to make some sort of mark, whether it was Stanley to make himself famous or Thomson to cross Masailand, but these aspects of ego were overshadowed by much larger purposes that at the time, at least, seemed sensible. What were to come were safaris that had cut their link with the sensible, at least as most of the (perhaps stuffy) people who comprised the safari's world were to judge them. These were the 'stunt safaris', expeditions that, by method or intent, were so bizarre that they called attention to themselves.

Cranworth pretty well summed them up when he wrote disgustedly of 'the man who procures his game with a lassoo, a trap or from a balloon', for it was examples of two of these things that provided the oustanding examples of the lunatic fringe of the safari. Had he written a few years later, he would have included two others. (The trap was never made a stunt, at least until the efforts of Frank Buck. Trap guns, in fact – fixed so lion or leopard or hyena actually got the muzzle into the mouth before activating the trigger – were commonplaces of farms and, it is said, of some less than scrupulous trophy hunters.)

Some primitive symptoms of stunts appeared almost as early as Nairobi itself (perhaps because, in the eyes of some, Nairobi was a stunt). Richard Meinertzhagen, for example, went out on the Athi Plains with a man named De Crispigny to try some pig-sticking *à la* Indian lancer, but the pigs were warthogs and the lances were poles with bayonets lashed on, and the landscape was littered with animal holes. Worse yet, De Crispigny spotted a lion and took out after it, upon which his horse decided to go home and De Crispigny fell off. Undaunted, he shot the lion at close range with a pistol. 'No more lion-sticking for me,' Meinertzhagen concluded. 'The risk is not justified.'

Some years later, Lord Delamere and some friends had 'an elaborate tin castle' on wheels built, from which they thought they would 'cinematograph' lions. However, when the 'wonderful tin castle' was wheeled out on the plains, the cinematograph 'refused to act', and the camera-person locked up in it sat numbly while the lions admired the metal architecture. 'None the less it was a wonderful piece of careful workmanship'. Like lion-sticking, however, the tin castle was less a stunt than a whim of the moment; it lacked the necessary ingredient of publicity.

It is not the moon, but notoriety that brings out real wackiness. Thus, it is hardly surprising that the first certifiable safari stunt was thought up by a newspaper owner. Nor, perhaps, is it surprising that he was from Chicago, where stunts and newspapers had gone together for years.

W. D. Boyce was the owner and publisher of the Chicago *Saturday Blade*, which was to real newspapers what the tabloids that Americans find in their supermarkets are to *The Times*. In 1909 (as always, apparently) Boyce needed to sell newspapers. A moth looking for a flame, he was drawn to the bright light emanating from Roosevelt's safari. It would not be enough, obviously, for him to traipse after Roosevelt like any other visitor. (Besides, Roosevelt had pretty well muzzled the press.) What would now be called a gimmick was needed, and Boyce found one in the panoramic aerial camera. Thus was born the Boyce Balloonograph Expedition.

'UNIQUE IDEA WILL STARTLE THE WORLD', *Blade* readers found in June 1909. 'The two million [*sic*] and more readers of the Saturday Blade will experience a thrill of joy when they pick up their favorite paper this week and learn that W. D. Boyce, its publisher, is now arranging an expedition to Africa in their interests.' Managing to quote his own press release from the rival *Tribune* ('which is substantially correct'), Boyce announced that he was 'going to darkest Africa to hunt wild beasts from balloons'. His principal goal was photographic, not lethal.

By mid-August, the expedition was in England ('MR BOYCE IN ENGLAND/ FAME HAS PRECEDED HIM'), and by the end of the month Boyce had hired Will Judd ('FAMOUS GUIDE IS SECURED') and was off to Naples, Alexandria, and Mombasa. Copy flowed like molasses. Column after column of the Boyce journal was filled with the excitements of getting ready, especially the testing of the cameras and several huge box-kites. In fact, Boyce 'en route to the jungles' was experiencing what others sometimes do with sex: getting there can be all the fun.

On 25 September, Boyce was in Nairobi, and the *Leader of East Africa*, also eager to build sales, published a long interview and a photograph, in which Boyce looks genial and pleased, like a somewhat overfed Woodrow Wilson. The expedition had set itself up 'on the ridge opposite Mr McMillan's residence'. There, Boyce had already given an exhibition of a balloon ascent, the balloon filled with '[hydrogen] gas [generated] in the great vats provided for the purpose'. The ascents, after a two-day delay, went pretty well; two of the people to go up were the cartoonist John McCutcheon and the first wife of Carl Akeley, who thus 'had been the first woman to make an ascension in

British East Africa', which was probably not the achievement for which she wanted to be remembered. Boyce also put on two free film shows, one for 'fashionably dressed' Europeans and the other for Africans. McCutcheon's account shows that Boyce was taking movies and was able to process his own film quickly, for the show included his train trip and his safari's 'march through the city'.

In fact, much of Boyce's effort was very good, and there is no doubt that the undertaking was a big one that had been pretty well handled up to this point. He brought six other Americans; he had more than 20 cameras, box-kites, the balloon (or balloons; accounts vary), the gas generators, the photographic lab, and tons of gear.

The long-term judgement of him, however, was dreadful: 'a grotesque conception, that ended in ridiculous failure'.

For the fact was that Boyce's inspiration, like so many others that had their good points, failed. Like da Vinci's flying machine, it was an idea whose time had not come. Ironically, 'balloon safaris' are nowadays among the most chic of activities, and in the early morning you can see half a dozen of them floating over the Mara, heading for their champagne breakfasts somewhere downwind. Boyce's, however, is remembered as a 'grotesque conception' – because he failed.

Exactly what went wrong is not altogether clear. The party paraded out of Nairobi and went toward the Sotik country; the panoramic camera was run up on the box-kite and got a few really wonderful photographs of the safari and of a Masai manyatta. (The East African newspapers had already printed some of the panoramic pictures.) 'BALLOONOGRAPH EXPEDITION NOW IN AFRICA', the *Blade* told its readers on 2 October, but there is a hint of treading water to the report. Had something already gone wrong? Boyce cabled:

> I am leaving by a special train for Kijabe. I have twenty-five cars and two engines. The grade is very steep. From Kijabe our expedition starts over a barren, waterless desert in the Sotik country. This territory is closed and no white man has ever hunted in it. [This was untrue, of course.] Our party are well and anxious for the start to the wilderness. . . . The caravan numbers 350 people. [McCutcheon said 230.] No expedition in Africa has ever attempted the dangerous country we are going into. We must contend with hostile natives, and the country is literally infested with lions, tigers and leopards. [There are, of course, no tigers in Africa.]

At the end of the Boyce cable, his editors had appended a note to assure his 'millions of readers' that he was well and at the very moment 'is taking pictures and fighting the wildest animals there are in the world'. Immediately below this were two short articles, one headlined 'GIRL BITES A FISHHOOK' and the other 'SAVING BIBLE OLD WOMAN DIES'.

Three months later, the *Leader* noted as if in passing that 'Hughes and

Caywood of the Boyce Balloonograph expedition are sailing home via South Africa'. Boyce went on around the world, filing stories on this foreign scene and that but remaining strangely silent about his Balloonograph. If he had spent the intervening months fighting tigers with one hand while taking pictures with the other, his millions of readers did not learn of it. At the end of October, he had written that he was 'in camp at last', repacking the gear, 'entertaining Nairobi with balloon ascensions', before starting for 'the greatest game region in the world – led by noted hunters who piloted Stanley, Roosevelt and other famous nimrods'. Later articles were still about Nairobi. It was as if he never left the city.

What had happened?

In a word, nothing. It seems that the expedition got to Kijabe, actually got to the Sotik, but it was so beset by calamities that only humiliated silence could deal with the situation. No photos taken from the balloon have survived, and probably there never were any. The photographic equipment functioned, but the paraphernalia surrounding it did not.

Perhaps Boyce's enthusiasm for gadgetry got the better of him. In his interview with the *Leader*, he had described some of it: a telephone connection with a baited lion trap, so the lions could 'telephone when they are ready' to have their pictures taken. Long-distance flash photos. A balloon early-warning system for game.

A story that persisted in East Africa has the safari making its way along the windy edge of the Rift escarpment. The balloon, inflated, is being tugged along by a mule. The wind blows more strongly; the mule rises from the ground; and balloon and mule float off, never to be seen again. The story would seem hyperbole, for who would be crazy enough to tether a balloon to a mule? Boyce would, of course. 'It occurs to me that one good plan for transport', he had said in his interview, 'will be to fill the balloons beside the railway track, load them with stores instead of sand-ballast, and then float captive on a rope fastened to the harness of a mule.'

'It is scarcely possible to believe', Sir Frederick Jackson wrote, 'that a sane man could imagine that he could get the [contraption] within even telephoto range of game.'

But if he had succeeded – *Ah, if he had succeeded!*

Charles Jesse Jones was a Westerner who had got (or taken) the nickname 'Buffalo' from his days on the plains. By the time he had the idea of taking his skills and his showmanship to Nairobi in 1910, he was 65 years old, famous as a hunting guide and as a man who had 'lassoed' such animals as the American mountain lion.

Jones 'showed us something altogether new in the ways of hunting', one man said, and indeed he did: the use of the Western lariat on lion and rhino. With two cowboys, Marshall Loveless and Ambrose Means, and a string of 10 horses, he set out from the States after a meeting in Boston with W. G. Sewell of the Boma Trading Company. (One Nairobi historian remembered six cowboys and called him 'Tarpon Dick', heaven knows why. Another remembered 'forty splendid ponies', four times the number of rawboned horses he brought.) Just what had inspired him – aside from all the publicity being given Roosevelt, who was still in Africa – is not clear. Means said years later that a prominent Democrat, Charles S. Bird, sent Jones to discredit Roosevelt, a Republican, by showing that dangerous animals could be taken without all the killing that Roosevelt did, but this seems a rather daft notion. 'He truly believed it better, fairer, and in every ethical sense more creditable for a man to capture an animal alive than to shoot it', and there may have been some sense of pooh-poohing guns and killing, but probably not Roosevelt. Later actions, however – hiring Cherry Kearton to make commercial film, sending cables to American newspapers – suggest a more usual desire for publicity.

Jones also brought a pack of dogs to run the wild game, not in itself a 'fairer, better and ... more creditable' way of hunting. At a stopover in London, he bought 'collars and belts, chains, branding-irons, a block and fall, muzzles ... corkscrew picket-pins' and other gear for dealing with big animals.

The Jones safari was organized in Nairobi under the direction of a white hunter named Ray Ulyate. While it was being set up, Jones and his cowboys played Wild West in the streets. Later, one disgruntled Briton would say that Jones dressed up as Uncle Sam, but this was probably a dyspeptic memory of the elderly Jones's goatee and Buffalo Bill hair-do. The cowboys gave some public exhibitions: Jones himself was quoted as saying that 'the English Lords hired the natives to run one block, giving him a rupee, and if one of us failed to [rope] him ... he received two rupees. It was great exercise for our horses, but only a few received rupees.' Most of Nairobi had never seen roping before, and the spectacle was made more dramatic by general disparagement of the American cow horses. These were probably what we would now call 'cutting horses', which often work cattle with their heads so low to the ground that to anyone accustomed to only English horses they look exhausted, at the very least.

When, at last, the Jones extravaganza left Nairobi, it was with a triumphal procession to the railway station: Jones in the lead, in sola topi and buckskin shirt, followed by the American and Boma Trading Company flags, his cowboys, Kearton, the pack of dogs, and more than 100 porters. Jones said he was seen off by 'Lord Delmar' himself. They embarked on a 'special train' (but most big safaris got special trains, because they would have overloaded the 'up-mixed') that was 'loaded to capacity with horses and dogs, camp baggage, moving-picture cameras, cowboys, photographers, and porters'. They went down into the Rift and, near Longonot, began showing what they could really do.

'Riding lions' had been thought the most thrilling of East African sports for some years. Done on fast horses, it involved a cross-country chase of the lion on horseback, with a kill at the end by rifle, the hunter dismounted. It was fast, exciting, and very dangerous.

Jones, Loveless, and Means now carried this to a new level. Armed only with revolvers (which they rarely used), and with Ulyate protecting the cameraman, Kearton, they began 'riding' and, when possible, lassoing, a variety of animals. The procedure was somewhat like cattle cutting and roping: the two cowboys would select an animal, 'cut' it from the herd, block it between them, and the roper would throw a lariat. With the animal held (often by a rear leg), the roper would dismount while his horse kept tension on the rope, which had been snubbed down on the horn of the Western saddle.

The first animal cut and roped was a big eland. Loveless jumped down, at which point his horse got the novel smell of wild animal and bucked so violently that the capture was ruined. Then Loveless roped a giraffe, which presented a unique problem once they had it secured – how to get the rope off the neck. They finally had to throw the animal.

The big successes were a lioness and a full-grown rhino. Bayed by the dogs, the lioness was moved with firecrackers when it began to kill the dogs, and it was finally roped, not by a man from a horse, but by a loop that had been thrown and got hung up on tall grass above the animal's head; she jumped into it.

Jones is supposed to have served as a decoy for the rhino, causing it to charge him. Loveless and Means kept throwing loops on the big animal, and the rhino kept breaking the ropes. Finally, after four hours, the animal was too exhausted to run any more, and, the dangling ends of rope tangled in a stump, it simply came to a stop. One cowboy threw a loop under a foot, and the rhino let it stay there. It was caught.

'At last a cablegram came from Nairobi announcing the lassoing and capture of giraffes, cheetah, warthog, zebras and many other animals; and best of all, it told of a six-hours' fight and capture of a large rhinoceros.' The responses, even in BEA, were positive. 'They astonished the world', Sir Alfred Pease wrote, 'for not only did they rope a lioness, but a very large rhinoceros, as well as other game.' Former ranchman Theodore Roosevelt was approving: 'Buffalo Jones and his two cowboys, Loveless and Meany [*sic*] . . . are old-time Westerners and plainsmen, skilled in handling horse and rope. They . . . roped and captured a lioness, a rhinoceros, a giraffe'.

There was only one sour note. Many years later, the American naturalist James Clark, who was in Nairobi when Jones was there, wrote, 'Jones did lasso many animals . . . but he was brutally cruel with them. He tied them up and then horsewhipped them with a heavy bull whip.'

It was evidently in this way that the flamboyant Jones was able to 'tame' his catches before sending them off to zoos.

Stunt begat stunt. No sooner had Roosevelt returned home and Jones publicized his feats than a wealthy Mississippian decided that dogs were just the things with which to hunt lions. Paul J. Rainey was already known as the man who had captured a polar bear with a lasso; a fawning journalist called him a 'big game hunter, naturalist, millionaire, and sportsman extraordinary' who had hunted 'ever since he was in short dresses'.

A less admiring R. J. Cuninghame – Roosevelt's 'steel and whip-cord old boy' – didn't like him and 'despised his hunting methods', referring to Rainey in 1924 as 'this person. . . . His methods did not appeal to the sporting instinct of the Briton.'

In 1911, however, Rainey made a great first impression in East Africa. His success was little short of astonishing, and most people needed to recover from the shock of his lion kill – 74 in a few weeks, 9 in one day – before evaluating him.

'If my hounds could run a bear down and worry him until I came up and killed him, they could do the same with lions', was Rainey's reasoning. The same theory – weary the animal to near-collapse – had governed his lassoing of the polar bear, which he had let tow a motorboat until it was exhausted (although he had inadvertently strangled another bear to death that way earlier.) 'When a lion has been chased by hounds for thirty minutes, most of the fight is out of him.'

The method was in fact deadly: let the dogs exhaust the lion, then walk up close to it, keeping the dogs between lion and hunter, and shoot it at close range. A number of the dogs would be maimed or killed, to be sure.

'It was a great sport to see the hounds fighting the lion. . . . I shot him . . . a little far back, and he turned like a flash and charged. The hounds gave him too much trouble, however.'

Edmund Heller, who had been with Roosevelt in 1909–10 as a scientist, saw Rainey's methods up close. 'Rainey's chief interest in life is hunting with hounds', he wrote to Roosevelt. He went with Rainey into what is now the Masai Mara Game Reserve. 'On the trek out the hounds were carefully kept away from antelope and punished whenever they showed any interest in hoofed game . . . [Then] they were taken out on lion drives and used for hunting down wounded lions.' When the dogs were fully trained,

the method of hunting soon developed into laying zebra & buck kills for the lions to visit. These kills were visited every morning with the hounds as soon as daylight would permit. The dogs then picked up any lion trails. . . . Usually the lion was found within an hour . . . Then the dogs would fight him in the brush until the hunters appeared. With the dogs about the shooter had nothing to fear. . . . Usually Rainey crawled into the thicket & shot the lion at a few yards as he stood fighting the hounds.

The mortality among the hounds however was great. A month's hunting killed nearly all of them. Only two crippled bear hounds returned to Nairobi. . . . Only a few of the dogs were killed outright by the lions. Many were wounded and lost, others were affected by sunstroke & strayed away, while still others were killed by warthogs which they attacked.

The killing of so many lions in such a short time has caused some consternation in the game department. The warden is uncertain whether it is better to favor the settlers & let R kill as many as he can or put a limit on his bag & protect lions as game animals.

An article in *Literary Digest* credited this method with killing nine lions in 35 minutes, 'a feat unparalleled in hunting annals'. He 'shot seventy-four lions, breaking the world's record', whatever that was. The article opined that Rainey's 'exploits . . . outclass those of the great lion-hunter Selous'. Rainey, who was not afflicted with excessive modesty, said, 'I shot several times as much big game' as Roosevelt, and 'I think my plan of hunting lions with hounds will be adopted by nearly all the sportsmen who go to British East Africa in the future'.

He was wrong. Dogs proved useful to farmers trying to clear lions from cattle lands and to government hunters, but sporting hunters, especially British ones, rejected them. Rainey came back to East Africa several times to pursue his idea of sport, none the less, even buying a house there. He died of illness in the early 1920s.

Stewart Edward White's contemptuous judgement has prevailed. 'The same effect can be got chasing warthogs, hyenas, jackals – or jack-rabbits.'

Arthur Young and Saxton Pope were American devotees of the longbow. In the 1920s, their names were associated in the United States with a kind of hunting that was then unusual and always difficult. Trying to expand the limits of their sport – and to publicize it – they were drawn to East Africa.

Stewart Edward White, who was by the mid-1920s the *éminence grise* of the rugged, went with them on their safari. Before going, he claimed that what they intended was not a 'circus stunt'. Arthur Young said afterwards that it was the 'uncertainty of the feat' that attracted him, although he used the word 'trick' to describe the use of bow and arrow on big game: 'the trick can be done because we did it'.

Preceded by a shipment that included 2000 arrow shafts and 5 bows with pulls ranging from 65 to 95 lb, the two archers and White headed for the lion country of the Kenya-Tanganyika border. There, White and Leslie Simson (the man who had pioneered the use of the car in getting close to lions) served as white hunters, standing at each end of the car with heavy rifles while Pope and Young shot their arrows.

The arrow's range is short, and they had to get in very close. They missed a lot. On their first lion, after several misses, they scored some 'slight flesh wounds' and finally put two arrows into the chest. The lion, caught in a tree, had not been able to escape.

Others, encountered on the ground, charged. They were shot with the rifles. Of seven lions killed, only one was got without a rifle. Still, Young insisted that they had proved that 'the trick' could be done – 'not that anyone would ever advocate the bow as the proper weapon with which to hunt such animals'.

Predictably, British response was less than kind, especially when other archers tried the same stunt. There was criticism of 'American-style archers who come to Africa with super-bows and three-foot arrows fitted with steel "war heads". One of these modern Robin Hoods took more than an hour to kill a bull elephant, in which time he made a living pin-cushion of the animal.' A professional hunter later wrote of Pope and Young that 'the game wardens very rightly took a very dim view of that kind of cruelty [wounding but not killing] and stopped it'.

Even White, who had started out as a supporter, was critical. He admitted that African animals were simply too big and tenacious of life for bow and arrow, and 'the long bow suffered a signal defeat', the bag insignificant despite 'thousands of arrows'. Without the two men armed with rifles, and without the car for a close approach, there would have been no hunt at all. What Pope and Young had attempted was 'a stunt'. Barring what White called the 'special conditions' of the Serengeti – an abundance of lions; game in the open in full daylight; country driveable by car – 'lucky accident' was the only thing that would provide a lion kill.

The stunt safaris would be little more than aberrations, and they would have no lasting significance, were it not that they shared several common characteristics. It must already be obvious that all the hunters were American, for one thing. For another, all were in it for self-interest, whatever other reasons they gave. To be sure, self-interest drives almost everybody who goes on safari, even if the self-interest is only pleasure or recreation, but the self-interest that springs out from these accounts is publicity, combined in Rainey and the archers with the desire to prove a personal, even a crank's point.

Such a combination of nationality and self-advertisement had an effect, particularly in combination with Roosevelt's safari. The flag-waving, the parades, the newspaper releases, what would now be called 'hype', combined to leave on British palates a decidedly bad taste, especially when Roosevelt's high animal kill was remembered.

Yet, there was another common factor of perhaps more importance. Except for Boyce's Balloonograph, the stunt safaris all depended on an uncommon cruelty that even contemporaries remarked upon. Jones's use of the whip, his and Rainey's driving of animals to exhaustion, Pope's and Young's repeated wounding of game went beyond the accepted cruelty of hunting. In fact, the best hunters believed in hunting ethics of the clean kill and minimal suffering, and what the stunt safaris did was raise questions about that ethic and its boundaries.

They also raised questions about the role of humans in East Africa, above all humans with money, cars, and technological resources: did humans have all dominion to give pain and to kill? Were animals like the lion the 'vermin' that the statutes called them, to be chased, injured, hurt? Or were humans stewards with a responsibility for the preservation and the ethical treatment of wild animals?

Such questions were not debated as direct results of these safaris. The connections were not always noted. But, as debates about hunting, game, preservation, and the behaviour of safari clients heated up, the stunt safaris stood out more clearly as examples of one set of extremes.

THREE UNFORGETTABLE WEEKS
1940 to the present

'[To] Mount Kenya Safari Club ... William Holden, the movie star, is part owner ... and we saw him riding his scooterbike across the beautiful grounds.'

'The last night ... the Chuka dancers ... began a series of three tribal dances on the lawn beyond the patio ... It was an exciting, colorful finale to three unforgettable weeks on safari.'

Ruth Lothrop, *East African Safari* (1973)

I N 1945, the safari was the institution pretty much as Buxton, Roosevelt, HRH, and Hemingway had known it. By 1970, it was something they would not have recognized. The changes that had turned the world upside-down after the Second World War gave East Africa a good shake, as well, with the result that a quarter-century after war's end the safari itself was largely unrecognizable. Its landscape remained, and some of its animals, but the snake had again shed a skin and revealed itself as an almost different creature.

Yet, in 1945, no signs of immediate change appeared, and to some it looked as if things could be picked up where they had been dropped in 1938. There were, to be sure, ominous shifts in Europe: much of the continent destroyed, England in financial ruin. East Africa, on the other hand, had come through the war pretty well. It had not been much of a battleground this time, although it had contributed men and food and served, in 1940–1, as the staging area for the lightning conquest of Italian Ethiopia.

Hunting did not start up immediately in 1945 at its old levels, in part because again the game had been reduced by wartime activity – this time the killing of plains animals to feed thousands of Italian prisoners of war quartered in Kenya, and again the recreational slaughter of all sorts of game by soldiers with automatic weapons. Some years after the war, experts were estimating that 'large game' numbered only five per cent of its pre-1900 number.

By the 1950s, however, safari clients had started to pour in. A new phenomenon was beginning: mass air travel.

'Nairobi is the safari capital of Africa', Alan Moorehead proclaimed. 'Nairobi is the safari capital of the world', wrote John Gaunther. A woman visitor said, 'Everyone in Nairobi is safari-minded. . . . [The hotel lobbies] were packed with incredible duffel bags, canvas sacks, trophies, spears, washbasins, guns, cameras.'

Nairobi was on the verge of explosive growth. One cause was an influx of money for international tourist development; the other was a radical change in African life that would cause thousands – mostly young men – to 'come unstuck' from village life and gravitate to the capital. By 1960, ship travel would be winding down to its end, and the heat of Mombasa and the clatter of the 'up-mixed's' doors would disappear from the safarist's experience. Instead, big four-engined aircraft, the next generation of the Second World War's bombers, would land at the expanding Nairobi airport and disgorge their weary loads. A few years later, the planes would be jets – British Airways, KLM, Sabena, Air Kenya – and many of the passengers would have left their homes in the United States only the day before.

In 1950, Nairobi had 14,000 Europeans, 55,000 black Africans, and 40,000 Indians. Total Kenyan population was about 5 million. East Africa's Indians were a strong but distinct community, no longer the supposedly comic figures the British called 'baboos'. They expressed their new identity in phenomenal growth – '90% in 15 years' after 1948 in Kenya, Uganda, and Tanganyika. African population grew, too, with the result that total population in Kenya alone was 7.2 million in 1960 – a 40 per cent increase in a decade.

This growth was played out against social and intellectual change that was to leave the safari visitor for the first time a white guest in a cluster of black nations. The Depression and the war had obscured, for whites at least, a truth most did not want to face: the British Empire had been moribund for years, and Africans were not content to be ruled by a white minority.

The situation was most severe in Kenya, the historical centre of safariland. There, a 'minute handful' of whites had 24 per cent of the desirable land (the 'White Highlands'), while 'five and a half *million* Africans have to get along as best they can on the rest'. This status quo was maintained by a system that one educated non-European has equated frankly with South African apartheid. Tanganyika had neither such land inequality nor such a system; Uganda, with 5-plus million Africans and fewer than 8000 Europeans, was 'infinitely, beyond calculation or measure, more free [of the colour bar] than Kenya'.

The ultimate result was *uhuru*, which came to Tanganyika in 1961, to Uganda in 1962, and to Kenya in 1963. But the short-term result in Kenya was the movement, puzzling and frightening, called Mau Mau. Largely Kikuyu, it used mutilation, brutal murder, and blood oaths to try to isolate whites. Mau

Mau provided a new African menace for white writers and for films like *Safari* (1956), giving a novel fillip to the danger–manliness–violence notion of safari. First appearing in 1953, the Mau Mau required the British Army and Air Force to destroy them (along with a lot of habitat and game animals in the Aberdares, their final refuge). They were like the psychotic gesture of an individual, irrational and terrifying: the connection between Mau Mau and black repression was there, but it was indirect and the gesture was crazed and disproportionate. And it had a perhaps predictable effect on the European mythos: even today, Europeans point out the ranches where 'whole families' were murdered by their servants in the night (and such things happened), but the facts are that more than 13,000 black Africans died because of Mau Mau – as did 32 whites.

Mau Mau had its effects on the safari. Hunting guns had to be locked up with a Game Ranger every night. Rangers were diverted to paramilitary duty, and acting or honorary rangers – among them Ernest Hemingway, now on his second safari – were pressed into service. And many visitors went to Uganda or Tanganyika instead of Kenya while the Mau Mau threat existed.

Mau Mau was only a temporary obstacle, however, to a tourist migration that has proved unstoppable. Fed by the post-war American economic expansion, enabled by the air industry, it found its inspiration in a cluster of colour films whose impact was far greater than that of any of the pre-war black and white movies. One – the 1950 *King Solomon's Mines* – with its gorgeous Technicolor and a truly stunning animal stampede scene, probably did for African travel what *Three Coins in a Fountain* did for Italian. And it fixed for its audience a new image of the white hunter: the wonderfully handsome and aristocratic Stewart Granger. Mau Mau could not compete.

Safari travel became redefined economically to include a middle-class hungry for luxury. An introduction to hunting was made to cost less by splitting the old Kenyan Visitor's Full licence into per-animal licences: £50 for a 'major licence' that included a lion, a cheetah, a hippo, and plains game, and extras like £75 for the first elephant and £100 for the second; and £15 each for rhino, leopard, and giraffe. (At the same time, the pound was being devalued to $2.40. Britons, in their 'austerity programme', were not the gainers; Americans were.)

At the same time that they licensed this growing clientele, game departments were aware that the stock of game was shrinking. As early as 1950, the Kenya Colony and Protectorate Game Department reported that 'most visitors want to shoot a lion', but the favoured Masai district had already been closed because of over-hunting; the effect was to drive visitors to Tanganyika, where lions were 'tame and easy'. Visitors did not go after northern Kenya lion, because the new safarists were 'rather shy, to put it mildly, of such [difficult] hunting'.

By 1957, the department reported that 'licensed hunting has now reached such proportions that it could seriously threaten the existence of certain game animals'. Licence sales continued to climb, however, with an understandable transfer from Kenya to Tanganyika during the Mau Mau years: 89 in Kenya in 1952; 40 in 1953; 189 in 1958 ('as many as can comfortably be absorbed'); 163 in 1960 (plus 800 photo permits for controlled areas); and 205 in 1961. Tanganyika went from 66 in 1951 to 116 in 1953, to 200 in 1955, and to 237 in 1960, falling to 154 in 1961 – the year of *uhuru.*

Thus, the pattern was the same across East Africa: rapid growth in number of safaris, number of hunters, and amount of hunting pressure, with the safari tourists highly vulnerable to political events, i.e., Mau Mau and black independence. Their hesitancy should not be dismissed out of hand as racialism or lack of courage; the overwhelming message given whites in Europe and America by 'experts' (i.e., former colonials), books, and films was that the African states would prove incapable of governing themselves and that whites would not be safe in them. A drop in safari numbers at independence was thus inevitable, but what was not predictable was the alacrity with which safari tourists responded when it appeared that the new nations were not only safe but were also hospitable, rapidly expanding their tourist industries, with a democratizing emphasis on safari activities other than hunting – game viewing and photography.

By rebounding in such numbers, middle-class safari clients served as an unconscious stamp of approval of the new East Africa. For their part, the new governments encouraged changes that removed the most egregious symbols and memories of racialism. These changes were brought about by emphasizing game-viewing rather than game-killing; by building lodges for numbers of visitors rather than safari-camping facilities for a few; and, above all, by bringing hunting to a full stop. The safari thus showed what in fact had always been true of it: it was not merely responsive to racial and political policy, but was an at least symbolic instrument of such policy.

'In the 1930s only the really wealthy had hunted big game in Africa.' The key word here is 'hunted'. Only the well-heeled would *hunt* for some years after the war, too. 'A big game safari as now conducted remains a millionaire's pastime', the Kenya Game Department reported in 1950. John Gunther said that before the war, 80 per cent had come to hunt, 20 per cent to take photographs; 'now these percentages are reversed'. More and more, safari travel was becoming devoted to something other than hunting.

The post-war period was remarkably fluid, and percentages and estimates changed rapidly – Gunther's percentages may be inexact – but the overall shift was from wealthy to well-to-do clients, from hunting to photographic and game-viewing safaris, from safaris of a couple of months to safaris of three weeks. And, most certainly, the shift was toward more and more Americans.

Europe was broke; America was rich and getting richer.

'The great majority are Americans, some very rich, but most of them middle-level business people.' As jet travel became commonplace, the newly independent nations built new airports and welcomed thousands, then hundreds of thousands, of people who worked for very good livings but could devote only three weeks to pleasure. It remained – and remains – possible to spend a fortune, but such expenditure is now pretty rare, although one American convicted in the securities scandals of the 1980s was reported to have spent some of his gains on 'fishing and hunting trips' in Europe and Africa.

Despite the overwhelming popularity of non-hunting safaris, hunting continued to define the popular idea of the safari. '[At the New Stanley bar] they met and conferred with their white hunters', one visitor wrote in the 1950s of 'all' travellers, as if all were there to hunt. Paradoxically, it was only as hunting was fading that one of the American 'pop' hunting magazines declared itself 'the first outdoor magazine to send its shooting editor on safari'. This mission, whatever its literary goals, at least represented an acceptance of the safari as a popular vacation within the reach of a mass-circulation magazine's readers.

The firm of Safarilands disappeared; now the leaders were Ker, Downey and Selby, and White Hunters, Ltd, but there were more and more firms – many of them short-lived – as the number of visitors grew, and more and more after *uhuru* that did not deal in hunting. The hunting firms could lay on either hunting or non-hunting safaris, but the tendency always was to include a white hunter in the package. J. A. Hunter argued that a man with a gun was always necessary to protect the defenceless photographer, but this was in the days when visitors were still getting out of their safari cars and taking photos on foot. (Nowadays, it is against the law to get out of a car in a game park, and finding a place where you can walk can be remarkably difficult.)

In the 1950s, costs for a 'regular safari' – meaning a hunting safari – could run to £30 a day for two people. The Kenya Game Department reported 'up to £1,000–1,300 per month per person' in 1957. Alan Moorehead estimated in the late 1950s that 'with every luxury possible', £27 per day for one was adequate, with a second person added on for another £21. The New York–Nairobi air fare in those days was $1700 first class, $1100 economy – not far off its 1988 cost (but the dollar was worth three to four times as much). The Colonial Governor's salary had risen to £10,500 in 1957 (£28.76/day) including expenses; the Chief Game Warden now made £2300 (£6.30/day); such clerks as 'assistant auditors' and 'senior examiners of accounts' made about £900 (£2.46/day).

By the 1960s, safari costs had climbed to £50 per person per day, although a firm called Uganda Wildlife Development, Ltd, planned to offer three-week safaris for 'roughly twenty-six hundred dollars, including the air fare' at Uganda's independence. Denis Holman in the late 1960s printed a comparison of costs in the three new nations, with Tanzania (the old Tanganyika plus Zanzibar) the highest and Kenya the lowest, with per-person costs dropping as a second client was added. Costs varied from £55 to £60 a day for one.

The 1970s, however, with their enormous inflation, saw per-day costs go beyond £250 for a luxury safari, and in the 1980s £600 a day was a high, but not the highest, price.

Looking only at the amounts the well-heeled were willing to pay for hunting safaris, therefore, it may at first glance seem surprising that in the 1970s, first Tanzania and then Kenya brought hunting to an absolute halt. (Uganda's safari industry was swept away, as were a horrendous number of its people and its animals, by the violence of the 1970s and 1980s.) Tanzania subsequently allowed limited hunting again through its nationalized scheme, TAWICO, but Kenya has not allowed a visitor's gun to be fired since the day in 1977 when a Kenyan newspaper carried the banner headline, 'Farewell to Arms!'

The Game Department's estimated 1977–8 revenue had been 1,186,800 Kenyan pounds; the actual income after the ban was about 10,000. The loss would seem to have been enormous, and to this day various explanations are given for the turnabout, the World Bank, the IMF, and a conspiracy of animal-lovers being among the culprits. Whatever the reason – and there appear to have been several – Kenya does not appear to think itself the loser in the long run. It is apparently impossible now to reconstruct the political infighting that led to the hunting ban, but it is worth remembering the problems that the ban solved: first, the sequestration of large areas of land for use by a relatively small group of people, at a time when population pressure put land at a premium; second, reduction of the primary tourist resource, the game herds, at a time when increasing tourism wanted more of them; and, third, international disapproval of hunting at a time when the nation was seeking international favour.

A fourth factor is worth considering: that hunting represented one of the most vivid reminders of colonialism.

It can be argued that, from the 1950s to the close of hunting, people who went on hunting safaris paid more to get less. This is not to say that gear or service was any worse; quite the contrary (although there was a post-war shortage of quality camping materials until the early 1950s). But the geographical scope of the safari became limited, first by reduced client time and then by the 'block system', in which each safari was assigned an established area of land to hunt. Gone were the days of the two- or three-month hunt, gone the days of almost unlimited wandering. 'One of the most delightful things about sefari [sic] life is that there should be no hurry in it,' Rainsford had said in 1910. Now there was lots of hurry in it.

A sense of renewal runs through safari accounts up to the Second World War, a sense not of possessing Africa but of having the time and the peace to be possessed by it. It is contained in responses like Farson's 'being reborn . . . the world before Adam', and Dickinson's 'Let me live in the African wilds for absolute enjoyment, content, and peace'. The sense of a 'world before Adam' came not merely from the abundance of animals but also from the apparent suspension of time and of boundaries. When, then, time became a factor and boundaries were circumscribed, the experience was reduced. It became more difficult, in Vivienne de Watteville's telling phrase, to touch the earth.

This loss was mirrored in another – further loss of contact with the people of the safari. Less time meant less chance to watch and listen, perhaps to understand. The porters were long gone; now busyness and the press of time lessened the chance that the American visitor with three or even two weeks would come to know gunbearer or tent servant. The old feudal system was breaking down from other pressures, too; a safari workers' union was created. The atmosphere changed.

With no group was the change more apparent than the white hunters. Before the war, they had been a very small number, probably no more than 25 practising their craft at a time. In the 1950s, demands for their service rose phenomenally, and the rough-and-ready apprentice system that had trained and put an invisible stamp of approval on the former few broke down. Today, former professionals are rueful about those post-war days.

Eric Rundgren said there was a lowering of standards. Another hunter said some of the newcomers couldn't be trusted to stand firm if an animal charged; some couldn't even shoot straight. There were accusations of discreet blackmail (no tip, no trophy), of over-charging. It had all happened too fast, and trying to satisfy 400 licence-buyers a year with a professional cadre of a few dozen white hunters was impossible.

Some of the best white hunters had founded the East African Professional Hunters Association in 1934. They had 37 members by the war. They took in another 19 between 1947 and 1949, probably to fill vacancies (a number had been lost in the war; others – already near retirement at the association's founding – were gone). Between 1950 and 1960, they added 43 more members. Then, in the 16 years from 1961 to 1977 (the end of Kenyan hunting), they added 112 – more than their entire membership since its founding. Yet they refused admission to a considerable number who were not, they said, up to their standards; those rejected went right on offering themselves as professionals to an industry that needed them. The old-timers were shaken. They were forced to suffer the experience of medieval guildsmen when Renaissance mercantilism came: their elite had done its work wonderfully as a monopoly when supply exceeded demand, but it was an irrelevance in an open, eager market.

Bunny Allen has described his own experience in getting his first professional's licence in the 1930s – a meeting in Game Ranger Archie Ritchie's office, with a bottle of pink gin put out. 'It was like being in a very private little club,' Allen wrote, and those words might describe the white hunter's world until the 1950s. Men of good will, men of similar backgrounds and ideas, men good at their jobs formed a tight little group that was self-regulating and self-limiting, but when the explosive growth of the 1950s came, it was inevitable that good will and collegiality would not work as either a training system or a skills test. The result was a lot of bitterness.

The result was also a reduced experience for some clients. There really were inferior white hunters now, and some people paid a lot to hire them. 'The White Hunter racket' one disgusted professional wrote. 'Some of them are not qualified to be their own gunbearers.' There really was a movement toward the rushed, the impersonal, and, in a few cases, the 'positively unscrupulous'. You paid a great deal of money and you expected to get somebody like Stewart Granger, and now and then you got somebody who depended on his own gunbearer to find the animals and who overcharged you on car mileage and who demanded a tip in advance (up to £200). It was a system in decline – or, rather, a system self-destructing from too much stress.

'All-motorized, we simply rushed through the bush, and arrived at the other side of Africa before we had time or thought for hunting.' The car had become the essential ingredient of the shortened safari. The war gave it a new twist: four-wheel drive. The first four-wheel-drive vehicles were surplus Jeeps; then came the wonderful Land Rovers, and much later the Japanese versions of them. But to some of the old-timers, four-wheel drive is what really destroyed the safari. Now anybody could go anywhere. Now no little enclave of game was protected by gullies or mountains. Now not even the black mud of the rains was an obstacle to the three-week wonder from Chicago.

The stalwart East African landscape fought back, however. Farson averaged only 11 miles an hour getting from Isiolo up into the Northern Frontier Province. (In the mid-1980s, we drove at 50 mph over the terrible corduroy road and still couldn't keep up with the armed truck convoy that was supposed to protect all of us from bandits.) Tyres blew, and, in the rocky north, cars drove on half-deflated tyres to prevent blowouts.

In the midst of all this change, a few things held firm. As late as 1960, the Muthaiga Club had a rule that 'professional sportsmen' (including Beryl Markham's jockey) could not enter the club but had to wait on the verandah. Black tie was still worn in some places in the evening in Nairobi, but, astonishingly enough, the sun helmet had at last bitten the dust. (Roosevelt would have been pleased.) The tendency to seem something they were not still drove some Nairobi types to wear 'elephant-hair bracelets and leopard-skin hat bands' and still does, although now the leopard skin is plastic and the elephant hair is dyed grass.

The gorgeous excess of the 'champagne safari' was a victim of the war, but Americans who had known only American camping were none the less astonished. Jack O'Connor found a 1953 safari 'astonishing luxury for an old desert rat like me, who on most of his trips has been his own guide, his own cook, and his own skinner'. Progress had added a new touch: an evening message service from a Nairobi radio station for 'parties in the field'.

Ernest Hemingway came for his second gulp of East Africa in 1953, again with his wife (but not the one of 1933). Again, Percival was his white hunter. Perhaps it should have seemed like a repetition of the first safari, but too much had changed, most of all the writer himself. He had a block south of Kajiado, then another centred southwest of Lake Magadi. It was there that he shaved his head and dyed his clothes Masai red and went off with a spear and served as an honorary Game Ranger. It was there, too, that he had his Kamba 'fiancée'. He was a couple of years older now than Roosevelt had been for his safari, and perhaps age drove him to do things that now seem very foolish. It all ended badly when he and Mary Hemingway were injured in a plane crash in Uganda, then were injured again in the process of being rescued. European newspapers reported that he had been killed. It was like a nightmare about a safari, or at least a hung-over dream of one – attempting too much, going over the edge, seeing death.

While the hunting safari was suffering its decline, the kind of non-hunting trip pioneered by May French Sheldon and Mary Hall was at last becoming dominant. Attributes of the hunting safari persisted even when there was no hunting (the use of a white hunter with a gun most of all), but authorities were beginning to offer other possibilities. Most important was the national park movement, which had begun before the war but saw its greatest success in the decades after.

The Serengeti had been declared a national Park 'in principle' in 1940. It became so in fact some years later. In Kenya, the Nairobi National Park was created in 1946 as the result of years of work by Mervyn Cowie; it was followed by Tsavo in 1948, Mount Kenya in 1949, and the Aberdares in 1950. In Uganda, Queen Elizabeth and Murchison Falls Parks were established in 1952. Thus, by the mid-1950s there were large areas closed to hunting in which non-hunters could watch and photograph animals. Visitors were often suspicious, expecting little more than outdoor zoos, but they found, like an Italian visitor, that the great game parks were 'selvaggia, nel senso assoluto della parola' ('wild, in the fullest sense of the word'). You could be mauled by a lion or trampled by an elephant as well in one of them as in a hunting block; for the protection of both animals and humans, it became a rule that visitors could not leave their cars. Still, the elephant and rhino occasionally bashed a car to show whose parks they were.

In time, the parks were opened to camping. Visitors then found how *really* wild they were. One Park Ranger, camping in Nairobi National Park, was awakened in the night by sounds in his tent; flashing a light, he found a genet cat finishing his bacon. He drove the cat away, only to wake shortly after to the sound of it drinking his bath water. The bacon had been too salty.

Camping in the parks for the first time could be a shock. Putting up my first tent at Amboseli, I found I was standing in the midst of what seemed to be a field of elephant dung. The whole campsite appeared to be elephant dung. 'Oh, don't worry', I was told, 'you see, they've already come this way'. And, true enough, no elephants appeared. What came instead, on my first night in the bush, was a leopard that sneezed and wheezed around the perimeter of the tent and left its clear paw-marks.

Such sounds do not give confidence for night-time trips to the always distant privy. Hyenas, which seem to be ever-present at night, are noisy and close, and you remember the stories about their biting humans (usually sleeping drunks) in the dark, just as you remember that the hunting dog disables its male prey by biting off the testicles. As Negley Farson noted, it is a 'tickly job' to step out of a tent into the absolute darkness to relieve yourself, 'never . . . more so than when – Wa-yoooo!-woo! wooo – a huge hyena, not the little laughing variety, howled within ten feet of my bare behind'. My own tickly job came when I squatted over the slit in a long-drop privy in the dark and two bats flew up between my legs, acquainting themselves along the way with everything I thought of as private.

The camping safari is probably as close to the old safari as most of us can ever hope to come. Except for a few very expensive and intentionally anachronistic safaris (those of Abercrombie & Kent, for example), for which one pays well to evoke the old days, a group safari by minivan can come as near to touching the earth as East Africa offers nowadays. Companies literally put together walk-ins without reservations (although many such tours are reserved months in advance) for safaris of up to two weeks. African drivers and cooks often become the campers' first (sometimes their only) African acquaintances. Food is simple but good, cooked over big wood fires, eaten sitting on folding stools. Tents are small but adequate. Clients provide nothing but a sleeping-bag and their own beer, and, for about £24 a day they travel the old safari routes, sleeping on the African earth and waking to the sunrise on canvas – and trekking to the privy in the dark to the sounds of the African night.

It was because many visitors dislike tents and Wa-woos and long drops, however, that local and regional governments began to build other accommodation in the 1950s. East Africa had offered 'rest houses' – utterly simple, usually thatched, huts put up for the on-the-go ADCs – for as long as officials had gone on safari, and these had been available to visitors if not needed by the government. Government officials continued to have priority in 1953 in Tanganyika over such facilities as the dak bungalow at Itigi, which had a steward and a cook and running water, but visitors could use it otherwise. At Ngorongoro, there were seven single and four double huts – 'unfurnished, no staff' – two of each by reservation and the rest first-come, first-served, bring your own bedding and food. In Kenya, a number of locations had *bandas* (self-serve huts), but Ngulia Lodge at Tsavo and Ol Tukai at Amboseli were, in the 1950s, among those already offering hotel-style rooms.

The first 'safari lodges', as they came to be called, were very simple and were in fact much the same as bandas. 'Travellers . . . should carry with them bedding, food and cooking utensils.' The remnants of these are now usually run under concession, but they still offer some of the best bargains and the most pleasant living in the region. I remember with great pleasure a day and a night at a banda in Meru National Park in 1984, where we had to bring only our food; the beds had great swags of mosquito netting, and boiled water was brought in an oversize thermos jug, and while I cooked dinner a baboon came up on the porch to watch and two waterbuck grazed within 50 feet. I prefer to camp, but the East African banda is a wonderful change for a night or two.

In the 1960s, the safari lodges started to become the hotel-like structures we know nowadays. They ranged from 'tented camps' with big canvas tents under permanent thatched roofs, and attached bath and toilet tents 'after the Indian fashion', to clusters of luxurious cottages; to multi-storey hotels with *cordon bleu* dining-rooms and game-viewing over lighted pools and salt licks. Some of them – Treetops most of all – have become famous in their own right and offer experiences probably not available to the old tented safari.

Essential to a lodge safari, as to any other, is motor transport. Most vehicles nowadays will be either chauffeur-driven vans or big four-wheel-drive cars, all with viewing hatches in the roof. Big safari companies make up groups according to established itineraries to visit the major parks and lodges for £60 or so a day per person. Accommodation is equal to that in good hotels anywhere, and the pattern of the day is somewhat that of the old safari: up early and off for a morning 'game run', then back for lunch, sleep, a visit to the lodge gift shop, a swim in the filtered pool, and off on another game run before a multi-course dinner and, often, a get-together in the glow of a huge outdoor fire. Much can be said by traditionalists against the lodge safari, most of all that it can be so hermetic as to keep the visitor entirely from meeting East Africa; but it can be said in its favour that it has brought the safari into the present and made its rhythms and its sights available to a great many people who would never think of carrying a gun or sleeping in a tent.

Kenya remains the centre of safariland, such as it is nowadays. Nairobi-based safaris can be arranged well ahead of time through travel agents or international airlines but need not be so. The leading organizers of contemporary versions of the champagne safari seem to be Ker, Downey, and Abercrombie & Kent. The leading lodge-tour operator is United Touring Company (UTC). Small custom-safari companies may be harder to locate, but Gametrackers (Kenya) and Bushbuck are leaders in this area. Dozens – perhaps scores – of large and small operators run drop-in safaris, both lodge and camping, out of Mombasa and Nairobi. Intrepid travellers, most of them young, arrive in Nairobi with a backpack and a sleeping-bag and head out within a day or two for 3- to 14-day safaris that go all over Kenya.

The facts of international life, as represented by the borders inherited from colonialism, have restricted safariland even further than in the 1950s. John Bisley of Nairobi's Gametrackers told me he thought that a Kenya–Tanzania combination would be 'hard to beat', but such a combination was not usually possible in the 1980s. Nor was extension of a Kenyan safari into Uganda; indeed, once in the mid-1980s we could not even go into Kenya's Mount Elgon National Park because of rumours of armed intruders from Uganda.

Yet, even the more limited safaris of modern East Africa can be glorious experiences. Whether by chauffeur-driven Range Rover from luxury lodge to luxury lodge, or by jolting ex-military Bedford from campsite to campsite, they are like nothing in American or European experience. I, of course, prefer the second sort, with its resourceful cook and its tents and its outdoor existence. Others want the protection and the comfort offered by the first kind. Both are safaris – and both demand an appropriate attitude from the visitor; as Bisley told me, the most important thing would-be safarists can bring is 'an open mind – relaxed. Sometimes things take longer to do here than where most tourists come from. Rough roads and long journeys are part of it all.'

But, given that attitude, the safari can still enrich the visitor.

KAG

Clothes, gear, and edibles

SAFARIS were possible without lots of gear, but few went that way. Arthur Neumann was a great one for going off with very little. Others – Roosevelt's advisers, for example – never thought enough was as good as a feast. Indeed, theories of safari preparation broke down into two main camps: the Spartans, who kept trying to pare down until they had nothing but the clothes on their backs and a quinine pill; and the Athenians (post-Periclean Athenians, probably) who let the stuff accumulate and accumulate into ever larger piles, shouting like Sherman, 'Send in more men!' whenever the available porters were up to capacity. As Daniel Streeter said, the list for an Athenian's safari 'read like one of Walt Whitman's poems'.

The Spartan view, like so much that is sensible, worked against a basic human desire, or perhaps several human desires – the love of things for their own sakes; the love of gadgetry; the accumulation of souvenirs; fear of being 'not with it'. The Spartan view takes self-discipline, itself a rare quality in somebody spending an office worker's annual wage on a week's holiday.

Getting the gear for travel was the beginning of the journey. It was an act of sophistication, of being, in fact, not a tourist but a traveller. How close to travel itself it was to buy the tents and guns and folding baths, possession of which gave proof of being at home in this most foreign of foreign places, Africa. And how ultimately satisfying the buying and wearing of the clothes.

So, as a rule, newcomers took the Athenian route. The unvarnished truth might be that you could do a safari in your gardening clothes, with no more gear than you could toss into the rumble seat of a Model T, but fashion and advice and your own secret desires pushed you toward *things*, and you left Nairobi with a wonderfully satisfying collection. 'We had so much "kag" the springs groaned. "Kag" was festooned about us until we looked like peddlers.'

Clothes were the most important. Books, magazines, travel brochures, even personal letters, have always told us we could have our safari clothes made overnight in Nairobi, and they still do. The point is not that such a thing can be done – I suppose it can, although I've never tested it – but that obviously we all want it to be possible. We all want to be able to transform ourselves overnight in Nairobi, to arrive a caterpillar and leave a butterfly.

We take dressing very seriously; most of us are what we wear, or become what we wear. As the man in armour is vastly different from the same man in a bathrobe, as an actress in costume is vastly different from the same woman in blue jeans, so the safarists for the first time in bush shirt, hat, and boots, seeing themselves in the mirrors of the Norfolk, were transformed from the mundane creatures they had been in Milwaukee or Manchester.

Precisely what comprise 'safaris clothes' have changed over the years. Today's 'safari suit', in fact, has evolved so far from the safari that it is not worn by people on safari at all, but by African businessmen at work; it is an open-collared polyester suit whose jacket buttons from navel to clavicle. What we now define as 'safari clothes', on the other hand, are the product of a century of practical experience as amended by Hollywood costume design, and these vestments are worn not by the professionals of the safari industry but by their clients. (Professionals wear almost anything, it turns out.) Whatever tailor they came from, however, and whatever nods they make to current fashion elsewhere, it is safe to say that they are khaki or olive drab in colour, they are covered with pockets that button, they have epaulettes, and their vertical development is stopped with a hat.

The hat is crucial. A safari outfit without a hat would be a poor thing, indeed, unrecognizable to other tourists and confusing to the locals. The hat has an honourable past – so, for that matter, do epaulettes and buttoned pockets – but in its current avatar, with imitation leopard band and Aussie snap-up brim, that past is a little hard to find. Safari hats nowadays are a little like those raincoats that come festooned with brass rings – history explains them but does not make them sensible.

Europeans have always worn hats in BEA. A European without a hat was, until after the Second World War, a logical impossibility. The question was never until then hat or no hat, but what sort of hat, and what sort of decoration on it. We all know now that the only proper decoration is plastic leopard skin, but time was when settlers wore the real thing, or even gamier frills. Alan Black is supposed to have worn a hat 'with the tail tips of fourteen man-eating lions' dangling from it, whether as a sort of Spanish fringe or a band has not been passed down. Russell Bowker, an early settler, wore the entire skinned-out face of a leopard; other settlers made do with bands of fur. Obviously there are plenty of precedents for the modern plastic strip. The immediate one, however, is not a settler's hatband, but Stewart Granger's in *King Solomon's Mines* (1950) (although, oddly, Gregory Peck wore a leopard *print* hat band in the 1947 *Macomber Affair*).

Behind the hat (or under it, perhaps) was an abiding European superstition that the African sun would cook the brains in a trice. The observed truth that the sun had no such effect on Africans was taken as evidence that Africans were physically different. Several styles of hat were available: the rather Teutonic cork helmet of the sort Americans associate with London police, probably a tropical adaptation of the metal military helmet; the sola topi, or pith helmet, or Bombay bowler, lower in the crown and wider in the brim than the helmet; the double terai, a felt hat that looked as if the wearer had put somebody else's hat on top of his own (named, probably, after the tiger country of the Himalayan Terai); and the soft felt South African hat, hardly distinguishable from the American Stetson. Both the double terai and the soft felt were probably latter-day versions of the slouch hat of the eighteenth and early nineteenth century, often seen in sporting prints.

Other hats were tried, to be sure. Jackson urged the use in the bush of 'Ellwood's patent Shikar hat of felt and brown canvas' and had no use at all for the sola topi, which caught on every bush and which the rain 'reduced to a heavy shapeless pulp'. This was advice specifically for hunters, however, and Ellwood's patent never caught on generally. Perhaps a few people tried woven straw (Katherine Petherick had in 1861 in Sudan), which served well in the Caribbean, but it was probably not thought opaque enough.

In fact, the sun's potency was so revered that some people kept their hats on indoors, like the heroine at lunch in *Woodsmoke*. Mere corrugated iron was not trusted to keep the sun out. Lugard suggested going under a good, stout tree if the hat had to be removed. (This must have made tipping one's hat good exercise.) The elephant-hunter Bell wrote that 'when the solar topee [*sic*] was at the zenith of its power . . . it was still considered to be suicidal to be caught by the sun outside its enveloping shade'.

Many Europeans added a 'spine pad' to the enveloping shade, one early visitor warning that the parts to be protected from 'the deadly tropical sun' included 'the nape of the neck and the base of the brain'. Stewart Edward White said flatly that 'the protection of helmet and spine pad should never be omitted, no matter what the weather, between nine o'clock and four'. In that case, a sola topi and a spine pad must have been excellent things in the long rains, the one turned to mush and the other to a cold sponge laid against the back.

Cherry Kearton's films of Roosevelt's safari show a wide variety of hats, but they do show every European wearing at least one, both on the march and at the ceremonies staged for the great man. (One man is clearly wearing two.) Roosevelt himself is most often seen in a topi, although Cuninghame wore a soft South African felt. In Martin Johnson's 1923 film *Simba*, both the topi and the wide-brimmed felt are common. The double terai was never, probably, as popular, although it was still showing up in photographs of the royal safaris at the end of the 1920s.

The topi was Indian and sometimes came wrapped in a fabric scarf, the pugaree; this was sometimes let fall behind (as in some engravings of Stanley, and in the motion picture of his life starring Spencer Tracy). The wide soft hat from South Africa, Australia, or America was also supplied with a fabric band. Sometimes the band was a pugaree of pongee (raw) silk in cream or ecru (the natural colour), folded and twisted.

Why the hat became the locus of animal trophies is unclear; perhaps it was the most visible location because the highest. Perhaps it was part of the military legacy of the hat, both the helmet and the soft-felt types having wide military use; insignia always wound up on the hat. Medieval knights are supposed to have put tokens there. American Plains Indians, on the other hand, carried trophies at the waist or on a separate shaft; the Shifta of northern Kenya and Somalia are said to have worn the testicles of their victims on their belts, not on their hats.

Or perhaps evidence of a man's prowess (the implication of the leopard band is that the wearer has killed the leopard) went on his hat because men's hats tend to take on a good deal of individual identity; also, they are the item of clothing that is worn every day, so the trophy once secured to a hat need not be removed. At any rate, that hats took on an emblematic role is clear.

At the end of the 1920s, Game Ranger Archie Ritchie wore 'a brown Spanish hat', apparently without decoration. He made up for it on his car, however, which had a pair of rhino horns on the radiator. In 1950, Negley Farson was still being advised to wear a hat in the Northern Frontier Province or be 'struck dead'.

About the only people who wear hats in Nairobi now are tourists. On the other hand, I lost my hat up north and the next day was flat on my back with heat exhaustion. However, I hadn't worn a spine pad, either, so perhaps that was the cause.

The rest of the safari costume was beginning to take shape by the turn of the century, much of it again based on Indian or military fashion. 'Kharki [sic] Norfolk jackets with spinal paddings, flannel shirt, cummerbund, knickerbockers, strong shooting boots, and pith helmets', Willoughby advised in the 1890s; he meant by 'Kharki' both a colour and a fabric (cotton twill). One recognizes the fear of the sun here in the spinal pad and the cummerbund (later the flannel wrap or the abdominal belt); we should recognize a fairly practical shooting outfit, too, in the breeches and good boots. The Norfolk jacket, itself a form of shooting coat, was one forerunner of an essential of the safari costume – the bush jacket. (The other important forebear was the military coat.)

Clothes for safari wear were already being made in Mombasa and Zanzibar before the turn of the century and were cheaper there than in London; Jackson advised getting 'knickerbocker breeches' with leather knees in one place or the other, and leggings (gaiters) with 'spat' feet. We are inclined to forget nowadays that hunting really used to be hunting, with a good deal of the stalk done on hands and knees, for which leather facings were more than useful. Selous can be seen in one photo of the Roosevelt safari wearing knee-pads, which in thorn country would have made a lot of sense. Jackson also recommended clothes of 'Kharki and Indian shikar cloth', particularly a coat made 'Norfolk jacket fashion' with big hip pockets 'fairly large and roomy [with] a good deep flap [that] should be made to button'. He wanted a breast pocket on the left but none on the right so the rifle butt would have nothing to catch on, and two sets of cartridge loops 'for the cartridges of the two Express rifles most in use'. This was the bush jacket nearing adolescence – breast and waist pockets, button flaps, cartridge loops.

In 1900, Burberry's advertised a 'Veldt-coat' (the Boer War had begun) and said it was 'an adaptation of the Tennis Shirt to Field uses'. The Veldt-coat (shown 10 years later as the Gabardine Suit, same illustration) was made of 'Tropical Rainproof materials' and was for 'Sport in Hot Weather. Invaluable to Gentlemen who perspire freely'. It had the shape of the bush jacket, only without the pockets; descended from a shirt instead of a jacket, it had implications of looseness and light fabric. A 1900 photo of Sir Alfred Pease shows another prototypical bush jacket, belted with leather but with big waist and breast pockets and a shirt-like small collar. The Veldt-coat was shown worn with breeches and puttees, and this is the outfit we hear about and see until after the First World War – gaiters or puttees, breeches, and some version of the Norfolk or military coat.

After the war, puttees were gradually retired, perhaps because of the years of field experience with that hideously impractical invention. Breeches were kept, however, but more and more as riding breeches, and through the 1920s we see and hear about lace-up knee-boots for both riding and walking. Above them, either a flannel shirt or some version of the bush jacket was seen. In 1940, Negley Farson had made in Dar es Salaam two shirts that sound like unbelted bush jackets, with pockets that 'could almost carry a camp kit (although they did look like maternity jackets)'.

Although some men (and women, too) were beginning to wear trousers in the field in the 1920s, the common alternative to breeches for men were shorts. Selous is shown in an engraving wearing shorts in the 1880s, perhaps surprising to those of us who think of Victorian niceties about legs and limbs. Roosevelt said that a bare-kneed young Philip Percival wore a flannel shirt, shorts, puttees, and boots in 1909; Stigand found shorts 'comfortable and cool' a few years later, but shorts allowed 'an interminable succession of sores, cuts, and bruises on the knee', not to mention the horrendous annoyance of ticks in places like the Athi Plains. Streeter went one better than the shorts-wearers by doing without pants altogether: 'It was cooler.'

Women's clothes changed more radically and far more swiftly than men's, but they had much further to go. Katherine Petherick, in Sudan in the 1860s, wore 'yellow Turkish boots, very loose and uncomfortable; full Turkish trousers, but over them a brown holland skirt or petticoat, and a white flannel jacket with capacious pockets; upon my head an enormous straw hat, over which folds of muslin were rolled'. May French Sheldon and Mary Hall inevitably wore full-length skirts. In 1905, Ethel Younghusband was wearing wool serge skirts as 'the most useful things . . . for ordinary rough walking. . . . They should be made short, as it is so very tiring to hold up a dress in the tropics.' Her idea of short, however, as her photos show, was barely ankle length. She hunted in such skirts and walked with her husband an entire safari north of Naivasha, varying them with puttees and boots under khaki skirts, carrying a silk parasol.

Another woman who came to East Africa a year or two later to hunt, however, quickly got rid of the 'silly little skirt' that she was supposed to wear over knickers and gaiters. It caught on thorns and was a nuisance, and she chucked it. Still, in 1913, Billy White was wearing skirts, as well as a veil and gloves. Perhaps women travelling with men, even their husbands, were reluctant to put off their skirts. At any rate, until the end of the First World War, most women could still be found in skirts on safari; 10 years after war's end, it would be hard to find any dressed that way.

One handbook of 1900 had advised that '*wool* is the watchword of all who value health', but in fact almost everyone preferred cotton, usually in a twill weave. Flannel was recommended for underwear and blankets (Jaeger flannel, usually). After the war, these same preferences continued, with flannel underwear becoming less common.

The spine pad, however – like the hat – persisted. Stewart Edward White thought that spine pads looked like the hotpads used in handling hot irons; they were quilted, often lined with red or orange to absorb 'actinic rays'. George Eastman was still wearing one in 1928, although some people (including Roosevelt) had done without them decades before. It appears that fear of the sun even caused some men to dye their underwear black (that was the reason they gave, at least) and to line their spinal pads with tinfoil.

A few diehards even continued to wear abdominal bandages. Lugard had recomended a thick cummerbund made from a wool blanket, to prevent the fever, dysentery, and cholera caused by chilling the stomach, liver, and spleen. Others recommended flannel sashes to fight the heat. When I was a boy, dreaming over the Bannerman Brothers' catalogue of military surplus, one of the few things that I could afford was a flannel abdominal bandage, a relic of America's adventures in Cuba and the Philippines. I never bought one, however. Children have innate common sense: I knew those things couldn't prevent cholera. Anyway, what can you play with an abdominal bandage – Epidemic?

She was 'unspeakably slim and shadowy in riding-breeches and a skirted tussore coat'. This was supposed to be a woman on safari in 1914, but it was written in 1924 and actually reflects the taste of that time. This look for women would last well into the 1930s; in fact, the Nazi villainess of *Jungle Queen*, a movie serial of the Second World War, would wear it, but it was dated by then. Slacks began to appear in the late 1920s; they would in fact shortly become the most practical costume. Vivienne de Watteville, on the other hand, lived a 'Peter Pan existence' in shorts, high on Mt Kenya in the late 1920s.

It was also in the 1920s that American clothes began to show up in BEA. Some sportsmen now wore L. L. Bean's rubber-bottomed boots in the field instead of rope-soled shoes (descended from British India) or hobnailed boots (from British Britain). Aggressive merchandising by New York's Abercrombie & Fitch ('where the blazed trail crosses the avenue') had made it the premier

American outfitter, one that boasted that whole safaris could be put together without ever leaving the store. Many Americans did just that instead of doing their buying in London, and probably the influence of the more casual American sporting clothes dates from this time. In one important sense, American summer outdoor clothes were better adapted to BEA than either English or Indian ones: they came from a similar climate.

American or British, everybody still used mosquito boots. They are not seen any more, that I know of, but they lasted until the 1950s – thigh-high soft boots to wear with pyjamas in the evening.

By the 1930s, Maydon was recommending slacks instead of breeches (nobody much was riding horses, after all; cars were in wide use), with canvas gaiters and shorts or knickers. The fashions as we now know them were set, and the Indian tailors of Nairobi and Arusha would come to your hotel to measure you for custom clothing. It was remarkably cheap and remarkably good, and it was delivered next day, as a rule. Hats were bought separately.

When you set forth, you looked pretty much like the image we now carry of somebody on safari – lots of pockets, cartridge loops, slacks, stout walking shoes. A felt hat, probably flat-crowned and fairly wide-brimmed, or just possibly a sola topi; the helmet and the double terai had joined the dinosaur. Around your hat, a pugaree; you still had to earn the leopard band.

This image of c.1935 was raised to fashion stardom in the 1980s with the help of the film of *Out of Africa* and a rage for natural fabrics and 'authenticity'. Perhaps the only detail added by the Second World War was the epaulette, which bush shirts and bush jackets acquired in imitation of desert and jungle wear. Epaulettes themselves have a long history and were once made of metal, although even then they were vestiges of an earlier piece of shoulder-protecting armour. In cloth or cloth-covered board, they have long served to carry military rank on the shoulder. Now, like the brass sword-rings on the raincoat, they are inexplicable, although they do prove useful to hold purses or binoculars on the shoulder. They also have the great advantage of making the shoulders seem broader.

Most 'safari clothes' now go home as clean as they are first put on. Many spend their useful hours compressed between large bodies and safari-lodge barstools or minivan seats. It is worth reminding ourselves, however, that they are as they are because of now-lost practical demands of climate and of activity, particularly hunting.

On the other hand, certain safari clothes had a quite different, now lost, practicality. 'The clothing question cannot be left without emphasizing the absolute necessity of including evening-dress clothes in one's kit . . . At any station of any size in East Africa a dinner-jacket suit is certainly required.'

'I took with me a blanket, etc, and a little food, so as to be prepared for sleeping out.' This was Arthur Neumann, the Spartan's Spartan. W. S. Rainsford, who may be taken as a moderately conservative Athenian, recommended Jaeger blankets made into a sleeping-bag; hair mattress, pillows, and camp-bed; table and canvas chair; and dining table and mosquito net. The Athenian in full flower was McCutcheon: 'camping rugs, blankets, cork mattresses, pillows and pillow cases, bed bags, towels, lanterns, mosquito boots, whetstones, hunting and skinning knives, khaki helmets, pocket tapes to measure trophies, Pasteur anti-venomous serum, hypodermic syringes, chairs, tables, cots, puttees, sweaters, raincoats, Jaeger flannels, socks, and pajamas, cholera belts, Burberry hunting clothes, and lots of other little odds and ends'. In truth, such a list could be endless.

Probably the most important item was the tent. As Thomson pointed out, a tent was *home*; why skimp? Early in the century, Edgington's green, rot-proof canvas weighed 120 lb and, with poles, made three porter-loads. Roosevelt had both an Edgington and an Abercrombie & Fitch – or a heavy and a light – tent. The light seems to have had a sewn-in bug-proof door (unusual for the period), the heavy a bathing extension in the rear.

As early as 1913, however, safaris into the country far from Nairobi were trying to cut weight by using light tents because food for porters was so hard to find. Cuninghame designed one for White – quite possibly inspired by Roosevelt's lightweight – with sewn-in groundcloth 'and built to pitch with cross poles slipped inside a hem at either side'. This safari was a more or less Spartan one, for which White allowed himself and his wife only a couple of luxuries – 'golden syrup and a light folding camp-chair apiece'.

In that same year, Leslie Simson recommended to a visitor a 'very light tent, 24 lb weight, of paraffin oiled silk ... sold by Messrs Abercrombie and Fritz [*sic*]'.

Tents in the 1930s were still running to at least 40 lb, often to 60 lb, but these were full-size tents with eight-foot peaks, big enough for camp-beds and tables. In fact, these weights are about as light as such tents can get without going to very light fabrics, and many people like a heavy fabric when the night is noisy, for all that their logical selves know that a lion can rip the heaviest of canvas like rotten gauze.

Separate dining-tents were, and often still are, a feature of long safaris. The wind is sometimes bad in the evening in some locations, insects troublesome in others. The Johnsons in the late 1920s had a dining-tent lined with yellow to make it 'sun-proof'. Eastman travelled in Uganda with a gauze dining-tent against insects. In its later forms after the Second World War, the dining-tent became the camp centre, location of the radio, a refrigerator, gas lanterns, and tables and chairs, but in insect-free regions (and there are many) it shed two or three walls and its bug-proof net.

Toilets were highly varied. For one safari of the 1950s, a 'canvas comfort station' was set up 'discreetly behind the nearest bush'. Spartan safaris made do with a shovel and a thornbush. At the other extreme were separate little tents and all manner of elaborate devices like that 'Bush Thunder-box' in Waugh's *Men at Arms*, 'a mechanism of heavy cast-brass and patterned earthenware of solid Edwardian workmanship'. Nowadays, many East African campsites have privies, some very clean and workable, others so offensive they make you wish for the bush and shovel.

Although gadgetry – ice machines, folding wash-stands, patent camp-beds – occupied some visitors' attention, the focus of many turned, after the matters of clothes and tent, to survival: food and medical kit. Without exception in the hunting period, game meat made up the bulk of most menus, but this was augmented by canned and then iced goods as transportation improved. Again, of course, travellers took either the ascetic's or the sybarite's route. 'A sportsman . . . does not go to Africa to eat', said one, but another wrote that 'the party went on safari as though they took Fortnum and Mason in their hip-pockets'. Medicines, like foods, varied widely, with early travellers trying for self-sufficiency and recent ones relying increasingly on their outfitters.

The most important food item was water. Water was the great leveller: everybody needed it and nobody could carry enough of it. Parts of safariland are abundantly supplied with water, but many game areas are not. One result in the early years was that travellers didn't drink enough of it, and their constant fear of the sun was probably based on very real experiences with dehydration, which they blamed on the sun rather than their own chronic lack of water.

Lord Hindlip, for example, reported having his first water since morning at 6:30 p.m. after a day's hunting. Many would take only a pint of water for a full day in the heat. One medical theory even advised newcomers that they should learn to do without water altogether.

To be sure, available water was often unappetizing. May French Sheldon spread a waterproof canvas and caught rain, a relatively pure source, but she travelled in the rainy season; Martin Johnson did the same in season, using a copper still the rest of the time. In the mid-nineteenth century, Grant reported one waterhole that turned spoons black and litmus paper red, another where the water was 'nitrous, and nearly the price of beer'. Von Hohnel and Teleki made Lake Turkana's alkaline water potable by adding tartaric acid so it effervesced. 'This improved the taste considerably'. However, it also 'had a purgative effect, alike on man and the animals, which added to the weakness of our already enervated caravan'.

The elephant-hunter Sutherland, on the other hand, believed in alcohol, not water. 'To endure month in month out, year in year out, the arduous work of elephant hunting in a hot and enervating climate, considerable quantity of alcohol is absolutely essential to my physical well-being.' He drank whisky-and-soda and half a bottle of port each evening. He was a kind of bellwether: distillers have always been widely represented in all outlets for safari advertising.

When it came to actual, edible food, the abilities of a cook were critical. He (they were always men and still are) had to be able to cook complete European meals, including breads, on an open wood fire, and had to be able to improvise a kitchen without walls. One safarist had 'a vile cook, but on the whole a cheery fellow', not the arrangement most would have wanted for two or three months, where vile personality and culinary skill would have been preferred. Hoefler in 1929 had a more desirable cook who 'set up his establishment' in the bush, 'hanging his pots and pans from convenient limbs'. He improvised a 'regular system of shelves', then made a stove from a five-gallon can. Finch Hatton in 1919 had a 'real Swahili ruffian of the old safari type' who could 'devil chicken *à merveille* and is an expert baker. . . .'

The ability to bake was for many the test of the cook. Eastman, himself a camp cook of some skill, was disgusted with his second-safari cook's inability to find good yeast to make bread; he and Osa Johnson enjoyed baking over coals as a shared camp task. Probably what Finch Hatton meant by a cook of the 'old safari type' was that he had mastered such baking, as well as other aspects of English cuisine. The cooks with whom I've travelled in East Africa still cook as if their clientele were British, in fact; the last one specialized in mulberry crumble. And the baking of yeast breads remains a matter of great pride.

The other test of the safari cook was his ability to cope with fresh game meat, moreover to cope with the monotony of the same meat again and again. This was particularly troublesome with big animals, one of the drawbacks of elephant hunting being that when you were successful, you wound up with an elephant.

'We had to live for several days on the tongue and part of the trunk of the elephant . . . [which] is perfectly good, but excessively stringy and tough.' Elephant trunk appeared so many times at the de Watteville table that one day Vivienne's father 'flatly refused to look down those two holes, i.e., the nostrils, for another meal.'

Other big animals had the same drawbacks. 'The menu was:

Consommé (giraffe)
Tongue (giraffe's)   all good.'
Tail (giraffe's)

But, despite monotony, some game foods were prized. One *Field* correspondent found marrow-bone of giraffe, toasted in embers and split, so luxurious that he thought it brought on an attack of malaria. 'Tommy' (Thomson's gazelle) steaks were always welcome, but Grant's gazelles were believed wormy. Eland was and still is a prized meat. Buffalo was found excellent, as was wildebeeste. Some people like hippo – but, of course, if you liked hippo, you had to like a lot of hippo.

Zebra and waterbuck, on the other hand, were shot for the porters but were not acceptable for the European table. Rhinoceros, 'though sweet, requires very sharp teeth'.

Alternatives to this meaty diet were rare. Vivienne de Watteville and her father came on a tiny duka in the desert bush where they found a few cans of European vegetables; they might as well have picked up diamonds. Local fruit and some vegetables could be traded for, but these were seasonal and travellers could never depend on finding any. (Now, one of the pleasures of Kenyan touring is buying at local markets, which may be quite elaborate or no more than a few squares marked on the ground with stones; within these will be laid out the portions to be sold – four piles of three small tomatoes each, five thumb-sized bananas, two pawpaws.)

Fish was a welcome change. It did not always appear as one might wish it, of course; Donaldson Smith got it once cooked in Vaseline. Nor was it always a variety you recognized. Many East African fish are of the catfish family, others what Europeans call 'coarse' fish. Yet they are edible and often plentiful and big; Bronson, in 1907, caught 45 in the Ewaso Nyiro (south) and watched Outram catch five eight-pounders in a river he called the Lenderut (the Olgainet?). Osa Johnson was a great angler and caught big strings in the Ewaso Nyiro (north).

By the time she was fishing, too, many of Kenya's rivers had trout. Ewart Grogan had stocked some in 1906; Hildegarde Hinde wrote to Moreton Frewen, however, that Grogan's trout died but her husband's thrived, so the origin of the Kenyan trout fishery may be ascribable to him. At any rate, Osa Johnson outfished Daniel Pomeroy for trout on the Thika in 1927, and one of her husband's photographs shows her with a 5-lb and a 3-lb trout from below Mt Kenya. It is said a 16-lb trout was caught in the crocodile-filled Ewaso Nyiro around the Second World War.

The end result of it all, if one had a good cook, was that food became one of the highlights of the safari. The safarists' menus, recollected in tranquillity, suggest just such pleasure: 'Delicious giraffe tail soup, boiled buffalo tongue, and beans done as your Boston aunt used to cook them.' 'Precious sparkling beer ... slices of saddle of "Tommy" with fried potatoes and onions, then water biscuits and butter or jam to follow.' 'Soup, wild birds or game, meat, vegetables and canned fruit, bread, jam, tea or coffee.' 'Mallow-soup ... cutlets of gazelle and a spatchcocked ['split-open down the breast and spread out flat like a kipper', according to the Stigands] guinea-fowl, then curried venison and a marvelous pudding (cornflan from Glasgow, peaches from Australia or pine-apple from Natal) tea, [and] a final "tot".' 'Sandgrouse or Franklin [francolin] partridge ... or a bustard. ... Every five days we killed a topi and had fresh steaks and liver and roasts.'

The essential of all safari cooking is a good fire, and a good one is large. Safari cooks do not cook on a few twigs like American woodsmen; they create a varied topography of ash, coals, and flame that allows for a variety of heat as subtle as a good gas stove's. A proper safari fire is at least six feet across, for which the gathering of wood becomes a daily ritual. In much of safariland, the wood – often elephant-killed – is easily available, dry, and wonderfully fragrant, with the 'cedar' of Laikipia a personal favourite. Wood-gatherers, of course, need to exercise normal care of snakes and scorpions.

In this hot canvas, the artist does his work. Every meal inspires him, but evening meals of course bring out the best. A few recipies will have to suffice, with the first not prepared by the cook at all:

Sundowners

(Carveth Wells)

'This is probably the most important institution in Africa. The word is singular, but in practice there are usually sundowners of various kinds. Among others, I found French Vermouth and gin delightful, or a gin and gingerbeer (not ginger ale) . . . of course, a plain whiskey and soda makes a good sundowner, too. So far as I could see, the African resident likes a sunriser, an eleven o'clocker, an appetizer before lunch, a great many sundowners, and a few nightcaps.'

Bread

On a dry day, mix about four cups of white flour and one of Graham (whole wheat) with enough salt to mound in the centre of the palm. Use plenty of good yeast, perhaps double the normal (i.e., two packages of the dry). Let the yeast work with a cup of warm water and a little flour; when foamy, add it to the flour and enough warm water to mix into a firm dough. Turn out on some sort of flat surface – improvisation is everything in safari cooking – and knead for at least 10 minutes, adding flour to the surface until the dough can be worked with both hands without much sticking. Let rise for an hour in a warm place (a dark bowl in the sun is good, the upper surface of the dough oiled and then covered with a cloth to prevent drying). Knead down, form into a loaf, and let rise again for an hour or less. (The second rise is best done in the oiled baking container – a steel or cast-iron bowl or pan.) Rake aside very hot ash and some coals from the central fire; put the baking container on the ash and coals, then mound ash around it and pile ash and coals on the top. (Improvise a cover with a metal plate if nothing else appears.) The Stigands, on the other hand, recommended making an oven out of a hollow in a termite's nest, a questionable improvisation given the tendency of black mambas to take up residence in termite mounds. After 40 minutes, check the now fragrant bread, whose odour will tell you when it is almost done. Encourage a good brown upper crust with more coals on top in the final minutes. Try to keep people from eating all of it before dinner.

Ugali

For this East African staple, specially ground maize meal is best. However, the American corn product called grits is almost identical, and any corn meal that will make polenta will make ugali. Boil (for one) a cup of water; when it is boiling, sprinkle in three or four tablespoons of the meal. (If you drop instead of sprinkling, you will get lumps.) Add very little or no salt; salt spoils the sweet taste of the corn. Stir. Very quickly, the meal will absorb all the water and a thick batter will form. Move to a cool part of the fire – hot ash, if possible. Let cook slowly there until, when you stir, some grains stick to the bottom. Turn out on a plate and let cool to lukewarm. Eat, using the ugali as the medium to pick up other food.

My last cook reached into the cooking pot and actually picked up the mass and turned it over; the ugali was almost a loaf, and the pan came absolutely clean. I never found out how he did this.

Sukuma Wiki

The name is Swahili for 'end of the week', or bottom of the wallet. It is the cheapest and best of vegetables, but so lacking in status that one driver would not go with me to buy it at the market. Any good greens like collards will do. Boil with a little salt and perhaps an onion for half an hour or so; drain. Eat with ugali.

Steak Wapagazi

Or liver, kidney, or any other cut of game. Find a good 24-inch stick the size of a finger. Sharpen both ends. Skewer the meat with one end, looping the meat between skewerings. Push the other end of the stick into the ground close to the fire so the meat will broil, slightly aslant so the drippings fall on the ground. Turn the stick to cook the meat on all sides. Remove pieces or eat from the stick when you can wait no longer. (This safari classic is the centrepiece of the last section of Hemingway's *Green Hills of Africa*.)

Jugged Lion, Omohundro

(Alexander Lake)

'Skin and clean a young lion, preferably one about 6 months old. Save 1 cup of blood and add 1 cup of vinegar to it. Cut meat into stew-size pieces and mix with uncooked onions and celery. Pour wine (any kind) over the mixture and let stand for at least 12 hours, stirring occasionally. Drain. Season with salt and pepper. Put all together again in more wine with favourite spices. A spot of garlic goes well, too. Cook until fat rises. Skim. Bake until done, then add blood vinegar and take from heat without further cooking. Serve with stewed mushrooms and boiled onions.'

Elisa's Suet Pudding with Foaming Sauce

(George Eastman and Osa Johnson)

Mix together a cup each of suet (beef fat from eland or buffalo), molasses, raisins, and currants, with three cups of flour, two teaspoons of baking powder, a cup and a half of milk, and salt, cloves, and cinnamon. Turn into a buttered mould or bowl, cover, and steam for five hours. The result will be a dark, rich, artery-clogging thing my grandmother would have called plum pudding.

For the sauce, cream half a cup of butter and a cup of sugar in a metal bowl, then add the yolk of the egg and put the bowl in a longer container of boiling water to melt the butter. Add a bit of boiling water and as much sherry as the conflict of good judgement and desire will allow. Beat the white of the egg until it stands in peaks and add to the rest just before serving. The combination of sauce and pudding will finish the day so richly that you may not want to rise for the next and will give you a new understanding of the popularity of Epsom salts on safari.

After food, medicine: no early traveller seemed able to carry enough of either. Most food that was carried was a luxury; most medicine was a necessity. The contradiction early on was that medical science itself did not know much about many diseases or their cure, and so travellers carried all sorts of things. Without question, however, medical kits shrank as the twentieth century progressed; probably the greatest single cause was the discovery of an effective prophylactic for malaria; the next would be antibiotics. Between these events, various medicines and cure-alls, some effective and some daft, were carried.

In the beginning, the safarist had to plan to be physician to as many as 100 people; now, there are hospitals in safari country, and every travel agent knows about the two kinds of malaria. None the less, doctors are still welcome on safaris (and sometimes get cut rates), and far from the cities anybody with a pretence to medical knowledge can have an instant clientele by taking out a thermometer or a pill.

I travelled on a camping safari in the early 1980s with two young British doctors, who had brought a plastic bag of the sorts of emergency supplies an intelligent doctor would take. When they sat down under a tree in Masai country with this, Masai women drifted in as if a public-address system had gone up, and within minutes one of the doctors was treating a years-old panga (machete) slash that had, after healing over, again burst and begun to suppurate.

One need only bring the look of the West. In a Masai manyatta, a young woman with a baby on her back approached me. 'Pills', she said. (It sounded like an Italian calling for German beer: *pils*.) She pointed at the baby. '*Pills. Pills.*'

'Calomel and julep, quinine, the first thing in the morning, and strong soup or hot grog', Grant wrote in the 1850s. 'Fever' was a constant companion, the cause of malaria not really understood. Things were no better by Stanley's day: 'No quinine should be taken until [such cathartics as colocynth, calomel, resin of julep, and Epsom salts] shall have prepared the system'. Purgatives thus formed a large part of the medical kit, although Africa was not the cause; the British carried their anal preoccupations everywhere with them.

By 1900, however, a Major Ross was delivering a London lecture in which he laid out clearly the entire malarial cycle; by 1908, the *Field* was declaring malaria preventable and 'doomed to extinction'. Thereafter, safari travellers got advice on varying amounts of quinine to take, and the folk medicines and the quack cures disappeared.

Science and received wisdom mixed. Champagne was considered a restorative. Coffee or cocoa, first thing in the morning, prevented 'miasma, which . . . is worse just when getting up'. Infection was not preventable, so 'wounds which might contain poison must be kept open by inserting vaseline-soaked lint, and allowed to suppurate'. Cold baths prevented chills; then again, tepid or warm baths prevented chills. Sitting in draughts or sleeping on the ground was bad.

Until penicillin and the antibiotics, the common specific against infection was potassium permanganate, a ferocious salt that worked by destroying both bacteria and tissue. Carried in crystal form, it made up one leg of the medicinal triad – permanganate, quinine, and cathartics. When severe injuries occurred from animals or gunshots, the raw permanganate crystals were sometimes sprinkled directly on the wounds. More commonly, the crystals were dissolved in water and injected into the wounds, for which a large hypodermic was carried. When one was not available, anything that would get the solution deep into a puncture wound was used – a gun barrel, for example. More than one sufferer found the pain of the cure worse than the injury. The only argument in its favour was that it worked.

Severe pain was always a possibility. Early in the century, both cocaine and morphine were available; Hindlip used a five per cent cocaine solution to flush the venom of a spitting cobra out of a porter's eyes. This treatment was preferable to the rough-and-ready one of kneeling on the victim's chest and urinating into his eyes.

The early safari traveller might suddenly have to turn doctor. This role was increasingly assumed by the white hunters after the First World War, as their duties expanded and the clients' skills shrank; still, bush medicine was often called for. Petherick, in the 1860s, treated a man who had a spear through his back to below his collarbone. Barbed, the spear had to be pushed entirely on through; the wound was treated with sulphuric acid. The man recovered. One of Grant's servants blew off part of a finger, and Grant removed the rest with a razor without an aesthetic. May French Sheldon, who had some medical training, vaccinated her men for smallpox; both Barnes and Rainsford had seen instances of tooth-pulling in the bush. Decle stitched up by lantern-light the wounds of a man badly bitten in one leg by a lion. In the late 1920s, Finch Hatton advised Patterson to bring 'a medical outfit with which we could do a major operation if necessary'; ironically, it was on that safari that Finch Hatton was bitten in the backside by a crocodile and had to return to Nairobi. Most safaris did not have such dubious excitements, however, and fewer and fewer as the present was reached; most visitors were never called upon to dispense anything more powerful than the medicines recommended by Vivienne de Watteville – quinine, Epsom salts, and an antiseptic, for which she suggested Lysol, iodine, and Germolene.

Yet it is wise to be prepared. I carry a small kit of my own, ever since I looked into the first-aid box of my first outfitter and found only a few bottles and packages marked in Urdu, a language that nobody on the safari read. I was glad of my caution when I had to cope with my first safari injuries – not from a lion or a gun, but a car accident.

THAT GLORIOUS MADNESS
The hunters and the hunted

Y ESTERDAY'S work is today's sport. Set off from work by rules as a park
is set off from wilderness, sport requires leisure and some degree of
affluence, even if it is only the relative affluence of the person who does
not need to kill to eat. Sport has developed its own ethic and its own literature,
much of both devoted to emphasizing the separation from work (e.g., the dry
fly as a fishing tool to be compared with the net).

'The hunter is a death dealer', wrote Ortega y Gasset, one of hunting's
philosophers. Death is at the centre of hunting and gives the sport seriousness,
for death makes hunting an unnecessary and non-productive (that is, non-
labouring) giving of death. Hunting's moral importance, too, springs from
death, for it is only in the responsible acceptance of death-dealing that the
hunter can claim respectability. The hunter cannot be indifferent to the death
of the prey, or the hunter becomes morally contemptible; the hunter must will
the death and will to accept the consequences of the death. Paradoxically, this
seriousness has made the best hunters among the world's greatest lovers of
animals, and it has made the act of hunting the essence of life for them, what
Vivienne de Watteville called 'that glorious madness, when your heart beats in
your ears and you pant with fear and excitement'.

Not all hunters, and certainly not all East African hunters, have been of this
sort. There is a sense of mere habit to the killing ascribed to Lord Delamere
by Elspeth Huxley: 'The English seasons were marked off for him, as for
others of his tradition, by the species of animal it was appropriate to kill.
Success was largely measured in terms of destructive ability.' Others of his
class apparently hunted out of boredom: Archie Ritchie, the Kenya Game
Ranger, in explaining a drop in licences in 1933 and 1934, said that 'big-game
hunting is a fine antidote to the boredom of a settled civilization', implying
that the Depression was a more powerful antidote and kept them away. John
McCutcheon called it 'not an elevating sport', but found the 'by-products'
(scenery and wildness, presumably) 'delightful and inspiring'.

The urge to hunt has itself been given many explanations. Rainsford posited
a 'dark survival of barbarism', Negley Farson a 'lust to acquire beauty – to *get*'.
Most hunters would probably place themselves somewhere equidistant from
barbarism, acquisitiveness, and glorious madness, seeing in the hunt a unique

way of entering into a natural process in an otherwise unnatural world.

The ethic that is the boundary to separate sport hunting from work hunting has many quirks – 'clean kills', 'fair shots', 'giving the animal an even chance' – and is obvious in the difference between, for example, stalking and killing a lion with a light rifle, on the one hand, and putting out a lump of poisoned meat for it on the other. Most cases are not so simple, however, and in the particular the ethics of much hunting are difficult: the case, for example, of the American archers who made pin-cushions of their prey without killing it, which might be compared with the Kamba or Okiek hunter's killing of a large animal with a single arrow whose load of poison kills in minutes. These are made still more complicated by the facts that the Americans arrived by car, which the lion did not associate with danger, and were backed by men with heavy guns, but the Kamba works alone and stalks his prey sometimes for days.

The American hunting writer Warren Page stipulated three qualities of what we might call ethical big-game hunting: personal danger, difficulty of terrain, and cleverness of the prey. What he did not mention was hunting method, although this is implicit, perhaps, in danger, because the ethical hunting method must involve danger to the hunter. This qualification rules out traps, poison, and the like. Non-hunters would say that any use of a machine – the rifle – that pushes a projectile at the prey at 3000 feet a second removes the danger. Hunters do not agree.

However, they admit that technology must be limited if sport is to have boundaries: automatic weapons have always been unacceptable for (legal) East African hunting, for example. (It is significant that they are the weapon of choice of armed soldiery – since the First World War, the single greatest destroyer of game.) Military automatics from both superpowers have flooded Africa and are now the favourites of poachers.

The desire to hunt but not to kill overtakes many seasoned hunters; they find, of course, that a hunt without a kill is a logical contradiction. Vivienne de Watteville, who must have loved hunting as much as anybody ever did, put her guns away and gave it up. Agnes Herbert wanted to, but thought she could not 'forgo the shot'. The word love has been used to describe the relationship between the ethical hunter and the prey, and love is very hard to put aside.

For most hunters, however, something more tangible than love lies at the hunt's end. Most, at least most who go to Africa, seek trophies. Page described this as 'a sort of madness' (psychosis seems to be a handy metaphor to those who write about hunting) to get the biggest part (usually horns or head or skin) of the most unusual creatures. It is Farson's acquisitiveness, reduced to the mundane. Rowland Ward's, the London taxidermists, made the acquisitiveness competitive by publishing an annual record book, which at least one modern white hunter thought had done as much as anything to ruin sport hunting. Yet competitiveness runs through big-game hunting – you see it in Hemingway and Roosevelt, for example, and in Rainey; and if you talk to many hunters, you hear it in tones of envy and desire – and competitiveness ensures that a hunter's search will never be ended, for there may always be a bigger horn, a better skin. Competitiveness and love are not very good bedmates, however.

What happens to the trophy after the kill is another matter. Wealthy men have long paid big sums to have heads and hides preserved and stuffed; a small industry still revolves around doing these things. The trophies then go up on walls (although a recent hunter who considered shooting a big sable withheld his shot because his American house has only eight-foot ceilings). Some people devote entire rooms to the trophies. Later generations, however, may not share the same taste. George Eastman's elephant and white rhino were put away after his death, and the rats ate them.

Not all trophies were mounted, of course. One could get 'a nice gong out of a pair of [hippo] tusks', if one wanted a nice gong. 'Beautiful souvenirs, such as bowls, trays, paper knives, table tops, whips, canes, and the like' could be made of rhino hide. 'And, of course, the feet of one's first rhino are always saved for cigar boxes or inkstands.'

Yet true trophy hunting places another limit on the idea of the sport in that it (in theory) limits the hunter to only one animal of each kind – the biggest or best, defined in some fashion (usually male with the best horns or longest tusks, and so on). Taken toward its limit, this ethic rather quickly leaves the experienced hunter in the position of spending weeks in the field without firing a shot, looking for that one animal; this is the position, in fact, in which a few superb hunters have willingly placed themselves.

At the opposite extreme is the professional hunter; the pursuit in this case is not sport but work, although it is a contradiction in sporting literature that the accolade 'great' has so often been given to professionals because of the enormous number of kills they have made: 'the great' Karamoja Bell because of his hundreds of elephants, shot for their ivory; 'the great' Selous because of his many lions (hunted with dogs, at that). It happens that Bell and Selous were 'gentlemen', however, a not inconsiderable attribute in a hunter. (A game animal was once defined as one that a gentleman would pursue.)

Without gentility, the professional hunter becomes a mere killer. British writers have always been very hard on the Boers of South Africa because they killed in quantity, and 'biltong hunter' (Boer meat hunter) is a synonym for what Americans call a game hog. Such hunters are supposed to have what Alan Moorehead called a 'glee for killing'. It is not a good thing to have a glee for killing in the world of sport hunting. Yet Baldwin, a genteel English professional, is thought highly of for having killed, with three other men, 61 elephant, 2 hippo, 11 white rhino, 12 black rhino, 11 giraffe, 21 eland, 30 buffalo, and 4 lion (among others) on the Zambezi in 1860.

In fact, quantity is part of much big-game hunting – quantity of species and quantity of individuals. One white hunter tried to teach his clients to go where hunting was more difficult (Page's quality of terrain) and the experience more intense, but 'they wanted to kill things – the more the better. I took them where the slaughter was sure and safe.' The desire to make big kills has resulted in some discouraging African scenes, like that of the 'prince from central Europe' who shot 600 sand grouse in a morning, or the European who had preceded Neumann (probably Donaldson Smith) and shot antelopes that he simply left dying, unwanted.

It is part of the psychology of quantity hunting that law replaces ethic; indeed, it can be said generally that legal rather than ethical limit is what many hunters recognized. East African limits were generous, despite complaints of over-regulation from the very beginning. Streeter said in the late 1920s that the licence 'appeared to give me permission to kill everything but the Governor General'. Many hunters took this not as a permission, however, but a goal: as Bronson said of unknown animals, 'Whatever they were I wanted one.'

It is human to move quickly from 'want' to 'need'. Thus, White felt justified in killing 'the twelve [colobus monkeys] *required* between us' [my italics]; Hindlip wrote of 'one or two specimens I still *required*' [my italics]. The result in many cases was an enormous kill, Roosevelt's and Rainey's being among the best publicized. This publicity, combined with a widespread sense of diminishing game, led to more stringent limits, but nothing changed the idea that the limits represented a goal and not a definition of greed. An unexpected result was the proliferation of 'scientific' hunts in the 1920s, when hunters with the glee for killing got the numbers they wanted by representing museums. They did not say, probably did not see, that in doing so they moved their activity from sport to work and thus challenged the ethic of their own actions.

Earlier East African hunters had often been young men, many of them military officers on leave or men taking a flyer at ivory hunting. With the railway and the development of the safari industry, however, it appears that the average age of sportsmen increased. Bronson and Roosevelt may be seen as typical – fiftyish, portly. Even more extreme types existed: William Northrup McMillan, who weighed more than 300 lb; George Eastman, who made his first safari at over 70.

Such people were not given to the all-day stalk on the belly or an 18-mile pursuit of an elephant of the sort that Judd made one morning. They were more like Kearton's and Barnes's 'armed tourists out to kill'. Increasingly after the First World War, their trophies were as much testament to technology (powerful weapons, the car, the aeroplane) as the hunter, and as much to their white hunter as the other things put together.

The perception of such a hunter by Africans – as the middle-aged armed tourist who could afford the best in technology and help – led to feelings that would surface with independence and that would show that the sport itself was not free of racial, or at least national, resonances. 'The killing of the animals has been largely carried on by foreigners who . . . are out to exploit our natural heritage', one Kenyan wrote in 1977. They were people who 'do not care for the future of this country and her people'.

Hunters, however, came in many guises. Some were crack shots, like Stewart Edward White; some were fierce competitors, like Ernest Hemingway; some were butchers, like Paul Rainey; some were gentlemen, like E. N. Buxton.

But relatively few of them were women.

And none of them was black.

The technology that made a middle-aged fat man the equal of a 400-lb lion found its perfect expression in the gun. It was the gun that made modern sports-hunting possible; it can be argued that it was the gun that made European penetration of Africa possible in the first place.

Guns have been coming to Africa for a long time. Grant found African hunters in the 1860s with 'Tower' muskets (flint guns with Tower of London marks) 'looking as perfect as when new'. They may well have been new; the gunmakers of Birmingham and Liège had long been turning out perfect copies for trade. Spanking new ones were still being offered by Germany's Alfa company in 1911, and muzzle-loaders continued to be found in East Africa: 30,000 of them were registered in Tanganyika in 1936, 39,000 in 1953. Europeans, however, had already surpassed the flint gun by the time Grant saw it, and they surpassed the percussion muzzle-loader by the time it got into African hands in large quantities.

Hunting rifles for Africa were big and heavy in the nineteenth century, the most famous being Sir Samuel Baker's 'Baby', which reportedly shot an 8-oz explosive shell and weighed 20 lb. 'Baby' was a response to a genuine problem: the killing of such game as elephants with relatively weak 'black' powder (a mixture of sulphur, saltpetre, and charcoal). The usual answer was to make bores enormous and guns weighty, so that a sizeable charge of powder could be placed behind the lead bullet. No one gun, however, sufficed for African game: one heavy enough for elephant would blow plains game apart; a big ball slowed too much for long-range shooting; a gun with enough metal at the breech to contain the explosion of a big charge of powder was too heavy to carry all day, and so on. Thus was born the idea of the 'battery' – three to five guns to cover a wide range of needs.

Stanley in 1870 recommended a 12-bore (12-gauge in America) shotgun, a 10- or 12-bore double rifle, and a 'magazine', or repeating rifle, 'for defence'. A 10-bore gun was one the circumference of whose bore would accept a lead ball whose weight ran 10 to the pound; a 12-bore would accept 12 to the pound, an 8-bore, 8 (i.e., balls of 2 oz each). Modern shooters are more comfortable with calibres expressed in hundredths of an inch, however. A 10-bore gun is .775 calibre, a 12-bore .729; thus, Stanley was recommending rifles with bullets of about ¾ inch diameter – smaller than 'Baby' but still huge by modern standards.

The 'magazine rifle' was a relatively new development in Stanley's day, represented mostly by the fast-firing but fairly puny Winchester lever-action rifles. They were not muzzle-loading but breech-loading, and used not loose powder and ball but a brass 'case' that held powder, ball, and priming charge. With the brass cartridge (made commercially feasible at about the time of the American Civil War), guns of all kinds, including sporting guns, made a quantum leap, for the cartridge was fairly weather-proof and fast to load.

In the 1850s, the British gunmaking firm of Purdey had picked up a faddish expression of the day and called one of its powerful rifles the 'Express Train'. The idea caught on; for generations after, powerful rifles were to be called 'express' rifles. Large in bore, after *c.*1870 they used long cartridges that one sportsman compared to Corona Corona cigars – in both size and price.

By the end of the 1880s, von Hohnel was recommending a .577 express, two .500 express, a 10-bore, and two double 8-bore rifles as an African battery. Like Stanley – like everybody – he believed in taking many guns.

Von Hohnel's guns were made by the great London firm of Holland & Holland. They also supplied him with another gun that was a brief African rage, the 'Paradox'. Paradox guns (similiar to W. W. Greener's 'invisibly rifled' or 'choke rifled' guns) were shotguns with short sections of rifling near their muzzles to give the ball the spin of a rifle bullet. They had the weight of shotguns (lighter than big rifles) but the accuracy up to 100 yards, it was said, of rifles. (The rifled slug for shotguns was a later invention. Franklin Russell also describes a one-inch-bore Paradox for Indian tiger, short-barrelled and weighing only 7 lb. but powerful enough to kill an elephant.)

Weapons technology was now moving too fast for sportsmen to keep up. Before von Hohnel could be widely read, a new explosive was becoming generally available. Called 'smokeless' gunpowder because it did not put out the clouds of dark smoke of the old black powder, it was made of different chemicals (nitrates – nitro-glycerine, cordite, axite, and so on) and often gave double the propulsive force of the same weight of black powder while producing far less smoke. Its immediate effect was to blow up the breeches of a lot of older guns; its long-term effect was to transform guns and hunting and to bring a new expression into use: the 'high-velocity' and 'high-powdered' rifle. Although smokeless powders were being used a decade earlier, the gunmaker Jeffery cited 1897 as the year when black-powder express rifles no longer held their prices and Jeffery went to the .450/.400 cordite (i.e., smokeless) express.

Express rifles made the transition to smokeless powders in the same calibres, but new sporting guns closely followed the development of military guns in reducing bore sizes. (An obvious affinity exists between military and sporting calibres, sporting generally following military's lead. One result was a nationalism of hunting cartridges: British shooters favoured the .303, Americans the .30-06, central Europeans the German 7mm.)

From the American Civil War until the Boer War, then, military – and sporting – arms moved from muzzle- to breech-loading, from single- to multiple-shot, and from large- to small-bore (see Table 1).

Table 1. Decrease in military bore sizes (after W. W. Greener)

Year	Country	Calibre (inches)
1850	England	.750
1852	England	.577
1871	Germany	.433
1871	England	.450
1886	France	.315
1889	England	.303
1892	Rumania	.256
1893	United States	.300
1906	United States	.30 ('.30-06')

This diminution in bore size was made possible by two developments: first, the 'bottle-neck' cartridge, in which the bore (bullet) size was smaller than the chamber (powder-holding cylinder) size; and second, smokeless powder. In 1860, the typical cartridge was cylindrical and rather fat and filled with black powder; by 1900, the typical cartridge was bottle-necked and fairly slim and filled with a smokeless propellant. A number of the new cartridges were 'necked-down' versions of older ones – a .450-calibre bullet, for example, placed in a resized .500 cartridge, giving such new designations as .500/450.

Thus, at the end of the nineteenth century, sportsmen were caught up in a swirl of new and old technology that led to spirited controversy. Smokeless powder gave the power that Baker had sought with 'Baby', but it blew up the old guns. Unless the hunter was going to throw out all the guns and start over again, either a mixed battery or an argument with other purists was inevitable.

Old calibres hung on, in new uses. By 1900 there were .577 smokeless cartridges, for example (and new 'fluid steel' or 'nitro steel' barrels to contain them). In 1908, Holland & Holland were even offering 16-, 20-, and 28-bore smokeless Paradox guns with steel barrels.

The idea of a battery of guns persisted, however. The guns used by Arthur Neumann on elephant are a case in point. Neumann shot a great deal, and his life depended on his shooting well. In the 1890s, he said he was 'laughed at' for not shooting anything *larger* than a .577 (as 10- and 12-bore rifles would have been). On one trip, he had a battery of a double .577, a single .450, and a 'common Martini-Henry' military rifle in .577/.450. On another trip, he carried a 10-bore Holland & Holland and a Lee-Metford military rifle in .303. In 1902, he had a double Rigby .450 that was 'wonderful' but that got so hot he had to wear a glove to shoot it.

Neumann's was everybody's experience, albeit intensified. There was no progression, only change; the breadth of choice was great and no single weapon had pushed itself above the rest. With the appearance of the new kind of hunter, however, the field would begin to sort itself out.

With the brass cartridge had come the bolt-action rifle. In sporting use, it soon rivalled the breech-loading 'double' rifle – two barrels, two shots. Bolt-actions were rugged and fairly cheaply manufactured; double rifles could be made to last for ever, but the alignment of the two barrels to a single aiming point and the nature of the double-gun market made bolt-actions cheap and doubles expensive. The result was that, as Jim Carmichel has pointed out, 'the unromantic fact is that from the turn of the century onwards, the bolt-action has been *the* African action by a factor of hundreds to one'. Wealthy sportsmen none the less used, and sometimes continue to use, the double.

The bolt-action has certain advantages: it holds more cartridges; it is cheaper; it is sometimes lighter. The double has its advantages, too: its two shots can come together or almost so; it does not have a bolt to jam.

Bolt-actions are somewhat limited in the length of cartridge that they will accept, however, because of the structure of the human hand and arm. Doubles do not suffer this limitation. This difference meant that, generally, express cartridges longer than three inches went into doubles, not bolt-actions. Doubles, however, were relatively slow to reload; some hunters therefore carried two cartridges between the fingers so they would be instantly available. This is not so easy as it sounds with a .500 express cartridge.

By the first decade of the twentieth century, then, controversy centred on two issues: bolt-action versus double, and express versus high-velocity (or large- versus small-bore). The real question of *who* was handling the gun was fundamental but slower to emerge. Thus, the (small) Dutch/Rumanian .256 cartridge for the Mannlicher bolt-action rifle became enormously popular because some veteran hunters (Blayney Percival among them) swore by it for even dangerous game. The (small) German 7mm (.276) cartridge was similarly popularized by the elephant-hunter Bell. But it remained to be seen what less experienced hunters would do with such cartridges on dangerous game.

These small calibres did have certain advantages. Both guns and ammunition were comparatively light and cheap. And they offered long-range accuracy; in shooting parlance, they 'shot flat' or had 'long point-blank range'. This meant that the bullet, unlike that of the express cartridges, came out of the muzzle so fast that it didn't have time to fall very far before it hit something several hundred yards away. The shooter could set the gun's sights for a hundred yards and know that the bullet would hit within a lethal area (the heart-size of an antelope, for example) at any range from 25 yards to 200 or more (see Table 2).

The high-velocity rifles offered one other huge advantage: their recoil was comparatively small (see Table 2).

Table 2. Sample trajectories and recoils

Calibre	Trajectory (to hit at 200 yards), inches above line of sight	Recoil energy,* ft-lb
.256	3.5	12.8
.303	3	14.4
.30-06	2.5	15.3
.500 Nitro Express	8.5	58
.600 Nitro Express	11.4	99

*Felt recoil is subjective, but many shooters would agree that 20 ft-lb is the threshold of discomfort.

Recoil had been the inescapable nemesis of the big-bore shooter. The heavier the bullet, the heavier the 'kick' given the sportsman, all things being equal; on the other hand, the heavier the gun, the lighter the kick. Baldwin in the 1850s put 3 lb of lead into the stock of his muzzle-loading rifle to try to reduce the recoil, 'as my right cheek and bone are nearly cut to pieces, and the blood at every shot runs into my mouth'. Selous's shooting was not better, it is said, because he had injured his shoulder with his early big-bore guns. Neumann in the late 1890s, 'dared use no other' than the .303 'for fear of the recoil'; he had 'nasty wounds on my fingers' from a 10-bore where the trigger-guard struck, and constant headaches. When Roosevelt in 1909 used a .450 cordite express while standing on a log with Cuninghame, 'the blast . . . made Cuninghame's nose bleed'. Barnes in 1910 saw a man knocked across a shooting blind by the recoil of both barrels of an 8-bore smokeless. (One can imagine the effect, therefore, on the gunbearer whose hunter used his shoulder as a rest for a .577).

For a time after 1900, the popularity of both express and high-velocity calibres meant that the battery usually included *both* sorts of rifles. Cotton in 1902 took a .256, a .400 cordite double, an 8-bore double, and a 12-bore Paradox. Pease in the same year was using a black-powder .500 express, a 10-bore Paradox double, and a high-velocity .256. Selous recommended three guns for Roosevelt: the (high-velocity) .30-06 Springfield, the American .45-70, and the .450 cordite express. Many hunters added a fast-cycling Winchester lever-action, despite the modest loads; Roosevelt and White used a Winchester Model 1895 in the more potent .405 (as did the Johnsons as late as the mid-1920s).

By 1910, black-powder guns and the Paradox, even for smokeless powders, were fading. Selous called the Paradox 'a very inferior weapon' for Africa, and Buxton said it was 'rather out of fashion', with second-hand examples available for £8–10. Still, 'nothing could be better [for lion] *as a gun in reserve*'.

John McCutcheon comically summarized the theory behind the battery of 1910. 'The presumption . . . was that we should first shoot the lion at long range with the .256, then at a shorter range with the nine-millimeter, than at close range with the .475 cordite, and then perhaps fervently wish that we had the paradox or a balloon.' (He called the Paradox a 'cripple-stopper', a common BEA expression for any gun to use close in on dangerous wounded game.)

The First World War showed the effectiveness of the small-calibre, high-velocity cartridges on men. It did not remove growing doubts about them on big animals. Despite the much-publicized success of people like Bell and Blayney Percival, the fact was that the small calibres had to be used with considerable accuracy or big game would not fall to them. Bullets were perfected – Spitzer (pointed), hard, soft, expanding, penetrating, jacketed, hollow, split – but the fact was that a 150-grain (about ⅓ oz) bullet did not do to a dangerous animal what a 500-grain bullet did.

High-velocity small calibres were not merely a fad, for their flat trajectories and tremendous penetration had a real place in hunting, but it became clear that in the hands of the average hunter, they could not be used accurately enough to ensure kills on dangerous game. And the new safari client was (often at best) an 'average' hunter, in whose hands the flat-shooting, high-velocity rounds did not always hit their mark. And if you failed to kill a lion or buffalo with the first shot of a small-calibre rifle, the chance of killing the animal with the one shot you were likely to have before it reached you was very slim.

Also, it is part of the ethic of hunting that animals should not be wounded and left, and that they should not be wounded unnecessarily. Thus, a buffalo that was killed with seven .30-06 and two .470 bullets (Eastman's 1928 safari) was hardly a more ethical piece of hunting than the Pope–Young lion bristling with arrows. Sutherland insisted that the small calibres were 'thoroughly unsuitable and unsportsmanlike' for this reason. Even Blayney Percival, 'though a firm believer in the .256', thought it too light for buffalo. (An experienced hunter like Hemingway, however, could still use the .30-06 to advantage; he killed lion, buffalo, and rhino using 220-grain bullets, although he wounded and lost some animals.)

By the 1920s, then, the controversies that had begun at the end of the nineteenth century were partly resolved by the admission that armed tourists should not use small-calibre rifles on big game. From this admission came the search for a new cartridge – the all-killer 'magnum'. (The word probably comes from the big champagne bottle.)

Such a cartridge had several requirements. It must be a sure killer in the hands of a modest marksman – but it must not be an *absolutely* sure killer (that is, a grenade or a machine gun would not do). It must, if possible, have modest recoil so that the relatively inexperienced hunter would not flinch and spoil the shot, or complain after of a hurt shoulder. And it must, if possible, be an accurate killer at long ranges, for both client and professional hunter agreed on wanting no charge of close-in, wounded animals.

The search took two paths. One was the development of high-velocity mid-calibre cartridges, the other the development of high-velocity, short-cased replacements for the big expresses. What was wanted in both instances was a cartridge that would cycle through a bolt-action – one between about .350 and .400 (medium), the other well above .400 (heavy).

One result was immediate: the acceptance of Holland & Holland's .375 'magnum' cartridge. Created in 1912, it established itself by the 1920s as a flat-trajectory, hard-hitting round with a bullet big enough for lion (see Table 3).

Table 3. Comparison of modern medium and heavy cartridges
(after Burrard and Rice)

Calibre	Bullet weight* (grains)	Muzzle energy† (ft-lb)
.338 Winchester	250	3927
.358 Norma	250	4353
.375 H & H	300	4263
.400 Jeffery	400	4100
.458 Winchester	510	4712
.460 Weatherby	500	8095
.600 Nitro	900	7600

* 1 oz. = 437.5 grains.
† Many factors limit bullet energy away from the muzzle; energies at the muzzle are given only for comparison. A very rough rule of thumb, however, might be that dangerous big game require ½ oz of bullet leaving the muzzle at 4000 ft-lb.

The magnum age did not really begin until after the Second World War. Then two innovations appeared: slower burning, more powerful smokeless powders, and new primers. The result was a series of cartridges whose best-known symbols are the Weatherby line of rather flashy American rifles. Somewhat baroque in their styling, they have the look of the large-finned cars of the 1950s and 1960s. The Weatherby guns, however, are only the outward expression of the real revolution – the line of cartridges whose biggest example, the Weatherby .460 magnum (1958), is for some the most effective big-game cartridge ever created.

Others would argue instead for the Winchester .458 (1956), a somewhat smaller magnum. The two magnums are probably now the most common and the most sought-after calibres for professional hunting in Africa, a sure sign of their practicality. For the amateur going after buffalo and elephant, they provide the necessary accuracy and power, albeit at the price of 'tremendous' recoil. At the end of the 1980s, as well, manufacturers showed a new interest in large-bore cartridges. The Remington Arms Company created a new .416, with a new rifle to match; Federal issued an entire new line of 'safari' cartridges; and buyers showed interest in old ones like the massive .505 Gibbs.

Thus, a three-tiered battery has evolved since the end of the First World War, which can be summed up by a Kenya Game Department advisory of the early 1970s: for elephant, rhinoceros, buffalo, and hippo, nothing less than .400; for lion, leopard, and eland, nothing smaller than .375 (with a shotgun loaded with buckshot for wounded lion or leopard in bush); for the large antelopes, .300 or larger; for smaller game, larger than .22.

The reasons for the big (over-.400) bores, despite the weight of the rifles that must contain them and the recoil they administer, can be summed up in Chauncey Stigand's remark after he was mauled by a charging lion: 'For a springing or charging lion . . . and for the violent animals at any close quarters one wants a 15 pounder or a large bore howitzer'.

We might also remember a wise man's counsel: 'It is far better and safer to over-gun than to under-gun'.

Good guns have never been cheap, but the bolt-action rifles of the 1890s and after were so comparatively cheap, and so well made, that they became part of the democratizing force that changed safari hunting. The London-made double rifle has remained the *ne plus ultra* of East African hunting, but its status is in good part nostalgia, for the good bolt-actions – even the good, plain bolt-actions – are excellent guns.

Three military bolt-actions dominated the early scene: the superb German Mauser, whose many models, climaxing in the 1898, are still enviably simple and strong; the Austrian Mannlicher, whose full-length stock and short barrel became enormously popular; and the British Lee-Enfields. In 1903, the Mauser design was made the basis of the American Springfield, which became by the 1920s, according to Leslie Tarlton, the best sporting rifle in the world.

Generally, these rifles were used in sporting and not military models, although some shooters (Neumann, for example) liked the full military stock with handguard. 'Sporterizing' was done in the United States by such custom houses as Griffin & Howe of New York, and Sedgley of Philadelphia, who provided checkered half-stocks and new sights for the military actions. Mauser manufactured its own sporting models, as did Springfield Armory after the First World War. In London, the established gun houses – Holland & Holland, Rigby, Westley Richards, Gibbs, Evans, Jeffery, and others – built their own versions of the Mauser or the British military actions, so that 'Rigby Mausers', for example, were seen. London's heart, however, remained in the beautiful and expensive doubles.

In 1937, Winchester brought out the bolt-action rifle that has become the standard for many American shooters, the Model 70. Although twice redesigned since its introduction, it remains a major American sporting rifle.

In 1902, a *second-hand* Westley Richards double in .303 calibre cost £57/10 – about the same as a month's supply of porters for a big safari. By contrast in 1908, a .400 cordite Jeffery bolt-action *with 400 cartridges* was advertised in Nairobi for only 250 rupees – about £16 – and in 1907 a new Jeffery Mauser was advertised in the *Standard* for £15, or £12/12 without checkering or pistol grip. About the same time, a mass-produced German Mauser was on sale for only 100 rupees – less than £7. In the 1920s, second-hand bolt-actions were widely for sale in Nairobi for less than £10, but used double express rifles cost from £50 to £100 each. It is probably safe to say that throughout this period, double guns held a value of at least seven times that of plain bolt-actions.

Finding ammunition for these rifles in Nairobi was not always easy. One difficulty of the London proprietary cartridges was that all makers' were different, even in the same calibre (that is, the cases were different). 'Nyoka' cited an example in 1909 of four men, all with .450s, none of whom could use any of the others' ammunition. On the other hand, the Nairobi gunshops built up a stock of odd ammunition as hunters sold off their extras before leaving. Partly in this way, American ammunition reached BEA as well, although it could not be counted on until after the First World War.

The multiplicity of calibres continued until the Second World War, when existing British stocks and tools were 'stripped out, scrapped, modified, or simply lost'. Time and money were needed to retool after the war, and by the time the new safari clients began arriving in their remarkable post-war numbers, American rifles and cartridges had taken a big piece of the East African market. These were joined by resurgent European names after the 1950s – Mauser, Sako, Husquvarna, Fabrique Nationale. Many of the British proprietary cartridges disappeared or became extremely hard to find (and expensive), and increasingly a few international firms – Norma, Winchester, Remington – provided ammunition for many makes of gun. At the same time, rifle-makers increasingly bored new models for a small range of what had begun as proprietary cartridges – the H & H .375, the Winchester .338 and .458 magnums.

The search for the ideal cartridge and rifle has continued. Warren Page suggested in the 1970s that what he called the 'one-gun safari' was possible, and that the 'three-rifle battery' was outdated in an age of short safaris and 'total kills per hunter [of] fifteen to twenty-five heads'. He suggested the .338 Winchester or .375 H & H magnum for his one-gun safari, but both law and ethics have made bigger guns essential for elephant and buffalo, with the smaller high-velocity cartridges preferred for game at the small end. No ideal rifle exists, therefore, although some hunters with one eye on airline baggage limitations have been drawn to interchangeable-barrel guns.

At the end of the 1980s, a typical mass-produced bolt-action rifle in a heavy calibre cost upward of £400; lighter calibres were cheaper, but a three-gun battery would run to £1200, not counting accessories like telescopic sights.

One Holland & Holland 'best quality' bolt-action, on the other hand, cost about £3800, while their Royal Double Side-by-Side Rifle was quoted at £26,250. A London-made Rigby .416 Magazine Rifle in .416 Rigby or one of the big international calibres was just over £3300; their Best Quality Sidelock Ejector Double Rifle was £19,500 in all major large calibres except .600 Nitro Express, whose price was 'available by quotation only'. Between these extremes lay a wide choice of guns in bolt, double, and over-and-under configuration, with some Spanish and German double rifles available at about £1700, and some high quality bolt rifles at the same price.

Probably, the mass-produced magazine rifles of today are better than any rifles available in 1900 – safer, more accurate, and more powerful for their size. Probably, as good a piece of machinery as the typical hunter could want can be bought for less than £1000. Beyond that, woodwork, engraving, and cachet are what is being bought – along with a good deal of history, to be sure (and not a little snob appeal).

The primary objects of the East African hunter's search were five: elephant, African or Cape (never 'water') buffalo, rhinoceros, lion, and leopard. These were the Big Five, the animals that provided the requisite danger to the hunter.

Other desirable game existed: the bongo and okapi; the big eland; the startlingly beautiful greater kudu, sable, and roan antelope. Not normally dangerous, they were none the less difficult to stalk and lived in interesting and challenging terrain. Smaller plains game – the high-leaping impala, the awkward wildebeeste, the Thomson's and Grant's gazelles, the topi and the hartebeestes – were not 'royal' game and were often shot for meat, but finding big or unusual specimens appealed to some hunters.

All African animals die hard. Their lives are perpetual challenge, and if they have survived they have done so because of superb conditioning. Most will continue to run with the heart stopped; the brain does not know until the blood has been emptied of oxygen that the pump is dead. Lion, leopard, and buffalo can run 100 yards and kill a hunter after an apparently fatal shot. Tenacious of life, they exist in the environment where 'kills' are in fact only a pause between the chase and the banquet; many plains game are at least partly eaten alive. Life is appallingly hard.

The elephant was for centuries the most sought-after of these animals because of the two tusks that curve down from its upper jaw. Ivory has always been the goal, yet it was not until the last few decades that because of it the elephant's extinction seemed not merely abstractly possible but likely. Ivory has no essential usefulness; indeed, most things made of ivory these days are supremely tasteless, but it is ivory that has none the less doomed the elephant.

The biggest tusks were probably a pair of 214 and 226 lb, now in the British Museum. From early days in BEA, the legal minimum weight was 30 lb per tusk, so it should be clear how large the record ones are. They are over 10 feet long, too. The pair that weighed 256 lb *together*, shot by Cockburn and Hoey in 1907, were certainly large enough.

Elephant-hunting is dangerous work and has become more dangerous as much elephant habitat has shifted from the open plains to forest. Elephants have killed or maimed many hunters; when an elephant kills, it does so with an air of rage and vengefulness, often mashing the body so thoroughly into the terrain that it is not identifiable. The tusks are used to impale, the knees to crush, the trunk to rend. The numbers of elephants killed by individuals are, then, remarkable: Teleki killed 'his first ten ... with great ease' in days: Delamere's companion in 1897 shot 21 in as many days on Marsabit; Neumann shot 14 in one day, scoring at least one 'right and left' as if he were shooting driven birds; Bell shot 18 in a day, 180 in six weeks; Sutherland shot 1000 in his lifetime, as did at least half a dozen other ivory hunters before colonial governments made such kills more trouble than they were worth.

Yet it has never been easy to kill an elephant. Most hunters are advised to shoot for the brain, which is small and protected by many inches of spongey bone. Roosevelt got a cast of an elephant skull so he could study the structure. Bell had elephant heads sawn in half for the same reason. Yet Bell killed them with the .276 (and a lot of luck, some said; they said he left a lot of wounded, too).

The aftermath of an elephant kill was often more remarkable than the hunt itself. Europeans unaccustomed to hunger were astonished at the Africans who appeared to sit in circles around the pile of soon-to-be meat. Sometimes they had to be physically restrained from attacking the carcase. The actual skinning was itself phenomenal; as Bronson described it,

> the moment the abdominal wall was punctured, high up on the elephant's side up out of the opening rose an intertwining, writhing mass of colossal intestines, each at least eighteen inches in diameter, all tightly distended with the gases of dissolution until, beneath the bright rays of the declining sun, they reflected every brilliant and soft neutral tint of an opal, rose up and up, six feet or more above the carcass, ever slowly gliding and writhing.

If the sportsperson wanted the skin, the corpse had to be rolled over; the assembled crowd was needed then. The tusks were chopped out. Then, at a signal the crowd was let loose, swarming over the animal – Percival saw this by torchlight with Eastman's elephant, an astonishing spectacle – and people were actually inside the huge carcass, cutting, slashing each other, throwing meat to those who waited in a ring. Such a scene was described by Bronson, Clark, Streeter, and others. Clark saw a man blown off his feet when he put a knife into the gas-filled innards.

Neumann wanted only the tusks and missed all this, of course. He did not bother to chop them out, but left the beast to rot for a few days, when the tusks pulled easily. Modern poachers, armed with the best that 'developed' governments can supply, shoot rights and lefts with M-16s or AK-47s and remove the tusks with chain saws.

The lion, on the other hand, is little poached; rather, he or she is poisoned and starved. The poisoning may be actual, as along the boundaries of Nairobi National Park, where the farms are beginning to press close; the starvation is long-term and symbolic, standing for the removal of habitat and lion prey by another animal that cannot control its own population.

A lion is a fine animal. Small or large, young or old, it has a pure wildness. Yet it seems playful at times, affectionate at times, convivial and loyal. I have seen a young adult male allow itself to be bowled over by a cub, even pretend not to have seen the cub coming. I have seen lions comatose with over-feeding, the flies a disgusting black network on their bellies. I have seen lions stalking through the evening grass, ignoring me so as to watch their prey. I admire lions for the qualities of all cats; independence, self-interest, brutal honesty.

Lions were at first classified as vermin in BEA. As vermin, they did not 'go on the licence' but were shootable at sight, like hyenas, crocodiles, and leopards. J. A. Hunter hunted them as such to clear them from farm and ranch land. Martin Johnson was incensed by the vermin kills; he said that a man named Grant had killed 80, Stewart Edward White 60, Leslie Simson and Al Klein 100 each. He was wrong about Simson; his count was 232 by 1925.

'The death of a lion is a fine sight', White wrote. Lions die hard. They want to keep coming. There is a bit of silent film from Eastman's safari, probably shot by Martin Johnson. You see a lion at some distance, perhaps 60 yards. Suddenly the lion comes. Four seconds later, he is dead, but in that time he has crossed the intervening space straight at the cameraman, has flinched to the right when one heavy bullet (Eastman's Westley Richards?) hits him, come on, and then been slammed down to the left from another heavy gun there. Only 1.2 seconds separate the first shot and the death.

Lions make many false charges – 19 out of 20, Klein estimated. The twentieth, however, is as they say, a sonofabitch. For this reason, hunters are encouraged to use the biggest of the mediums (the .375 H & H) or the heavies on lion. It was when a lion was charging that the double gun was a comfort: you could keep the express sight on the beast and fire, wait for the barrel to come down from recoil, and fire again. The bolt-action might just jam, and then . . .

Having a safari broken up by a rhinoceros was part of the early BEA experience. So many of them existed around Kilimanjaro and down on the plains that they were a nuisance, dashing through the line of porters and sending loads in all directions as men scrambled for trees or cover. Yet the rhino seldom, if ever, had malicious intent: near-sighted and stupid, it was merely choosing a response from a very narrow range of possibilities. In the cafeteria of the rhino brain, the menu is very short. The animal could be dangerous; a few people were stepped on or gored.

This reputation for menace, however, made the rhino an easily justified kill. Account after account tells us how the rhinos charged and *had* to be killed.

When later safarists let the charges finish their course, they found they usually petered out and nobody was the worse for them, but the early visitors found ample justification for multiple kills. In fact, rhinos were fairly easy to do away with; you walked around until one snorted, put its horn down and charged, and then you shot it. Ranges were short, the hunters' aim inevitably better than the rhinos'. And there were lots and lots of rhinos.

Yet Selous saw early on that 'the rhinoceros will probably be the first of the wild animals still existing in Africa to disappear'. They were simply too stupid. And they were too desirable, not for their beauty or their cunning, but for the pointed mounds of hair that grew from their noses – their 'horns'.

Cranworth – on foot – saw as many as 60 in a day in the early years of the century. White saw 14 in two hours, but he, too, knew that the rhino would be the first animal to go. Archie Ritchie said in the 1930s that you could find one in an hour if you really cared.

Rainsford thought they should be 'shot on sight'. A Colonel G. E. Smith apparently did just that; he shot 17 in one day, back before Roosevelt's safari. J. A. Hunter shot more than 150 in a few months of 'control' work in the Kamba country as part of a scheme that killed 1000 or so to clear the land for farming. (The farming idea didn't work.) Poachers have hunted them almost to extinction in the last decade.

Nobody has had a safari broken up by one in some time.

The leopard is far more beautiful than the rhinoceros but even harder to see, the reason not reduced numbers but secretiveness. Its beauty is thus unregarded, for it is mostly nocturnal and very, very wary. Yet I have seen one lie in full view by a waterhole, staring over the dull brown surface with the baleful eye of a tiger. Leopards *look* dangerous.

And they are. Like lions, some leopards kill human beings for food – mostly children and small women. Then, with a strength the slender body belies, the leopard will lift its 100 lb burden effortlessly into a 20-foot-high tree crotch. Leopard can leap walls with their prey, haul big antelopes high up into trees.

Most people who have had encounters with leopards have done something to the leopard first, although not always. Harold Hill was 'roughly handled' by a wounded one in Roosevelt's time. Carl Akeley killed a small one by kneeling on it and crushing its lungs; so did Eric Rundgren, and so did a Nairobi resident who, early in the century, found the animal on his verandah. A man named Rattray, who was devoting his life to domesticating zebra, almost died trying the same thing during the Johnsons' time.

The leopard, once wounded, goes to cover and waits for the hunter. It can be dying, but it will try to get its own back. When it comes, it comes in a streak of sickening speed and sinks its front claws like hooks into the human's neck, its teeth into the face; then long rear claws rake the hunter's abdomen, opening it like a gutted fish. It was for such encounters that white hunters used to wait with dread, entering the grass or the donga or the reeds with a double shotugn loaded with buck. Not to be afraid in such a situation would have been idiocy.

The leopard is mostly shot over baits nowadays from well-made hides. And no wonder.

The buffalo, unlike the leopard, is a very easily seen animal, and a very large one that looks mean. Five feet at the shoulder, it has a way of looking with lifted head and beetling brows that is reminiscent of the sort of people who wear chains and tattoos and long hair. On its forehead it carries a massive 'boss' with two horns that curve out and down. Unlike the bull of cartoon drawings, it charges with its head up so that it can see exactly what it is aiming at.

The buffalo is unpredictable. It does kill human beings, goring and stomping them. It does not necessarily charge on sight, although it may. One evening I was on a road in the Loita Hills with John Bisley; we were walking off some local honey beer. John is a very fast walker. It was dusk, and finally I said, 'When should we turn back?' At that moment, we both saw the buffalo that stood 30 yards off the road. 'Now', John said firmly and did a military about-face. We sped back down the road, which was thickly lined with bush that looked impenetrable, although I know I could have gone through it that evening like a cricket ball through a window. But the bull did not charge.

It is buffalo that the doomed hero recovers his manhood by killing in Hemingway's 'Macomber'. It is buffalo that many experts say is the most dangerous animal in East Africa. It is buffalo, they say, that have maimed and killed a few tourists on 'walking safaris' in recent years. Although related to the domestic cow, therefore, the buffalo is a fitting game animal for the hardiest hunter.

Nothing small or medium is used on buffalo if the amateur hunter is wise. Like other big African animals, it can go a great distance when badly hurt, and it may decide to turn and use the end of its vitality on the hunter. In the charge, it must be *stopped*. It is no good hitting it so that it will die of blood loss or drowned lungs if it is coming at you. It has to be *stopped*. It is for such moments that the .458 Winchester and the .460 Weatherby Magnums were made, and even then the shot must be placed so that the bullet does not lose its force on the huge boss or skid along the massive bone of the forehead. It must go 'up the nose', or it must break something essential to forward movement.

These, then are the Big Five. Hunting them has become hideously expensive and, in some cases, rather unrewarding. Leopard went for £2800 each on the southern African game ranches in the late 1980s. Peter Capstick estimated in the late 1970s that the actual cost of shooting a rhino was then about £14,000–15,000.

As a result of a combination of scarcity, expense, and a complex of things I will call 'reduced experience' (for example, 'one of the most deplorable mockeries of sport', the reduction of the experience of shooting a white rhino to walking into a closed pen with a heavy rifle and shooting the captive animal), much hunting emphasis has shifted to other game. 'Who wants a giraffe?' Barnes asked back before the First World War, but the sad answer is that some people will shoot anything. Barnes put it exactly right when he said there was nothing in the way of trophy you could take from a giraffe, although he had heard of a man who had had a set of dining-room chairs covered with one, 'but he probably had an enemy who was getting married'.

We might also ask, 'Who wants a hippo?', but shooting hippo is still done. Hippo at least are dangerous, although seldom to the hunter, and we need to remember that it is danger to the hunter (not to passing boats and swimmers) that is important. Hippo are also large. Will Judd predicted that hippo would 'become as extinct as the dodo owing to its being the possessor of splendid fat', but other sources of fat have come along. Streeter was asked to shoot one by a woman who wanted to make soap: 'It sounded ridiculous that such a vast, independent animal should end up as a cake of soap'. Indeed, indeed – but less ridiculous than that it end up as a 'nice gong' or one half of a colour photo, the other half being a balding chap with a cannon.

In the supermarket atmosphere of some modern hunting, all sorts of animals have been made saleable to the armed tourist. The warthog is one; why anybody should pay to shoot a warthog, I don't know, as they have none of Page's qualifications of a game animal. (Although they may be like the javelina, which, as I heard one Texas park ranger say, might be dangerous 'if you got into a telephone booth with one'.) The jackal is another; the jackal is an essential minor predator and a cog in Africa's garbage-disposing machine, but hardly a game animal. Ditto the hyena, the striped, the spotted or the brown, all three of which are not at all the cowardly, charnel-house creatures of Hemingway's fantasy life (he hated them and shot all he could) but useful and fascinating creatures. They do kill other animals, and they do eat them before they are dead (as do lions and leopards), and they do very rarely attack humans, and they are pests in a camp for their thievery – we have had one steal two tea-kettles – but they are not 'game' and they are hardly trophies.

The actual hunting of game, especially the big five, was accomplished in the early days by the veterans of India and South Africa with pleasurable difficulty – the 'stalk'. Increasingly after the First World War, however, the armed tourist did his stalking by car and trusted his rifle to close up whatever distance was left.

Shooting distance became a debated aspect of the hunting ethic. 'I never fired a long shot in my life, and no real sportsman of my acquaintance does so', harumphed G.E.B. in the *Field*, asserting that such unsportsmanlike acts were best left to the Boer and the Cockney. Dickinson said that 'one should never fire at over 100 yards or 150 yards', which Cotton said could be reduced to 60 to 70 'with a little trouble' – that is, some stalking on hands and knees. White, however, said that his shots in 1913 *averaged* 245 yards (but he was an exceptionally good shot), and Rainsford found a few years earlier that most shots were longer than 150, with many over 200. To a degree, of course, the length of the shot depended on terrain and target: Taylor said that any shot at elephant over 40 yards was 'a very long shot', on rhino, 25, with most 'from 2 or 3 feet to 10 or 12 paces'. These are rather heart-troubling distances, especially if the animal in question is headed toward you.

One argument against the long shot was that it was 'unsporting' because it unfairly reduced the shooter's risk. The other was that long shots by poor marksmen left wounded and suffering animals. None the less, long shots on some animals became usual, especially as the telescopic sight (now almost universal) became common in the 1930s. With the shortening of hunting safaris to their present 7- or 10-day length, long shots have become desirable because they save time: a 300-yard shot with a 9X telescope is possible to most armed tourists with a magnum rifle, whereas crawling 250 of those yards might take a precious hour.

The leaving of wounded animals, whether the result of long shots or not, was unsportsmanlike. Yet it seems to have been done with appalling frequency. Ethical white hunters refused to let their clients 'brown the herd' – fire at a group of animals in hope of hitting one – and they made serious efforts to track and kill wounded dangerous game, but animals got away with wounds, none the less. Hindlip hit a rhino with a .450 'too far back' and was 'eventually forced, much to my disgust, to give him up'; he hit a lion twice with a .256 but 'I was reluctantly compelled to leave [him]'. Bronson broke a roan's hip, then its shoulder, but lost it after five hours; 'I was heartbroken'; he hit a waterbuck with a .405 but lost it; 'this was annoying, but I knew there were plenty more like him'; with the poacher John Alfred Jordan, he hit four elephants with .405 and .450 bullets, of which they killed one. Von Hohnel staggered a rhino twice, followed it for 'some distance, [but we] lost it'; another 'went off apparently mortally wounded but it was too late to follow him'. Barnes's companion shot a lion at 200 yards and left her to die overnight. Clark, protecting Dugmore's camera work, let several rhino go off wounded. Bernard de Watteville came on four buffalo, shot 'the nearest' with a .318 and 'followed up' only next day; he put one bullet into an elephant, after which his gun jammed and he never saw the animal again; he and Vivienne shot two buffalo that went into a swamp where they would not follow; he broke an elephant's shoulder and followed it into papyrus, where he thought he killed it but found he had killed a cow, the wounded one escaping; he 'shattered both fetlocks' of a hartebeest with long shots before realizing he had misjudged the distance, and the animal got away. Chapman 'crippled' an impala 'with a straightaway stern shot' but it ran off and 'I never saw him again'; he put seven shots from three different rifles into an elephant that was later seen 'very sick' but never found. Will Judd wounded a lion but thought it 'imprudent' to follow her until she had 'stiffened' and never found her. Margery Perham told of a lion shot by a Game Ranger and not followed up in darkness; it ate away 'half of his own front leg' in its pain.

Some of the emphasis put lately on heavier guns has come from precisely such incidents. Both hunters and game managers (including private ranch owners) want kills nowadays, not wounds, for, in contemporary African hunting, the hunter pays for the animal if he or she hits it, and the animal is then subtracted from the licensed total. Lost animals are thus wasteful of both money and opportunity – more persuasive arguments with most of us than humane ones based on the animals' pain.

Probably, as Bronson's comment about 'plenty more' implied, it was the apparent plenty of game that persuaded hunters to let wounded animals escape. It seemed that there were always more, and animals were not counted on the licence unless dead (unless a particularly rigorous white hunter – or a spy from the Game Department – was close by.) In actual fact, the game stocks were dwindling quickly while people like Bronson were hunting (1907), and, Africa-wide, more than half the mid-nineteenth-century herds were already gone. Few individuals saw the decline, however; to the newcomer to Africa, there were always 'plenty more'.

Franklin Russell has shown the political meaning of the astonishing decline of Indian species – barasingha, Kashmir stag, even the tiger – after India's independence. These animals had become victims of political change: the world turned upside-down, and the animals died. Preserved by the former masters, they became the surrogates for the masters. They were hunted almost to extinction by people whom the masters had not allowed to hunt.

Hunters should not be surprised that the glorious madness is a political act.

Ownership of game animals came with ownership of land, as the British and Germans saw it when they took East Africa. Such ownership pertained to the government (ultimately the Crown, hence 'royal' game), then to the landowner. There was never any real question (among Europeans) about the game's belonging to the original inhabitants. Nor was there any real questioning of the concept of ownership: man shall have all dominion.

However, although it was logically clear to Europeans that 'ownership' of game automatically shifted from them to Africans on the day of *uhuru*, it was not emotionally clear. They continue to view African animals as their own, if not by ownership of the land, then by claims of higher stewardship (claims that Africans had not been allowed to make, although the severe decline of animal numbers began only after whites arrived (*c.* 1880), and 'it was not until Europeans introduced fire-arms and . . . wire . . . that the slaughter of game on a large scale really began').

A claim of higher (white) stewardship played into racial ideas, and many whites said that the new black nations would destroy East Africa's animals as India's animals had been destroyed. ('The game is doomed. . . . The game hasn't a chance for survival' under African rule; 'only in Portuguese Angola and Mozambique will the game survive'.) Yet some of what seems racialism in such predictions was an inability to surrender emotional ownership. And, contrarily, much of Africans' stated vexation at whites' hunting (in the reactions to the Kenyan ban, for example) was a long-delayed expression of deep resentment of white claims to ownership.

From almost the beginning (1902 at the latest), Europeans rented (licensed) ownership of animals to other Europeans and called African claims of ownership, poaching. Game would remain plentiful, as Selous put it, 'as long as natives were not allowed to become possessed of firearms, and all traffic in the hides and horns of wild animals . . . is strictly forbidden'. Yet denying Africans the right to kill animals flew in the face of millennia-old cultural patterns. Relatively few Africans were subsistence hunters, although some (the Okiek and the Kamba, for example) were highly skilled, but they and others also hunted for trade (mostly ivory). Such hunting appears not to have lowered animal numbers until the 1880s, and it is impossible to separate now the double-barrelled effects of European firearms and the voracious European ivory market. It appears true, however, that blaming only Africans for the lowering of animal numbers is misplaced.

Africans' hunting was work and not sport. We should not wonder, then, that resentment was created among Africans when this work was denied so that non-work (sport hunting) could be done by people from far away who did not even stay (i.e., licensed visitors.) Nor should we wonder today that whites show intense resentment of Africans' resumption of an old form of work (killing animals for meat, hides, and ivory), for what the Africans are doing is triply offensive to certain *mazungu*: asserting ownership, which arouses deep competitive emotions; replacing sport with work, which violates an ethic by which many of these whites have lived; and poaching, because African governments have kept colonial game laws.

It is no wonder that hunting is political.

Peter Hathaway Capstick has said that the Kenyan hunting ban came about because legal hunting funded a game department whose anti-poaching activities were too effective to please those people in power who were profiting from poaching. (This argument at least gives the lie to the notion that Africans could not protect game.) I have heard versions of this explanation from others, all *mazungu*. Whatever its truth, it casts a revealing light on the politics of hunting, suggesting that African governments, in adopting European ideas of legality and licensing, may none the less need a way around their own laws to satisfy an older, pre-European form of work. (This is quite separate from the simple crassness and greed of wanting a way around the law so as to make money.)

We like to take firm stands against poaching. It comes morally pre-digested for us: as a form of theft, it is wrong; as a cause of death, it is callous and profligate. Poaching is inevitably presented in terms of violence and gore – the thunder of automatic weapons fire, the roar of the chain saw. And of course it is true that modern poachers leave carcasses, kill females, wound animals that later die horribly. Who cannot feel righteous, inveighing against it?

Yet we should remember that Jim Carmichel properly called the 'great' Karamoja Bell a poacher. He might have said the same of a number of other 'great' ivory hunters, many of those same Europeans who shot 1000 or more elephants each. The first reason for calling them so is that they often violated law (European law) and were not licensed; the second is that they killed in such immense numbers, with such numbing effectiveness, that no decent claim of ownership can stand; their work was ownership by piracy.

Pirates do not do their work in an economic vacuum, however; their thefts are useless unless they have a market for their spoils. In the case of ivory (the goal of most of the 'great' hunters), that market was mostly European and American: 'In the early 1900s, the ivory trade killed more than 100,000 elephants *a year* to feed a growing market for piano keys, billiard balls, and trinkets' [my italics].

What, then of the 'Game Department Black List' of game-law violators forwarded to a District Commissioner in 1926, which included the names of three members of one of Kenya's best-known white-hunter families; one reverend person; one famous English hunter; and only two non-European names among the 42 people 'in the habit of committing' offences?

Or what of one J. S. Finnie, who in 1912 shot six elephants, only one with a tusk over 30 lb?

Or what of the white hunter who urged a client to shoot an elephant although he had no licence?

Or what of the 'sportsman' who, in 1926, wounded an elephant without a licence and explained that 'my idea was to take out a licence if he died'?

Or what of the 1910 statement that 'in Uganda [British] officials consider the profits from their ivory as a compensation for the expense of living [there]'?

Or what of the sometimes tragically misguided policy called 'control hunting'? Is this exercise of governmental ownership – J. A. Hunter's killing of 150 rhino for a land-clearance scheme that didn't work – good and moral because official policy declares it so? Or is it, in a larger moral sense, a kind of poaching?

Or what of the 'written requests from army officers to allow them to shoot animals for weddings and other ceremonies' in Uganda's Murchison Falls National Park in the late 1980s?

Or what of the widely reported hunting safari made by wealthy Middle Easterners *inside* Masai Mara Reserve, almost certainly with official connivance, in 1988?

Is a poacher merely somebody who kills without a licence? Or is a poacher somebody who kills for personal benefit? Or somebody who kills beyond a level of decency? Or somebody who kills with disregard for the hunting ethic?

What we are taught most to hate about poaching is its supposedly direct and inevitable connection with the disappearance of animals like the elephant and the black rhinoceros. There is no question that the animals are disappearing. It is estimated that about only seven per cent of the game that Thomson and Stanley and May French Sheldon saw remain. There is also no question that there is widespread, often out-of-control, poaching. Therefore, the argument goes, poaching is bad because it is directly and solely responsible for the disappearance of the animals.

Cloudsley-Thompson estimated, in 1960, that the 1860 population of African elephant had been about 3 million. 'Between 1880 and 1910, over two million elephants were shot'. However, it was not the shooting, horrendous as these figures seem, but another matter altogether that really concerned him – loss of elephant habitat. '[*In 1960*] *there is food and space left for some 300,000*' [my italics]. There is far less food and space than that left now; there will be far less left in the year 2000.

Poaching is horrible, but it may be over-population, not poaching, that is going to do for the elephant. However, highly organized poaching (sometimes using aircraft and trucks) is now so murderous that many experts believe the elephant will be all but extinct before the year 2000.

Others think that elephants are not near extinction yet, but they have declined to a couple of hundred thousand and will continue to decline. Modern legal hunting plays no part in that decline. (Indeed, ethical hunting is now seen as a constructive management tool.)

Poaching is directly responsible for abrupt local population losses, including Uganda's '90 per cent ... in the last five years [before 1988]'. Although, ultimately, the fundamental threat to the elephant may be rampant human expansion, 'poaching for ivory is the most immediate threat'. The horror of poaching is unquestionable, but, regrettably, its very horror serves to obscure the less dramatic horror of human expansion. Governments espouse anti-poaching campaigns, which are popular among industrialized wazungu; governments remain 'pragmatic' about loss of habitat. 'The outcome ... will probably be a cultivated continent with a few thousand elephants kept in a handful of highly managed parks that are little more than game ranches.'

The rhinoceros *has* become nearly extinct because of hunting (before the 1970s) and poaching (mostly since then). It is poached horrendously. Rhino horn is supposed in parts of the world to counter impotence, and it is supposed in the Arabian Gulf to represent status when made into a knife handle. Therefore, since one human erection is more important than one ton-and-a-half animal, and one Saudi adolescent's vanity is more important than a creature whose presence is as strange and wonderful as a dinosaur's might be, the rhino will indeed disappear.

Tony Dyer estimated in 1972 that black rhino numbers had been reduced from the 600,000 of the 1870s to perhaps 22,500. Since then, hard work by the poachers has reduced that to a few thousand in all of Africa. Fifty-two hours of survey flying in 1980 turned up exactly two, both in the Serengeti. Poaching is said to be responsible for a 90 per cent population decline in the Mara *in ten years*. Tanzania's Selous Reserve held 3000 black rhino in 1981, 300 in 1986. There were mere handfuls of black rhino left in Kenya's game parks in the 1980s. (White rhino have been somewhat brought back in southern Africa, where they are hunted under highly controlled conditions.)

Modern legal hunting will not reduce rhino populations. Modern poaching will. Modern human expansion will reduce them to zero.

Many species would be vastly better off – their declines would be postponed

Women were not supposed to be up to the rigours of a safari, but many did it better than men – despite clothes that men would not have tolerated (c. 1914)

Women's safari clothes got more sensible by the twenties, and after World War Two they were as functional as men's. Fashion, however, was another matter

THE BIG FIVE: *Left:* Buffalo, with Roosevelt and his son Kermit; *right:* lion; *Below:* elephant, with Roosevelt again; *opposite above:* rhino, and *below:* leopard

Illustrators exaggerated the perils of Africa by over-stating the relative size of animals. This hippo appears able to gobble up Roosevelt, boat and crew

It is dangerous enough to shoot buffalo out on the plain, but sheer hell to follow one into dense reed and mud

The python is so rare that most Africans have never seen one. These four seem less than happy with this one, which was *supposed* to be dead

Never under-estimate the danger of a vegetarian. Hippo are territorial and aggressive and can kill a man with one bite

'Who wants a giraffe?' one sportsman said, but they were once an acceptable target. Drying the skins was a major camp chore, and the need for skilled Africans to skin and cure trophies raised safari costs

'A typical sportsman's Kenya bag' was the photographer's caption. These were the days when lion were 'vermin' and any number could be shot

Taxidermy and outfitting extended the safari's economics to London and New York and represented the greater part of the total cost. Relatively little of the money spent on safaris stayed in black Africa

The first step in building a piano – shooting an elephant (c. 1890). The gunbearer's flight, often shown by white illustrators, was in fact rather rare

Whites' sport (and the profit from ivory) was impossible without cheap black labour. Here, tusks, skull and skin are being carried to the railway

About a ton and a half of ivory, worth about £1,000 to the white professional. His black workers got about £2 each for the two months' work

Hamburg, where good elephants went when they died (c. 1900). Ivory 'factories' were also located elsewhere in Europe and the USA

'The One-Night Stand'
Sex and safari were often linked

'Buffalo' Jones, the stunt safarist who 'lassoed' rhino and lion

Shooting a buffalo with a percussion rifle was an act of courage. The dense cloud of smoke at least gave you a chance to dodge the charge (c. 1860)

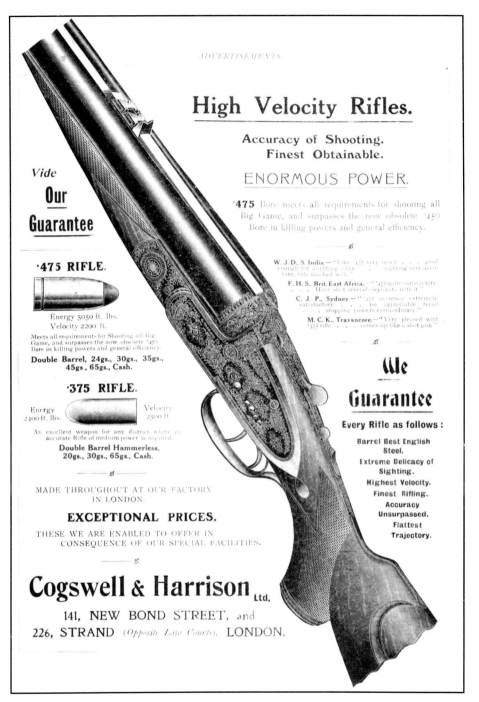

A London double rifle for smokeless powder (c. 1910), the *ne plus ultra* of hunting weapons
– 65 guineas, cash

HOLLAND & HOLLAND'S SPORTING RIFLES

·240 BORE 'APEX' Regd. SUPER EXPRESS

MUZZLE VELOCITY 3000 ft. sec., STRIKING ENERGY 2000 ft. lbs.
PRACTICALLY FLAT TRAJECTORY at 250 yards.

	Muzzle	100	200	250
		1·9	0·0	
Line of Aim				
	0·75		0·0	2·5

MEMO.—Measurements above and below the line of sight are given in ins.
Great Accuracy, Extreme Lightness, Freedom from Recoil.
An Invaluable Weapon for Use in all parts of the World.

NEW "SUPER-THIRTY" RIFLE

The only Rifle actually giving 3,100 f.s. velocity with a 150 gr. bullet. Striking Energy 3,210 ft. lbs.
Extreme Accuracy, Flat Trajectory, Great Striking Energy.
For Shooting Animals of the Softer Skinned Variety.

·375 BORE MAGNUM

MUZZLE VELOCITY 2850 ft. sec., STRIKING ENERGY 4250 ft. lbs.
BEST ALL-ROUND RIFLE YET PRODUCED.

·465 BORE RIFLE FOR BIG GAME

MUZZLE VELOCITY 2125 ft. sec., STRIKING ENERGY 4820 ft. lbs.

HOLLAND & HOLLAND, LIMITED
Gun and Rifle Makers to H.M. King George V
98 NEW BOND STREET, LONDON, W.1

Big game cartridges, from the Lilliputian to the Brobdingnagian (c. 1930). Recoil rose with powder charge and bullet weight

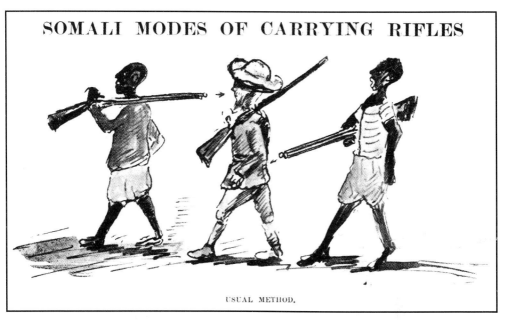

SOMALI MODES OF CARRYING RIFLES

USUAL METHOD.

An African 'battery' comprised several guns, for which gunbearers were needed. Sir Alfred Pease had trouble teaching them gun safety

Left: Fascination with the Masai marked the safari's history. This studio shot (c. 1905) shows a 'Massai Moran warrior' in full regalia. *Right:* A Masai on safari, probably as a scout. The animal is a Grant's gazelle (named, of course, after a European)

Black and white. This Masai scout later saved the sportsman's life 'by spearing a charging rhinoceros'

A safari headman (c. 1900). A manager and linguist, he kept things running smoothly

Safari workers were usually young, often playful, and hungry for entertainment

'My two trackers, Simba (on left), Tumbo (on right).' Africans had multiple names that often identified them by clan and parentage, but for safari use they got nicknames like these – Lion and Belly

'A "shari"' (*shauri* means talk). Such contacts with un-Europeanized Africans were a positive aspect of earlier safaris, now mostly gone

Local people got the meat when an elephant was killed. Many whites have described the remarkable scene as the animal was butchered. Here, for example, two people are inside the elephant

– if poaching was stopped. The emphasis on stopping *poachers*, however, is like the emphasis on solving the world's drug problem by stopping the farmers who grow coca and opium: it attacks only one of the at least three responsible groups.

Poachers, no matter how highly organized and how mechanized, are little people making the least amount of money from the poaching pyramid. If we hate poaching, the real objects of our disgust should be brokers in East Africa and Switzerland and Belgium, and dealers in the Middle East and Taipei, as well as every curio and trinket shop from Cairo to Fifth Avenue that sells ivory. And the real object of our attempts to crush poaching should be ourselves, or others just like us – consumers who buy the junk that is made from ivory and rhino horn and who are identical to the consumers who buy the junk made from coca and opium.

But no amount of poaching control will counter the effects of human population growth. 'The real threat to the wildlife of East Africa lies in the recent population increase', Cloudsley-Thompson wrote in 1962. Warren Page called it 'the octopus of population spread'. Well before that, Ortega y Gasset had pinpointed the same problem: '[Efforts to conserve] do not succeed in checking the rest of human progress, which, as it continues "humanizing" the planet, takes away from it, like it or not, the spontaneity of Nature'.

So, maybe some elephants will remain into the twenty-first century under 'ranch' conditions. Rhino, no. Lion, perhaps. Leopard, perhaps. The cheetah, that dazzling daylight hunter easily put off by tourist vans, will withdraw to whatever inaccessible pockets population growth may chance to leave it. Some remnant of the great herds of buffalo and wildebeeste and zebra will remain. But, for all their seeming numbers, they will be so reduced that the hunter's 'quality of experience' – Ortega y Gasset's 'spontaneity of Nature', Vivienne de Watteville's 'glorious madness' – will be utterly lost. There will be, quite simply, too many of us and too few of them.

Unless of course. . . .

AN EXPENSIVE LUXURY
The white hunter

As essential to our idea of the hunting safari as yeast is to bread, the white hunter was, as we have seen, a response to a consumer need, his title probably a conscious invention for commercial purposes by Leslie Tarlton. This is not to say, however, that he (the hunter was always *he*) sprang from Tarlton's head, complete down to his bush shoes and leopard hatband, utterly without precedent.

The great question is, of course, what did Tarlton mean by 'white hunter'? Newland & Tarlton's 1908 catalogue defined the new term as a 'white man who knows the ropes and speaks the language. Such a man would, in addition to looking after the "safari", give the benefit of his experience in the ways of game, and thus ensure good sport.' Cranworth, an authority on Kenya's early years and a director of Newland & Tarlton, described the white hunter in his first three or four years as a man who 'speaks Swahili . . . acts as go-between . . . oversees all the detail and routine of the camp'. In 1909, 'Nyoka' defined the white hunter as a man who 'runs the safari entirely', adding that he was 'quite a new idea'. It is significant that Tarlton, Cranworth, and 'Nyoka' did not include backing the client with a heavy gun as part of the white hunter's job, and they limited his involvement in hunting to '[giving] the benefit of his experience in the ways of game'. On the other hand, Millais said in a 1907 eulogy of Neumann that the great elephant-hunter had shot more elephants than 'three white hunters', but it is not clear from the context that he meant anything more than 'three whites who hunt'. In 1908, 'B. J. L.' defined the term (in inverted commas) as 'a white man, who is an experienced big game shot, and can be relied upon in any emergency'.

The term, then, invented *c.*1908 (the first use in print is apparently B. J. L. 's *Field* letter of that year) seems to have had two meanings until about 1909, the year of Roosevelt's coming. Almost immediately, however – that is, with Roosevelt – the two meanings conflated and the white hunter became both a white headman and a crack shot who protected the client; and, in the person of Tarlton, he became companion and social equal, one tolerable for two or three months of close contact. What we now call a white hunter appears to be a composite of functions originally separate, the 'big game shot, [who] can be relied on in any emergency' and the 'man who knows the ropes and speaks the languages'. Different early (pre-1910) white hunters in fact did one or the other – one in 1906, for example, not even carrying a gun in the field.

A manager, then, who was a hunter, a man of courage, a linguist, and a social charmer.

His forebears were in fact both white and black. The early existence of 'black hunters' is obvious; whites called them 'shikaris', the term the British had picked up in India, or trackers or even gunbearers, for in the last third of the nineteenth century, sportsmen in East Africa used as gunbearers men who were also translators and guides. That black professional hunters existed before 1900 is also clear; Abel Chapman encountered them, 'each with his attendant gun-bearers'.

The organizational side of the job was performed before he was invented by the early white visitors themselves. They were men who had hunted in India and South Africa. They did not need and certainly did not want to spend money on another European to do what they could perfectly well do themselves. Day-to-day management was turned over to an African headman.

The white hunter's social attributes had their precedents in pre-colonial African traders. These were men who had to exercise authority far from normal controls, yet men who had to be able to charm and entertain. 'There was a marked element of the theatrical in the trader. *Kivui* [a pre-colonial trader] . . . is still highly regarded for his debater's zeal, his ability to regale groups.' A marked element of the theatrical would prove handy to most white hunters, and regaling groups became an essential skill.

For actual examples of Europeans who took other Europeans into the bush, we have to look no further than the advertising columns of the *Field*. In 1898, a 'Gentleman with unique experience in the Iceland rivers' offered to take fishermen to Iceland, camping gear provided (for a fee); another wanted to guide two or three to the Rockies, 'no remuneration except personal expenses.' Another wanted to lead a party to India; a 'Gentleman owning an up-country store' in South Africa offered to outfit shooting parties. Such ads continued and, by 1905, included 'BIG GAME SHOOTING – Small Exploring, Hunting, Trading EXPEDITION shortly starting for Central Africa can TAKE FIVE GENTLE-MEN, each subscribing £500'.

These *Field* advertisements were symptomatic of the change from the veteran, do-it-yourself sportsmen to the neophyte who wanted help – the same change that brought Newland & Tarlton into being. The new sportsman did not want to go out into the bush alone, speaking no Swahili, the only white face in a party of 40–100 black men. That the reason for this attitude was racial is inescapable, although the racialism took several forms. Simple fear for physical safety was one. Fear of loss of face or of authority was another; the military experience, for example, that had typified so many of the early-comers was often absent, and fear of keeping discipline among 40 or 80 or 100 people whose language one does not speak and whose culture one does not understand should not be underestimated. And simple fear of loneliness (racial loneliness, perhaps) was another.

Newland & Tarlton could have used 'white safari leader' in their catalogue (the term was used by others). If they had, the history of the safari might have been rather different. In fact, in a 1906 advertisement they simply said 'Men who know the Game'. But with 'white hunter' they dramatized the new visitors' fears and calmed them – gave the drama a hero, as it were. And the white hunters they employed, and the freelancers of the period, quickly became 'the most colourful group of men that ever lived', although the very parochialism of the remark suggests what a limited world they occupied.

When Roosevelt began, in 1908, the correspondence that led to his safari, the two white hunter functions had not yet come together. The division is clear in the Roosevelt correspondence, existing in Roosevelt's own thinking and in the views taken by his correspondents. Roosevelt's original choice, as we have seen, was M. A. DaSilva, the Goanese hunter, whom Roosevelt had been advised to take 'simply as a hunter' because he was 'a first-class shot and knows the game'; Roosevelt's adviser (Arman Sanderson), however, thought him not 'fit to run the caravan, altho [sic] he can speak various native languages'. Roosevelt's fear in engaging a white to run the caravan was that he would feel 'as if I were being personally conducted in a kind of Cook's tourist party'. Clearly, Roosevelt believed that if the conduct of the caravan were elevated by giving it to a white, Roosevelt himself would be one of the things to be managed – he would become a tourist, in effect.

If, on the other hand, he had to follow Selous's advice and hire a white (at this point the only name in the pot was Will Judd's), then 'I should want it distinctly understood . . . that Judd was not expected to go hunting'.

In other words, if he could have a non-white (by his definition) social inferior who would do as Roosevelt told him, that man could carry a gun and back Roosevelt or his son in the field; but if he had to have a white social equal, that man could do no hunting.

It is fair to point out that other ideas were being offered Roosevelt at the same time, particularly that of hiring nobody at all and using government officials in the bush (mostly ADCs) to provide hunting advice, with local African guides picked up at each new location.

Significantly, Roosevelt's own ideas (gained from books) were already out of date, so fast had things moved in BEA. He spoke in one letter of wanting somebody to 'tell me what trade goods I would be apt to require', for example, as if it were 1890 and not 1908. In fact, when writing about the matter of a safari manager he referred specifically to the Willoughby safari of 1888, not understanding that East Africa had turned upside down since then. However, it is also significant that his idea of what he wanted in DaSilva was the 'Maltese or Portuguese named Martin, who was with [Willoughby and his companions] to take charge of their caravan'. Martin, who had also been with Thomson, was his model for a safari manager who would be socially inferior – i.e., bossable. (The assumption, of course, was that Portuguese, Maltese, or Goanese were socially inferior. Racial implications are inescapable.)

Roosevelt's solution – a solution to some extent forced on him by two sets of advisers – was finally to hire two men, Cuninghame and Tarlton, who more or less divided the white-hunter functions along the manager-hunter line. Cuninghame, however, served as a hunter when with Kermit, and Tarlton served as manager when Cuninghame was away, so the lines were quickly blurred. What posterity would remember was that Roosevelt had had two white hunters; subsequent safaris would have white hunters who were both managers and hunters.

It remains debatable who the first white hunter in fact was. Finding 'firsts' is mostly a mug's game, anyway, generating petty facts instead of knowledge; in this case, however, it forces us to examine the question itself – or to examine ourselves.

A number of people have suggested Roosevelt's correspondent, F. C. Selous, as the first white hunter. It is true that Selous had been in South Africa long before Nairobi was thought of, and it is true he was a renowned professional hunter, and it is true he had guided expeditions – Cecil Rhodes's Pioneer Column, for one. He may even have been a model for Haggard's Allan Quatermain. What he lacks as a candidate for actual, rather than metaphorical, white hunter, however, is any instance of serving in that role in East Africa in the relevant time period. 'Professional hunter' and 'white hunter' cannot mean the same thing. (Neumann was a great professional hunter but in no way a white hunter.) To be sure, the first white hunters were qualified because they had been professional hunters – that is, men who had made their livings from hunting animals, usually elephant (for ivory) but sometimes plains game for meat and hides. Indeed, if every biltong and tusk hunter is to be defined as an East African white hunter, then there are many, many – Baldwin, for example – before Selous.

The always outspoken Rainsford underlined Selous's ignorance, in fact, of East Africa. 'If Mr Selous knew the [situation], as he doesn't and can not, for he has only been one fortnight – long ago – here, he couldn't possibly write any such nonsense' as the advice he was giving Roosevelt. Rainsford was right; Selous did not know East Africa, and it was he who wound up with Judd as his white hunter, in fact.

Judd himself appears to be one of the likeliest candidates for 'first'. Another is Jack Riddell, one of the founders of Boma Trading Company, who 'arranged a lion hunt' for Winston Churchill in 1907. A. C. Hoey was often mentioned in the *East African Standard* (so often, in fact, that the conclusion must be that he was sending out what amounted to press releases); in late 1907 he was out with R. C. Cockburn, the safari organized by Newland & Tarlton, when Cockburn killed an elephant with 256 lb of ivory. Probably earlier that year, Hoey had been with Rainsford. (J. A. Hunter, whom Bull makes by implication the first, was in fact doing his early professional, not white, hunting throughout this period.) Alan Black, according to the *Globetrotter*, was a hunting 'guide' as early as 1907.

We simply do not know how early Cuninghame was a white hunter. We do know that by 1908 he was thought the best and was recommended to Roosevelt by Percy Madeira, who had employed him in 1907. Carl Akeley was taken out by him in 1906 'to teach [him] to hunt elephants'. In 1905, he is said to have 'accompanied' H. Holmes Tarn on a gathering trip for the British Museum, but what he did is unclear.

Nor do we know how early DaSilva was working, only that another Roosevelt contact, Arman Sanderson, had engaged him in 1907. One oddity of that relationship was that Sanderson had also been 'out', on the same trip to East Africa, with J. H. Patterson, famed as the killer of the man-eating lions of Tsavo; but whether Patterson and DaSilva served on the same safari is not known. This was not, however, Patterson's first outing as a white safari manager: at the very beginning of 1906, he took a party of five (including Moreton Frewen and the Earl of Warwick) to Laikipia, Uganda, and Eldama Ravine. Patterson is never referred to as one of the first white hunters, however; Anthony Dyer does not even include him in his lists. One reason may be that Patterson became Kenyan Game Ranger in 1907 and 1908 (although he served at least two safaris as white hunter while holding that post), but the real reason is probably his scandalous fall from grace.

Judd was referred to in a 1906 letter to the *Field*, the actual hunt possibly in 1905. The client had got a letter from Judd 'offering his services as a guide', but there is no way of knowing how Judd knew to send the letter in the first place. Judd himself had an article in the *Field*, however, that same year that shows he was performing some white-hunter functions in 1905 for a Dr Clifford Brookes ('to show him the different game localities in British East Africa').

Therefore, we know that Judd was at least guiding one hunt in late 1905, Cuninghame was teaching Akeley about elephants in 1906, and Patterson was both managing and guiding in very early 1906 (actually having brought the Frewen party to Mombasa in December, 1905). These, then, are the earliest candidates for the first white hunters – except for that James Martin mentioned by Roosevelt and the DaSilva whom he first engaged and then, apparently, let go. The historical record is clear that Martin – who was Maltese, not Portuguese – managed the Willoughby safari to Kilimanjaro; both Willoughby and von Hohnel said so. This fact would seem to make him as much an East African white hunter as Judd or Cuninghame or Patterson, and 24 years earlier. As for DaSilva, he was well established by mid-1907, 'a good shot and a capable elephant hunter' who had already guided Sanderson.

The 'first' white hunter, then, was James Martin. Purists of a certain mind-set may object that Martin was not as white as they would like; that, after all, was Roosevelt's point. In that case, the first white hunter was Judd or Cuninghame or Patterson, or perhaps Hoey or DaSilva – but DaSilva presents the same problem as Martin.

The search for the first white hunter, then, leads not to a name but to a reminder of what the term meant above all: that the hunter was white. Until well after independence, this same crucial significance would remain: in defining the white hunter, the primary criterion would be race.

This 'colourful group' numbered no more than a dozen when the First World War put a stop to the safari business. Their example would influence the profession for generations, however, and several of them would continue as white hunters after the war.

Pre-eminent, probably, was Cuninghame, 'lean, sinewy, bearded, exactly the type of hunter and safari manager that one would wish'. Cuninghame (born in 1871) had Eton and Cambridge in his past (though apparently no degree); he was already nearing 40 when he took out Roosevelt, yet he appears to have been universally respected for his bushcraft and his grit. He was associated as hunter or manager with some of the great names of the period – Roosevelt, Akeley, White, Babault – and was admired by Selous and Rainsford. Babault referred to him as a 'collègue ... du British Museum', perpetuating the tradition that Cuninghame was a trained naturalist. (Although Akeley implied that he was not. He became a member of the Royal Zoological Society. The British Museum connection may have resulted from his going out with Tarn in 1905.) He had been a professional elephant-hunter. As he set off on a six-month foot safari in 1914, he wrote that 'I am fairly fit but realize I am nearing the end of my usefulness in the sphere of African activities'. This was probably the 'huge safari in many respects and most unwieldy to handle' for Prince William of Sweden, which found him in Portuguese East Africa when war broke out. He went to London and tried to volunteer, wound up at 42 as a lieutenant in the American Field Ambulance, 'fishing for wounded', as Tarlton said in forwarding a sad, weary letter in November 1915. Cuninghame had been turned down for service because he was 'quinine fast' – filled with malaria but unable to use quinine any longer. In 1916, he was in a convalescent home in Nairobi after a 'mysterious mission to Zanzibar and Mafia. I fear he won't be fit for any more hard work in Africa.' He appears by then to have joined General Smith-Lorien's staff as political and intelligence officer, work for which he was awarded the Military Cross. And he did not return to BEA, but at war's end inherited a large Scottish estate, married, and lived his last few years as a wealthy landowner. By 1924, his eyesight was failing 'such that I cannot clearly see the backside of a rifle any more,' and he was 'absolutely certain I shall never return to Africa again'. He died of a brain tumour in Kirkcudbrightshire in 1925.

After Cuninghame, probably the best-known of the early white hunters was Judd. He was generally respected, with the signal (and vocal) exception of Rainsford. 'Probably the most experienced and capable hunter of African big game now living', one visitor said, and Jackson called him 'celebrated . . . a good hunter . . . dressed immaculately in hunting kit with shiny brown boots and highly polished gaiters, a *maradadi* [*maridadi*, Swahili for dandy] in fact'. Judd in 1913 was keeping a 'trading store' on the Mara River, presumably while continuing as a white hunter in the season. He stayed in East Africa after the war and was killed by an elephant in the late 1920s.

Leslie Tarlton is remembered better as founder of Newland & Tarlton and of Safarilands than as a hunter, but it was as a hunter that Roosevelt hired him. A noted rifle shot, he none the less said 'he was through with dangerous game' as early as 1910: 'I've had enough of it', he was quoted as saying. Roosevelt and Kermit apparently called him 'Bwana Safari', perhaps because they picked the name up from the Africans, although 'Safari' was the Newland & Tarlton cable name; Tarlton even jokingly referred to his wife as 'Mrs Safari' in a letter. His health was poor because of gallstones in 1910–11; he considered emigrating to America. But he stayed and became a pillar of the colony, serving as a founding member of the East African Professional Hunters Association in 1934. He had had to give up Safarilands the year before, however: 'the financial depression has knocked me pretty badly'.

Another man who would become legendary among hunters was Alan Black. Only 20 when the first white hunters came into being, he was a Newland & Tarlton employee and 'guide' by 1907, and he was mentioned as 'a hunter friend of Judd's' who went north with a party, but he was refused entry into Laikipia because his name was not on the official permit. He was a white hunter with Rainey before 1912, and Stewart Edward White said that 'his name might as well have been Quatermain'.

The man ultimately considered the *beau idéal* of white hunters, Philip Percival, was just starting when Roosevelt visited. He did some transport work for the Roosevelt safari, but (as 'Percival junior' – his older brother was A. Blayney Percival, the Game Ranger) he was listed as 'hunter' for the Duke of Connaught's safari, probably under Riddell, in early 1910. His great days were to come after the war.

George Henry Outram was 'an old Australian prospector of wide experience' who had hunted in South Africa and had been a member of the 1894 Anglo-German boundary survey. He was with Bronson in 1907 and with Rainey in 1911.

A. C. Hoey's publicity was so successful that he had been recommended to Roosevelt by 1909. On one hunt reported in the *Standard* in 1908, he shot 10 lions and 2 elephants, but this was apparently professional and not 'white' hunting; no client was mentioned. According to Tony Dyer, he turned his time entirely to farming after the war.

Jack Riddell – Captain Riddell, MVO, then Major Riddell in the Second World War – is perhaps best remembered as one of the founders of the raffish Boma Trading Company, but he was the most widely advertised of independent white hunters in 1907. How many clients he actually took out is uncertain, but he appears to have been white hunter for the Duke of Connaught's safari. He apparently left East Africa when war came.

These eight, with M. A. DaSilva, of whom I have been able to learn nothing else, were the principal white hunters between 1905 and 1914. Mention should be made again of J. H. Patterson, who took out at least three safaris before mid-1908 but left East Africa for good that year. Other white hunters of the period were Ray Ulyate, who handled the 'Buffalo' Jones party, and Fritz Shindelar, remembered by some for his dash but by Jackson for his lack of ethics: the worst of the hunters, he said, ignored the game laws, and 'of these an Austrian named Fritz was a bad example' for encouraging his clients to shoot more animals than the licence allowed, keeping the best trophy heads and throwing the rest away. An American safari of 1909 was led by a 'Seth Smith', first name not given (Donald?). Harold and Clifford Hill are sometimes cited as early white hunters, but they appear to have been more of the order of landholders who could always drive up a lion when needed. A Major J. A. C. Kirkwood worked with Cuninghame at least once; an S. H. Lydford was identified as a 'young white hunter'. A Major Ross was offering his services to sportsmen through the *Globetrotter* in 1907.

The first American white hunter was James Clark, who went to East Africa in 1909 to protect Arthur Dugmore from animals while he used his camera. Boma tried to hire him to work as white hunter for the Duke of Connaught but he declined; he did, however, serve the Colonial Governor and his wife in this capacity. When he left BEA in 1910, he returned to the American Museum of Natural History in New York, where he told another man, A. J. Klein, about what he had seen and done. Klein left the museum and came to Nairobi, where he became one of the notable white hunters between the wars.

These men were widely different – age, nationality, education – but they had some things in common. Some (Cuninghame, Clark, Klein) were naturalists. Most were experienced hunters, some cynically so. Most had previous or current other professions (storekeeping, farming, and professional hunting; several had done military service). Either their white hunting was sporadic or it was only intermittently recorded, or both.

The conclusion that may be drawn is that white hunting in the early days, although a new opportunity, was not a full-time job. Nor did it pay bountifully for excellence; 'they all drew the same rate of salary in spite of the difference in their qualifications and reputations'.

Jackson's remark about Shindelar suggests that the problem of ethical standards had intruded almost at the beginning. If so, it was not generally noticed; far more common was denigration of professional, rather than ethical, standards. C. H. Stigand warned the newcomer to 'carefully avoid the professional hunters' who offered themselves in Nairobi. 'These men know practically nothing about hunting and bushcraft'. 'Nyoka' gave the same warning: because 'the demand just now is very much greater than the supply' and there were only 'two or three excellent men', inexperienced people were jumping in and 'offering themselves'. Rainsford cautioned readers about 'several professional hunters hanging round Nairobi always looking out for a job', but recommended hiring a *good* white hunter 'unless you have reasonably complete command both of your nerves and of your weapon'.

Responses to the white hunter divided into two camps: those who, like B. J. L. thought him 'an expensive luxury', and those who were glad to be 'relieved of all camp worries [so that] you have nothing to do but enjoy yourself'. The debate continued until the war and was resumed sporadically after it, but the 1920s turned the 'expensive luxury' into a near necessity. By the late 1920s, no person of means who wanted to boast of his or her safari would have set out without one.

The ethical question, which had not seemed important before the war, became paramount 10 years after it. 'A white hunter is a man who wears a big hat and shorts, speaks Swahili, and takes tenderfeet out into the blue, eats their grub, drinks their liquor, and keeps them away from the game until their money runs out.' This cynical view at the close of the 1920s suggests how far the wheel had turned. The expensive luxury had become an expensive fraud – at least to the cynical.

'He was white beneath his beard and his tan, for it must be remembered that there are fashions in white hunters, just as there are fashions in Ascot gowns. The longer the beard of the hunter the greater the amount of romance that may be absorbed from Wild Africa – according to American heiresses.' This was 1929, too. Like the first remark, it suggests an institution in its maturity – fit subject for satire, fully equipped with caste marks (hat, shorts, beard) and supporting characters (American heiresses). Perhaps it should be pointed out that nothing can be satirized until it is successful, and the satire may not show real flaws so much as real success.

Yet a visitor like Margery Perham was not so much satirical as negatively analytical. She saw the white hunter as exploitative and perhaps immature, somebody who had 'made Africa a playground . . . [Somebody] not so much unscrupulous as unthinking. Africa was a glorious adventure, they roamed about it and killed off its animals and bought up land and drank with boon companions of their own kind, and fleeced newcomers, and engaged in all kinds of curious enterprises, and generally had a glorious time.' She described theirs as a 'not entirely elitist profession'.

John Taylor – never an admirer of white hunters, himself a professional ivory hunter – called it 'this racket'. He contended that things got so bad 'back during the twenties and thirties that a self-styled East African White Hunters' Association [*sic*] was formed with the laudable intention of putting a stop to it'. Taylor was probably right that problems within the profession demanded that it develop a conscience, although it seems too much coincidence that the conscience first found its voice during the lowest year of the Depression. Tony

Dyer said that 'a group of good and ethical hunters' created the association. [East African Professional Hunters, not White Hunters.]

It represented what may be called the moral centre of white hunting. The profession also had a far right – libertarian and reactionary insofar as it kept trying to return to the time before game laws – and a far left, or Happy Valley, wing – that did not join. In between were the solid names, 'better-known hunters [who] will stand no nonsense'. These included Phil Percival, by then the most sought-after hunter in BEA, Black, Tarlton, Klein, and slightly newer men like Pat Ayre, Donald Ker, Sydney Downey, and Jack Lucy. Before hunting closed down again in 1938–9, they had taken in more of the best and most promising: Bror Blixen, J. A. Hunter, Ben Fourie, and others. Before its 1977 dissolution, second and even third generations of names already known in the profession appeared: Hoey, Cottar, Seth-Smith.

And the organization appears to have had the effect it wanted. At the very least, it influenced the perception of the white hunter, and perhaps the reality, as well. The satirical and negative stabs of the late 1920s did recede in the 1930s, and it is really in the late 1930s and the 1950s (the 1940s being devoted to war) that the current idealization of 'white hunter' was formed. Whether this myth-making was the organization's doing is unknown; certainly there was a shift in perception from Perham's boyish exploiter to Hemingway's paternal guide.

It was a shift from the heirs of Fritz Shindelar to men who, in Stoneham's expression, stood no nonsense. The kind of 'nonsense' needs identifying. 'Men like Pat Ayre and J. A. Hunter cannot be bribed or intimidated.' That was one sort of nonsense – giving in to the rich client who could give a hunter an extra year's income just for leaving one small-tusked elephant to rot or for letting a lion be shot from a car. Another sort of nonsense was holding the client's trophies hostage to a tip. Another was pandering to the client, literally or metaphorically. What most of the nonsense came down to, finally, was breaking the law or the code for money. Clients were rich; hunters were not. The combination was potentially explosive.

The image of the white hunter, perhaps as a result of the Association, changed: 'not . . . Allan Quartermaine [sic] nor yet [a] Public School Jeeves . . . but a most polite and charming nursery governess'.

Image and actuality are often different. Some of the most famous white hunters between the wars created public personalities to enhance their employ-ability. One of these was Bror Blixen, Danish nobleman and former husband of Karen Blixen, who introduced Denys Finch Hatton as 'my wife's lover, and my best friend'. Blixen played very hard in a very fast set, was the natural choice (with Finch Hatton) to run the Prince of Wales's safari, and got himself lots of publicity with the international moneyed. He was said to have made £200,000 out of hunting, a remarkable figure. He cultivated a reputation as a womanizer. Bunny Allen wrote that he never 'missed a chance, whether it be for a grand trophy, the hand of a lovely lady, or the collection of golden shekels'.

Denys Finch Hatton was similar in some ways. Allen called him 'one of the first "great" white hunters', but surely he was thinking of Finch Hatton's reputation and not his achievement. One client asked him how he became a white hunter and he answered with studied casualness that it had 'just happened, if you know what I mean', but in fact his decision was a very deliberate one, to make money, as a letter to Kermit Roosevelt shows. Finch Hatton was an aristocrat; he asked that 'if you know of any pleasant people who want a shoot put them in touch with me. You know the sort of people I should get on with *and* the ones I should *not*', and in another letter he mocked his forthcoming client, the same Patterson who would laud him as 'fearless . . . popular with everybody, hard working, well educated'. Beryl Markham, who was briefly his lover, implied that he was bisexual and thought him 'brilliant . . . Intelligent and very well educated. He was a great hunter and a great, a tremendous personality.' One gets a picture from these varied sources of a much romanticized figure, a man able to seem different things to different people, with, at the centre, a boyish exploiter of the sort Perham had described. We know him now mostly as Karen Blixen's and Beryl Markham's lover, in which roles he may well have been that same boyish exploiter. (When Blixen got pregnant and sent him a cable to tell him so, calling the yet unborn child Daniel, he cabled back brutally, 'Suggest you cancel Daniel's visit'.) He was killed in 1931.

The making of one's own image became a probably necessary part of the most successful white hunting. Word of mouth was almost certainly the most important source a hunter had for new clients, as Finch Hatton's letter to Kermit Roosevelt shows. To get among the wealthy, to have them talk about one, these were important goals. Here, it is probably best to distinguish between an upper layer of those who were sought by name and a lower strata of hunters who were like contract players, taking out parties for the safari companies as they came along.

For all this image-making and very hard and dangerous work, most white hunters were not royally paid. In 1908, Riddell got £3 a day, all found. Cranworth implies that top hunters got £250 a month before the First World War, but other sources show that he must have been thinking of the very top figure in the 1920s when he wrote this; £40–75 was more like it in 1920. J. A. Hunter, who started after the First World War, said that £50 'gradually raised to two hundred' was the top. By the late 1960s, Holman said that 'the big names' made £7500 a year; the 'upper bracket of sound, reliable top-liners' £5000; journeymen £10 a day during what had become a nine-month season.

For these amounts, never more than an upper-level white-collar worker could have made, they risked their lives and worked hours as long as a working mother's. Babault describes Cuninghame's two-hour ride to find water, with two hours back, then hours more to ride back along the safari route and find lagging porters – all this after they had stopped for the day. Again, he was up and off at dawn to find porters who had not found camp.

J. A. Hunter described the white hunter's normal duties as including, besides camp management and hunting, auto repair, doctoring, driving, entertaining the clients, and, 'never under any circumstances [losing] his temper'.

He also had to teach some clients how to shoot, cure other clients of terror, and keep yet other clients from doing things like blowing up dik-dik with elephant guns. And then there were the unpredictable tasks. 'He has been called upon to perform the task of lady's maid, and it has been rumoured, I trust libellously, that even more intimate tasks have been required of him.' The last words imply sex, and it is certainly true that sexiness has come to surround the white hunter's image. It is worth examining why.

The fictional model that almost everybody mentioned was Haggard's Allan Quatermain, who was not presented as a sexual man; rather, Haggard's highly ambivalent notions of sex, especially in *She*, clustered around the English amateurs. (The 1950 movie version of *King Solomon's Mines* gave Stewart Granger's Quatermain a sexual interest – Deborah Kerr – who is not in the Haggard novel.) The real-life Quatermains, the men with whom the comparison was made, were people like Selous, Cuninghame, and Black, about whom no sexual musk lingers. It is absent in a novel like Young's 1924 *Woodsmoke*, even though the novel is about adultery. Indeed, we come forward to the 1950s – the signal exception is Hemingway's 1936 short story, 'The Short Happy Life of Francis Macomber' – before we find the white hunter regularly presented as sexually active and sexually irresistible to women; then the image is everywhere. It is overt, for example, in the books of J. A. Hunter, Holman, and Bunny Allen. It is also a cliché in Hollywood after the Second World War.

The image may have come from some of the white hunters themselves. J. A. Hunter and Bunny Allen put it into print; others undoubtedly talked about it. The prime means of transmission for the white hunter was always word of mouth, and long evenings, long days in the hunting car, long hours in the shade waiting for the game to appear, provided ample opportunity for story-telling. It was on some such occasion that Hemingway heard the 'Macomber' story from Percival; the actual incident had happened a generation before, is repeated in *Hunter*, and is a good example of its kind. It may also have been from Percival that Hemingway heard about the white hunter who took the double campbed on safari to be able to accommodate randy female clients. The stories must have been good telling; gossip, especially sexual gossip, with the names removed, must have been part of the good white hunter's act.

And some hunters *were* sexually predatory. Female clients seem to have been more common in the 1920s and 1930s than earlier; wives, as Hemingway so strongly suggests, may have been opportunists. This was, after all, the first high period of belief in sexual 'fulfilment' as an article of psychological faith, both male and female. 'Of course I made love with [Blixen] . . . sometimes when we were out there, there was nothing else to do but make love.' But this was Beryl Markham, hardly a typical safari wife. Blixen's name, however, is apt; an aura of male potency surrounded him, as one of rather romantic sexuality did Finch Hatton. (Hemingway spent a lot of time with Blixen after his safari and may have heard his tales, too.) Also, the perception of Kenya as an extended Happy Valley probably attached itself to the safari and then to the white hunter as its central figure.

One source of the sexy image, then, was the white hunters themselves. Another was their male clients, who appear to have seen their hunters as larger than life – in every way. The means of transmission was also perhaps the male clients by word of mouth, not least because, in masculine environments, sexually embellishing one's hunter increased one's own value by what lawyers call 'adhesion'.

And it was worth remembering that the white hunter was created to serve as the hero of a racial-sexual drama. He was 'a white man who knows the ropes and speaks the language. . . . Where a lady accompanies the party, it is often found to be advantageous'. *Advantageous* is not a double entendre here, although the late white-hunter image might try to make it seem so. The word does seem, however, to be code, and rather obvious code at that: a white female will be sexually safe from black men if the white hunter is along. This was reassurance for white women, purportedly; it may have more importantly been reassurance for white men.

The hunting ethic that had evolved in Roosevelt's day and that worked pretty well right up to the end involved the hunter in difficult and dangerous work. Its essence was that the trophy belonged to the client. No matter who really shot first or who really killed the game, it belonged to the client. Both ethics and self-interest dictated a second rule: no wounded animal could be left, at least no wounded dangerous animal. Perhaps the toughest part of the white hunter's many jobs became the one of going into heavy grass or tangled reeds after a leopard or a buffalo gut-shot by a client. The white hunter Eric Rundgren was almost ripped apart by a leopard that the client had managed to nick in the leg; the only thing that saved him, aside from his own great strength, was the rifle that got caught crosswise between him and the leopard. He managed to strangle the leopard, but it clawed him so badly he almost lost his arms.

A client could funk the responsibility of going in after wounded game. The hunter could not. The law said so; his own ethic said so; and self-interest said so: if word got out that he had left an animal, if an animal that he had left killed somebody, he was through.

Non-hunters, especially non-hunters who have never been to Africa, may not understand what this responsibility means. First, it means going into cover where you may literally not be able to see the end of your own rifle barrel. This cover may be 15 feet high, high enough to hide an elephant. Second, it means going in after animals that, when wounded, do not run away; they turn and attack. The buffalo is famous for twisting and turning and then lying in wait. Third, it means dealing with animals of great size and astonishing speed. A lion can run 100 yards in four seconds; a buffalo can come almost as fast. An Olympic champion takes a bit under 10. A fully clothed man with a 9 lb rifle would take depressingly, perhaps fatally, longer.

And it means killing, with one shot – two if there is time – animals that are very hard to kill. They come so fast, and have to come such short distances sometimes, that only one quick shot is possible. Hence the bone-crushing big-calibre rifles that are used for such work. And hence the white hunters who have died doing their jobs.

Yet, this dangerous and vexing job seemed worth the mediocre salary so long as the indefinable extras were there. These were independence, and great pride, and the sense of being a very special sort of person – of participating, as it were, in a myth. When, however, the myth began to crumble, the job seemed underpaid.

'Some of the younger ones get rather disillusioned when they find that the work consists mostly of disciplining and controlling an unruly client who wishes to break every law in order to get a record trophy in the shortest time', the Game Department noted in 1950. Patrick Hemingway was quoted as saying some clients treated him 'like a goddam butler'. Another white hunter was quoted as saying that sometimes 'he'd rather be a men's room attendant'. These remarks are symptomatic of a fundamental change in the way white hunters saw themselves. In fact, after about 1950 the profession started coming apart. Many forces were at work on it, and the hunting bans in Tanzania and Kenya should be seen only as symptoms of those forces, not as the forces themselves. The vastly shortened hunt (now a week to 10 days), the enormously changed world attitude toward hunting, the disappearance of empires – these were truly changes that inverted the world. White-hunter self-esteem suffered.

Yet, while they lasted, they were heroic figures. 'Clients tend to see their hunter as a father', John Heminway wrote. 'They boast of him. . . . He looms in the imagination.'

One can ask why. Why did men from the cities, often soft men, too old, men of power in their own worlds, make fathers of often younger men who carried the twin banners of *white* and *hunter*? Was it some atavistic memory, insubstantial now as smoke, something made of sweat and booze and the bang of the gun, to be carried like an icon back to the boardroom and the brokerage office? *My* hunter. *My white hunter.* Was it an affirmation, encoded for the white and the male and the powerful?

'Within a few years [after *uhuru*] the Chief Game Warden of Kenya had granted full professional licenses to fifty-three so-called professional hunters to whom the [East African Professional Hunters Association] could never have given even probationary membership.' They tried to hold their self-defined line. But East Africa was changing. In 1971, the association admitted Henry

Kibiego, its first 'African full member'. In 1973, there was a question in the Kenya National Assembly about translating the game laws into Swahili. There were other questions about the proportion of blacks to whites in the guide business. The White Hunters Bar and White Hunters, Ltd, were caused to drop 'White' from their names. In Tanzania, 'when [the hunting ban] was lifted ... the dashing white hunters ... were replaced by Africans – fully-fledged professionals in their own country'.

The East African Professional Hunters Association more or less closed up shop in 1977. The white Kenyans and Tanzanians who had been white hunters retired or went elsewhere – Southern Africa, Texas, Sudan. Now there are hunters in Africa, and there are whites who are hunters in parts of Africa, but everywhere outside South Africa they are called 'professional hunters'. Even the *term* white hunter has become something of an embarrassment or worse, and two recent books have insisted that the 'white' in white hunter had nothing to do with race. Are we to think the word was put in for its rhythmic value?

Where there is no hunting, as in Kenya, the task of safari management has passed to people (mostly men) both black and white; their primary technological skill is not with guns but with vehicles. I asked one – John Bisley of Gametrackers – if he was the modern version of the white hunter. The idea amused him. 'The white hunters were much closer to nature', he said. 'Definitely, a minibus driver is not at all like a hunter.' The admission, with its implied respect for a craft that has gone from Kenya, was given value by my awareness that John is himself an amateur naturalist. It seemed important to him, too, that the white hunters 'did plenty of walking' in comparison with current tour leaders: 'Everybody has been driving around Kenya for years with disastrous effect to the ecology of the parks.' Perhaps he didn't realize how long the car had been in use in the hunting industry. Or perhaps that respect for the vanished craft includes something unstated – a respect for men who, whatever else they were or did, lived within a code that included the preservation of wild nature.

So the white hunters are gone. They came in all shapes and sizes. Some were elitists, like Finch Hatton. Some were rascals, like Shindelar. Some were businessmen, like Tarlton. Some were naturalists, like Cuninghame. A few, like Philip Percival, were comprehensive professionals, the *gentils parfaits* knights of the bush.

But none was ever a woman.

And, until years after *uhuru*, none was black.

QUITE SIMPLY THE WHIP
Black workers and the safari

'**M**R Roosevelt will have to close his eyes or accustom himself to occasional severe floggings . . . for without it no safari could be held together a fortnight.' With these words, the American visitor Edgar Bronson sought in 1908 to lend presidential authority to the safari's most overt reminder of the realities of power. Bronson may be called an enthusiast of punishment, in fact, one who mentioned it often. That he was himself from a nation experiencing its own demonstrations of racial supremacy (the Klan and lynchings) perhaps explains him.

When another visitor – French, this time – questioned the use of the whip on his safari, the white hunter R. J. Cuninghame told him it was the only way to get '*les indigènes*' to obey. When he questioned further (Babault hated '*la terrible punition*'), Cuninghame said, 'See for yourself'. It was the standard answer of experience to naïvety.

It remained for another American to raise this answer to dogma: 'As for punishment, that is quite simply the whip'.

On 14 March 1907, three black men were flogged by a number of whites 'in front of Nairobi Court House, in the presence of a large crowd'. The 'Nairobi flogging incident', as it came to be called, was so paradigmatic it can almost be seen as a morality play of BEA colonialism. It had everything: racism, violence, sexual paranoia.

An official report later said that many in the crowd of 100 were armed and that 'they disregarded attempted intervention by a European police officer and magistrate'. The magistrate had 'heard the sounds of blows apparently by some thick thong upon the bare flesh'. The results for the three black men were that two received what official jargon called 'simple hurt' and one received 'severe hurt nearly amounting to grievous hurt [and] was in hospital a considerable period'.

The crime the three men had committed was said by the whites to be sexual offence to a white woman, including touching. The leader of the whites was the same Ewart Grogan who had endeared himself to Cecil Rhodes by walking from Cape to Cairo and publishing a book about it. Kenya was still under the Indian Penal Code, so the law could not support flogging; Grogan, by lifting the whip, quite literally took the law into his own hands. He gave the first man 25 lashes.

Two later fans wrote that Grogan was a 'fine example' of the 'typical upper-middle-class young Englishman of the Victorian era' and also said that 'there were many young men like Colonel Grogan in the England of fifty years ago'. Another writer has said he was 'anti-Asian, anti-Semitic, the type . . . who regarded [non-Britons] as undesirable aliens'. In binding and flogging three black men for insulting a white woman, and getting 100 white men to follow him, he confirmed both views.

The insult to the white woman in fact turned out to be 'impertinence' amounting to 'rudeness and disobedience' and the shaking of the shafts of a rickshaw that the black men were pulling at the time. There had been no touching and no lifting of skirts, as flash-fire rumour had had it. Grogan was not perturbed. 'As it has always been the first principle with me to flog a nigger on sight who insults a white woman, I felt it my bounden duty to take the step I did, and that in a public place as a warning to the natives.' The Africans had in fact told Grogan the truth from the beginning, but 'I would not anyhow take the word of a native against that of a white lady'. After all, it had been Grogan who had written that 'the Boer method of treating niggers as vermin is . . . the only one they deserve'.

The colonial government moved against Grogan and the other floggers, as it had to if a pretence of law was to be kept up. The reaction in BEA was hysterical; the *Times of East Africa* used up its stock of exclamation marks, plastering its front page with two and three at a time. 'THE BEGINNING OF THE END!' it trumpeted: white dominance was doomed. In London, the *Field* found the flogging 'repugnant to the instincts of men of British blood' but allowed that if Grogan *et al* were protecting white women because the government would not, something had to be done. The underlying message of both responses was clear: the white hold on East African power was fragile, very fragile.

What followed was a serious of indictments and a trial, with punishments the white colony saw as ghastly and the African community must have seen as laughable. Grogan got a month's imprisonment and a fine of 500 rupees (for 'unlawful assembly'), but the sentence could not be served because the Nairobi jail was 'medically condemned as insanitary *for Europeans*' [my italics]. Grogan, already president of a settlers' organization, became something of a hero in BEA, the holder of a 50,000-acre forest tract called 'Grogan's Concession', and the deliverer of an impassioned and popular recruiting speech in 1915.

The Nairobi flogging incident has a direct relevance to the safari, because flogging was the virtually unquestioned mode of safari discipline. So ingrained was this idea that the Swahili word for hippopotamus, *kiboko*, became, in European dictionaries, the word for 'whip'. The best – that is, harshest – whips were made from hippopotamus hide. Colonialism has its own language, and, in that language, kiboko became both a noun and a verb ('I kibokoed him'), so that in (for example) F. H. Le Breton's *Up-Country Swahili*, kiboko is defined as 'a hippopotamus-hide whip, a raw-hide whip, a hippopotamus'. (Words define reality, but reality defines words, too; since independence, kiboko means only hippopotamus.)

Arabs must have used the whip, but Europeans did not need that example; it was in the culture, especially the military culture. Grant excused one man a third of his lashes because he 'roared for mercy' and named an accomplice. It is with Stanley, however, that we find flogging really brought to almost a way of life. 'The virtue of a good whip was well tested by me on this day. . . . A dog-whip became their backs.' 'I ordered that [13 men] should punish him with one blow of the donkey-whip each.' 'I was obliged to thrash Bombay with my dog-whip.' '[M]y cane was flying around Bombay's shoulders.' 'Snatching up a spear, I laid its staff vigorously on his shoulders.' 'There remained nothing else for me to do but try the virtue of my whip over her shoulders.' 'Shaw was ordered to administer to him one dozen lashes.'

Other Europeans were also free with the whip: 'Twenty lashes' (Decle); 'a few lashes from a whip' (von Hohnel); 'a whip made out of hippopotamus hide is the mildest form of chastisement [Africans] understand' (Lorimer); 'la terrible punition que l'on appelle en Afrique la "kiboko"' (Babault); 'the African black is nothing but a grown-up child on whom no punishment short of a corporal drubbing counts' (Bronson again). French, British and American; male and female; settler and safarist – they were probably right: the only way for a minority to get a majority to do what they absolutely don't want to do is to use force. The question of why Africans didn't want to obey apparently did not occur.

What to some seemed like regrettable necessity ('the only way'), however, became with others a convenience: when Lord Hindlip had to wait at night in the tiny railway station at Naivasha for a train, he was kept awake by some porters and 'sundry other persons', whom he cleared off 'with the aid of two boots and a kiboko'.

A few Europeans objected. Meinertzhagen, 'nearly sick' over a man who was 'bleeding horribly' after a flogging, protested and was told that he was 'squeamish, that I did not understand the African'. (Be it noted, however, that it was Meinertzhagen who led a punitive expedition that carried out a massacre because of the torture killing of a white.) May French Sheldon at least tried to resist using a corporal punishment, but found habit and Stanley's example too strong; Barnes found 'very little need' of it, and so on. But by and large the Europeans in BEA, before the First World War, including safari clients, found that the logical answer to problems caused by the people whose lands they had occupied was 'quite simply the whip'.

After the war, flogging appears to have lessened. It would be pleasant to report that this was a new spirit of humanitarianisn, but the proper cause was probably the car. The law had always forbidden flogging, but enthusiasts of the whip had argued that out in the bush there was no other way, and Africans themselves, whites said (to other whites), preferred it to slogging back to Nairobi and facing time in jail. Once the safari was only a few hours from the nearest police station, however, it was easier to pile the accused into a lorry – but by then, the number of Africans (the porters) had been cut by 80 per cent, anyway.

Behind the accepted cruelty of flogging was a racial theory that justified it. We can see now that in fact the theory was not a theory, for it was not scientific; it was a wish, a dream. In its own time, however – from, say, 1900 until Hitler – it seemed scientific and theoretical, although in fact it was an alluring fan dance of white supremacy, naked racism peeping through the waving plumes of pseudo-science. This was the set of assumptions, assertions, and prejudices set down most tellingly by the American Lothrop Stoddard, seconded by Madison Grant. They were men of impeccable credentials – Anglo-Saxon heritage, good universities, good clubs, friends among the mighty up to Theodore Roosevelt, trusteeships on prestigious boards – and they spoke and wrote as if from the mount of authority. Whites listened.

'If this great ["Nordic", i.e., northern European] race, with its capacity for leadership and fighting, should ultimately pass, with it would pass that which we call civilization.' 'When I say "Man," I mean, so far as the nineteenth century was concerned, the white man.' 'The black race has never shown real constructive power. It has never built up a native civilization.'

These two ideas were inseparable and essential: that 'civilization' was a white creation, and that no such thing as a black civilization existed. Thus, 'bringing civilization' (sometimes 'bringing religion' or 'bringing Christianity') was an essential good performed by whites whether the recipients wanted these things or not (i.e., civilization was better than non-civilization, and the one should be imposed on the other). Civilization was the property of the 'great Nordic race' (Grant's buzz-words), and various sorts of decadence and rot ('the decay of ideals, rampant materialism, political disruption, social unrest, the decadence of art and literature') were the result of polluting Nordic 'blood' – in the case of early-twentieth-century society, with 'Mediterranean stock'. Worse was Semitic stock; worse than that was Oriental ('Asia, in the guise of Bolshevism with Semitic leadership and Chinese executioners'); and worst of all was black.

Therefore, the white Nordics had to protect their 'clean, virile, genius-bearing blood' from pollution by 'prepotent' blood like that of blacks, who, being more primitive, got the upper hand genetically when the stocks were crossed. (The use of pseudo-scientific jargon – 'superior germ-plasm' – gave this blather authority.) Stoddard, too, rained buzz-words: race-duty, call of the blood, coloured peril, the white species.

BEA and its safari clients got positive reinforcement from all this. First, they were allowed to believe that they represented civilization, an inherent good. Second, they were allowed to believe that they were inherently superior. Third, they were allowed to believe that their presence and their rule (and its extensions, such as flogging) were good because the African, 'having no past, welcomes novelty and tacitly admits that others are his masters'. Finally, their patriarchal 'protection' of white women was essential to 'the race-heritage, which should be defended to the last extremity'.

A rhetorical critic might say that it became necessary to dehumanize Africans in order to deny them human rights. Stoddard's 'white species' was a pseudo-scientific effort of this sort. In order to seize land, destroy cultures, and commandeer labour, it became necessary to declare over and over that black Africans were non-humans who had no rights of ownership, who created no culture, and who did no labour. The result in habitual white language was the reduction of Africans to sub-adult or sub-human status ('boy', 'childlike', 'savage').

The mechanics of dehumanization were fairly straightforward. At their crudest, they were merely the rote repetition of animalness: blacks smelled; blacks did not reason; blacks did not feel or show affection; blacks did not feel pain as Europeans did; blacks had abilities in hunting that were closer to animal instinct than to human intelligence.

Black women shared in such dehumanization because they were black; however, they were subject to a further level of it in a process in which black men themselves took part: they were rendered largely invisible. Then as now, they were seen but not noticed, present along roads and trails as the bent figures with 100 lb of wood or water on their backs, one hand raised to a forehead strap to ease the weight. As a toast that was reported at a recent Peace Corps gathering put it, 'To the farmers of Africa – and their husbands.' White men (and, by allowing it, white women) also removed black women from the white definition of the human by so often treating black women sexually as they never dared treat white ones. The *Globetrotter*, for example, published in a 1907 edition a large photo of a pretty black woman, nude from the waist up, titling it 'Nairobi belle'. The newspaper would never have published such a photo of a white woman; indeed, if it had, it would probably have been shut down, certainly would have been categorized with publishers of pornography and French postcards. The point is not that black women were not sexual objects to white men – we know they were – but that black women did not qualify for the structures that protected white women from at least some kinds of exploitation: they were not human.

Now, the evidence of the eyes and ears on any safari was that black Africans worked hard and long, but the inevitable complaint was that they were lazy. Similarly, the repeated observation was that they had no political organization, when a little analysis would have shown complex but non-European social and familial systems, but such analysis was rarely done; bizarrely inaccurate European words ('chief', 'king', 'witch-doctor') were used to avoid such analysis.

Visitors, including American visitors, seem to have accepted what settler Europeans told them about blacks without question. Safari clients rarely spoke an African language; their entire social intercourse was with settler Europeans, usually a very restricted group of settler Europeans, at that – outfitters and white hunters. Visitors asked questions; resident Europeans answered. Those answers were repeated in the books and articles the visitors later wrote.

'All African natives are overgrown children' (Mary Akeley). '[Porters] are only so many children' (F. A. Dickinson). Give 'a huge spoonful of castor-oil – mild treatment is wasted on a native's interior' (Ronald Barnes). 'Africans are slow in brain and action, never ready.... Their intelligence is of a low order' (Arthur Neumann). 'It must be remembered that the black is of a far coarser fibre than the white man' (Edgar Bronson). 'The native does not mind sleeping on the bare ground with only a piece of tanned sheepskin to cover him. [He] endures his discomfort like a wild animal' (Martin Johnson). 'The original racial impulse that started [East African blacks] down the years toward development has fulfilled its duty and spent its force' (Stewart Edward White). 'Allowance must be made for their indolent, carefree disposition. Why work, when they can pick a coconut off a tree and eat when hungry?' (Joseph H. Appel). 'The White Man hunts and travels and explores while the native does the camp work' (Martin Johnson). 'The East African is not a man, he is a child, and a child's education and discipline is what he needs' (W. S. Rainsford). The Kikuyu 'have the sunny good-nature and charm of children, and the unreasoning obstinacy' (Ronald Barnes). 'They are children, mentally, and they react very much as children do' (James Clark). 'The African blacks are children of the day. No emotion, hate nor love nor fear nor anger, lasts long' (Martin Johnson). 'It is a well-known fact that any native requires a triple dose of white men's medicine. Furthermore a native's sensitiveness to pain is very much less than the white man's. This is undubitable [sic]' (Stewart Edward White). 'No native, however efficient, is to be trusted with any responsibility' (Vivienne de Watteville). 'Slackers are no good in Africa, where success means a survival of the fittest' (Norma Lorimer). 'Three jumps ahead of the Pithecanthropus Erectus expressed their Anthropological status' (Daniel Streeter). 'It is best taken for granted that [Swahilis] all lie ... and they will generally steal if they get the chance' (Ethel Younghusband). A Kikuyu suffered 'a blow that would surely have broken a white man's neck' (Abel Chapman). 'Remember a savage has no brains. Treat him accordingly' (F. A. Dickinson). 'It would have taken more than Rawley's fist to damage an African skull' (Francis Brett Young).

Without these beliefs – and people really did believe them – it would have been impossible to maintain European control of East Africa; for that matter, it would have been impossible to maintain the safari. Counter-pressures and other ideas were very strong, especially the humanitarianism of the nineteenth century, so that, had it not been possible to believe that Africans were objectively inferior (even another species), seizure of land and two-tiered wage scales would have been impossible. Indeed, the division between beliefs in racial superiority, on the one hand, and notions of humanitarianism and equality, on the other, were roughly the same as the division between Nairobi and London, between settler and government. So severe was the split that the settler community once seriously considered kidnapping the London-appointed Governor to get its way; it remained severe enough to prompt cries of 'Betrayal!' when London made moves to grant majority rule to black Africans in the 1960s. It was already severe enough to cause Grogan to defy London's law in favour of settler racialism in 1907. (It should not be inferred, however, that London was entirely humanitarian and free of racialism; rather, it had other goals than the settlers.)

The cause of the settler beliefs, however, was not racialism pure and simple; it was, rather, a Gordian knot of racialism and the preservation of socio-economic privilege. At its crudest, it did make purely racial statements: Perham met a white hunter in 1929 who said bluntly, 'The white race must keep on top'; Meinertzhagen quoted the settler McQueen in the early 1900s, who believed that 'the white man is the master race and the black man must forever remain cheap labour and slaves'. Racialism took sometimes bizarre forms: White recommended carrying two thermometers on safari, one for blacks and one for whites; a European who had had a pair of trousers stolen by a black servant would have to get rid of the trousers, even if returned, because the black man might have worn them and 'it will be quite impossible for me, a white man, to use them again'; a white man struck a black because the black put his hands in his pockets while they talked. The contradictions were inescapable but necessary: a white man could put his private parts in a black woman's loins but not in a black man's trousers; a white man could buy a black woman, but a black man could not shake a white woman's rickshaw; a white man could chat with his hands in his pockets, but a black man could not. As day-to-day events, these add up to a kind of social pathology.

The language of racial contempt was also common, above all the word 'nigger', which, as a recent scholar has pointed out, 'appears in all the fiction' about the place and period. It is also common in safari literature, along with 'coon', 'boy', and so on.

'We were met by curly headed coons' (R. O. Preston). 'Two nigger witnesses' (the *Field*). Rickshaws 'propelled by two niggers' (Alonzo Hepburn). 'A faint but extraordinarily definite smell: the smell of nigger' (Francis Brett Young). 'The blackest-looking nigger I had ever seen' (Vivienne de Watteville). 'The coons themselves, particularly the women, are in large measure to blame' (John Taylor). '[E]verything from food to niggers' (Carl Akeley). 'It will be understood that the word "boy" refers to native porter or servant' (Vivienne de Watteville).

Some whites, however, were more circumspect (at least in print), perhaps more self-deceived; Roosevelt, for example, said that 'at least part of the high inland region of British East Africa can be made one kind of "white man's country"; and to achieve this white men should work heartily together, doing scrupulous justice to the natives, but remembering that progress and development in this particular kind of new land depend exclusively upon the masterful leadership of the whites'.

'White man's country' became a kind of battle-cry, and Elspeth Huxley used it as the title of her biography of its leading exponent, Lord Delamere. The expression assumed the beliefs in white superiority and black inferiority, and what it literally expressed was the European belief that only certain parts of Africa – cooler, healthier places – were suitable for European life; these would be 'white man's country', while the hotter, less healthy places would be black. In Kenya, the first white man's country was the Kikuyu highlands; it was extended to the Uasin Gishu Plateau, Laikipia, and other areas. But the expression also assumed the availablilty in those areas of cheap, i.e., African, labour.

According to Errol Trzebinski, in 1905 the white claims – 'white man's country' – amounted to a little more than a third of a million acres; by 1915, they amounted to 5¼ million. By the 1950s, the statutory White Highlands held 16,000 square miles (10¼ million acres).

Lord Delamere was the settler par excellence of white man's country. 'Our own people' – meaning whites – 'became one of his favourite phrases.' Huxley saw this as a 'form of white supremacy (benign, not tyrannous) essentially feudal in its inspiration'. The comparison to feudalism may have been partly naïve; feudalism was, after all, an institution based on force, one in which, as a recent historian has put it, power was treated as a personal possession. It is feasible only in an intellectual system, and among people, whose assumptions are not in the least troubled by vast inequity.

Huxley was herself a settler and shared settler views. She wrote of an African's 'simple mind' and 'the natural inability of the native to follow complicated currency changes'; she said that the African residents of the highlands 'had not even reached the stage of coherence when they acknowledged a tribal chief'; she accepted, most tellingly, the self-flattering white view that what became 'white man's country' had been unoccupied, that nobody had 'owned' it and so nobody stole it: 'the Uasin Gishu and Laikipia plateaux and parts of Nandi were practically unoccupied'. 'It was the empty spaces that were, in the main, filled by Europeans.' This idea, however, has been exploded by recent historians.

In a sense, the safari took 'white man's country' with it – it became a movable feast of whiteness. It did not lay permanent claim to any single spot, but it claimed the right to pass through or rest anywhere. The government segregated certain areas – the Masai and Kikuyu Reserves; the Nandi area during hostilities; a Northern Game Reserve – but by and large the safari claimed whatever spot it occupied, at least insofar as it exercised the rights to kill the game there, to take control of the water there, and sometimes to impress local labour there. Like it or not, the safari, for all its recreational nature, cannot be prised loose from the systems – intellectual, political, economic – that made white man's country possible.

McQueen's words – 'black men must forever remain cheap labour' – were of the essence of the white position. Cheap labour – cheap in the sense that the wage was disproportionate to both the work done and the Western wage scale for the same work – was essential to the white economy of BEA. Most of the early settlers tried farming, for which they had to break virgin land, plant crops often untested there, and wait up to several years for a return. Modern farming machinery was not available; human labour was everything.

At the same time, European investors were trying to recoup high profits from investments – many little better than gambles – in the area. Moreton Frewen and Lord Warwick were both trying to recover lost fortunes with Kenyan investment in 1906; their scheme was in timber, but cheap labour was as necessary to timber harvesting as to agriculture.

Nor were non-farmers exempt. Except for those who wanted to undertake to do everything themselves – the Indian duka wallah, for example – cheap labour was needed. This was as true of the independent ivory hunter as the investor. The *Field* reported that an Englishman had brought to Mombasa ivory 'to the value of £8,000'. This represented about 10 tons of ivory – the burden for perhaps 300 porters. Let us suppose a frugal hunter (like Neumann) as a hypothetical example: he would have gone out with 30–40 porters, picking up the rest to carry the ivory the month's journey to Mombasa when he needed them. If the 10 tons of ivory represented a year's hunting (and a very successful year it would have been), porterage would have cost him about £400 plus another £300 for the porters who brought the ivory out – almost 10 per cent of his gross. This would have been at £1 per month per man and does not include the higher wages for gunbearers, cooks, and headman, nor the cost of their food. None the less, it is obvious that any significant rise in wages would have cut into the profit that would allow him to live like a gentleman in England.

The 'labour question', of which safari labour was a part, was at the heart of settler arguments with London from BEA's beginnings. Sir Charles Eliot was a Commissioner (1900–4) liked by the settlers because he 'intends to confine the natives to reserves and use them as cheap labour on farms'. What settlers had in mind was something of the sort already law in Rhodesian Matabeleland: in Selous's words, '[the condition] that all the able-bodied young men . . . be required to work for a certain number of months per annum at a fixed rate of pay'. The rate, as Mark Strage pointed out, was 10 shillings a month.

Moreton Frewen in the *Irish Times* (4 June 1906), flacking his own schemes for BEA, said enthusiastically that 'in the dense Kikuyu population there is an abundant supply of cheap labour'. Rainsford saw by 1910 that a white would not survive without that labour: 'His fortune, his home, his all depends on a sufficient and staple supply of the labour, at the time he wants it, and at such a fixed price that he can estimate his profit and loss'.

Pro-equity forces in England, however, fought forced labour. This opposition led to such counter-attacks as '[Africans] are rapidly being spoilt through the way they are being pampered by legislation, goodness knows for what reason'. The colonial government, on the other hand, boasted of 'the increased prosperity of the natives under our rule and the lives of complete idleness spent by them'.

The result of the debate was that settlers did not succeed in getting a law requiring African labour and had to settle for paying low wages (10–15 rupees a month) and using the stick of the hut tax and the carrot of shoddy consumer goods to bring Africans, largely Kikuyu, to work. (Hut tax revenue increased, for example from £3000 to £97,000 between 1902 and 1908, probably as a result of more aggressive collection.)

The military did get forced labour during the First World War, however, when conscription to the Carrier Corps (labour corps) neared a million. The ironic effect then was a very real shortage of non-military labour at home; the harshest effect, however, was the disruption of African social structure. Whites who had not believed Africans capable of emotion were now treated to the spectacle of Kikuyu women 'weeping, mourning', as the men were taken away to war. 'There is every reason to believe that nearly all able-bodied men were recruited.' Of these, between 10 and 20 per cent died – more than 8000 black combatants from BEA, more than 42,000 'followers' [labourers]. Yet no pensions were paid to black troops.

Black troops were trained with the rifle. However, when a training school for black drivers was begun it had to be closed because of white, particularly South African, objections. The 'cheap labour' question had struck again: if Africans were taught high-paying skills, European dominance would be threatened.

The war experience gave the lie to the European contention that they had brought civilization to BEA and that their presence ended deaths from intertribal warfare; all the intertribal wars in the colonial period would not have taken as many African lives as the First World War.

In the 1920s, the *kipande* (work-card) and reserve systems kept the uneasy imbalance that allowed Europeans to improve their standard of living. Houses in the highlands were larger, better staffed; it was said that every white of whatever social level had a 'boy' to wait on him or her. Africans, trying to bring their families from the reserve to the white farms, 'squatted' on uncleared land, and temporary black communities grew up; Karen Blixen, for example, spoke of 'her' Kikuyu squatters. It was a new feudal wrinkle. The Europeans, however, apparently saw themselves still as benefactors: Frederick Beck Patterson wrote in 1928 that 'without safaris East Africa would be faced with an unemployment problem. . . . [The] increasing number of hunting parties is now taking care of a great many blacks who would otherwise have no means of support.' This remarkable statement was made in the face of the near-collapse of porterage (because of the car) and a safari wage scale only marginally above that for agriculture and set actually lower than in 1900. It may have been put in Patterson's noggin by his white hunter, Denys Finch Hatton. As for the notion that Africans would have 'no means of support', one need remember only Cloudsley-Thompson's trenchant comment that 'before the whites came, there was no poverty in eastern Africa'.

Such social and economic disparity could not go without upheaval. In the early 1920s, the 'Harry Thuku Rebellion' was quickly put down but presented an early Kikuyu response. The Kikuyu education movement and the circumcision battles of the late 1920s and 1930s were further instances of unrest.

Yet whites were trapped in their own economic dependence on inequity, even more so with the Depression. When the Second World War came, they could not resist trying to recover their recent losses with further inequity: minimum prices set at different levels for blacks and whites. 'Price manipulations, which brought great prosperity to many European farmers, contributed to a serious, and in some cases fatal, deterioration of the standards of life in the reserves.' After the war, the 'only' choice (the other was unthinkable) was to continue the old system, with the result that 'apartheid was very strong, much like South Africa's', and John Gunther found at the Nairobi airport separate toilets for Europeans and Asians but none for Africans. The situation was now intolerable and soon blew up.

It is perhaps hard – and unpleasant – to remember that safari workers were part of this labour picture. Europeans and Americans view the safari as a recreation; it suggests pleasure, not work. Also, images given to us of the safari in books and particularly films have made the safari labourer, except for the personal servant, invisible.

Yet the simple fact is that without African labour, the safari can never exist. Peters saw this in 1890: 'If my porters went off, the whole undertaking would prove a fiasco of the most ridiculous kind.' A. Blayney Percival, the Game Ranger, put it most succinctly in the 1920s: Africans are 'the mainstay of the safari'. Nor are we talking only about porters. 'Many a hunter is *made* by his African gun-bearer', Cotlow observed. Or, as one shagbag is reported to have observed to another about the life of a Depression-era white hunter, 'The niggers do all the tracking and hunting.'

Negley Farson summed the situation up for all of BEA in 1950: 'The white man's colonial life is parasitic upon the coloured man's'. (And woman's, one would say now.) The safari cannot escape this indictment. The white safari man or woman cannot escape inclusion in Farson's 'white man' category. The reason, again, is economic.

Before the First World War, porters earned about £1 a month, skilled safari workers perhaps double that – £12–25 a year if they could have worked all year, but the season increased from only three months in about 1903 to no more than five by 1914. At the same time, European female clerks made £110 a year and Goan male clerks about £160. If African skilled and unskilled workers had had to be paid at these rates – say £150 per year for a cook or gunbearer – the recreational safari cost would have leaped by 30 times £5 (number of porters times difference between actual and supposed wage), plus £10 per cook, gunbearer, skinner, and tracker – say another £30. The result – an additional £180 per white client per month – would have made the hunting safari industry untenable.

In 1954, average annual wages by race in Kenya were £940 for whites and £26 for blacks in forestry and agriculture; in industry and commerce, the figures were £950 and £59. Safari-industry wages probably approximated those of the second category (not because wages had gone up, but because porters, the lowest paid, had been mostly eliminated). Thus, if black-safari-worker wages had been raised only to a level between that of Indian males (£395) and white females (£525), they would have had to be multiplied by a factor of about 8. (White wages between c. 1910 and 1954 had gone up by a factor of about 4.) Assuming only 10 Africans per white on a safari, this would have meant an increase of £350 per month (10 times the monthly difference between real and supposed wages) per white at a time when the safari cost per person was about £2000 altogether. Again, this increase would have made the safari industry untenable, especially as this was the period when the less wealthy were becoming the primary clients. There is no avoiding it: the safari, like European society as a whole, lived on the underpaid labour of black East Africa.

Uhuru did not solve all of East Africa's problems, by far. It did not end all inequity and, perhaps what annoys whites most, it did not turn blacks into a continent of saints. But it had many good effects, not least of which was an abrupt end to any notion that blacks could go on being either invisible or dehumanized.

Some human actions have a symbolism that gives them great importance. Such was Grogan's when he seized the kiboko and 'took the law into his own hands'. Such, too, is the modern version of the safari. White visitors sit in zebra-striped vans, making game runs in the great reserves, and when they look at their driver – now their mentor, shepherd, and guide – they see a black man and perhaps understand the symbolism of 'sitting in the driver's seat'.

12

ZOO AFRICA
Myths and probabilities

O F the making of books about safari, there is no end – as this book
shows. The non-African idea of 'safari' comes from these books and
from the illustrations in the books, and from the more potent films
made, in their turn, from the books. If a single essential cluster of such books
can be cited as creating a safari myth, it need include only the books of Stanley
and Rider Haggard; if an essential cluster of films were wanted, it need include
only the films made of Haggard's novels and perhaps half a dozen others (of
which two are from Hemingway). From this small core of information comes
the 'safari' that has emerged in modern popular culture: the Safari Train and
the Skyfari of the San Diego Zoo, the waterborne safari down the Nile, Congo,
and Amazon of Disneyland. From it come unrecognized but powerful images
that still clutter the non-African mind: that Africa is a dangerous jungle; that
strong, white males are the defence against Africa's dangers; that black Africans
are faceless servants who speak unintelligible gibberish; that women are
powerless; that animals are to be killed at man's will.

Such ideas are usually unconscious ones, yet they have the power to stand
between us and the real Africa (whether we are talking of the Africa of politics
or the Africa of recreation) like concentric fences. They affect not only our
discourse about Africa; they affect our very thinking: they are the 'language'
in which Europeans and Americans mostly describe Africa to themselves and
each other. Yet it seems we could do better than accept our mental vocabulary
for a continent from a bully and a fantasist.

Stanley and Rider Haggard had such importance in creating our idea of
Africa and safari because they spoke so feelingly to the imperial psyche.
Stanley's embattled, brutal white man (whose brutality became, in Europe,
heroism) was of a piece with two-fisted Christianity and the peak of empire.
Even the valuelessness of his expeditions was made to take on the abstract
accomplishment of the crusades. What is more wonderful than a quest without
a genuine object?

'Let us go to Mt Kenia and look for a white race that does not exist.' One of Rider
Haggard's characters says that – not his hunter-adventurer Allan Quatermain,
but another man; and not in Haggard's first African book but in his third,
although he published these phenomenally successful novels only a couple of

years apart in the mid-1880s. They are a paradigm of the white experience: East Africa – the Africa of the heart, the Africa of films, of novels and popular journalism and dreams – is a place where whites go to look for a white race that does not exist – themselves. They are a paradigm of the search that found a white race in the White Highlands (by way of the Nairobi flogging incident and the Harry Thuku Rebellion).

Allan Quatermain comes after Haggard's *She* and his *King Solomon's Mines*, and, in all the history of glorious literary junk, few works exceed them in inventiveness or lunacy. 'You did not write *She*, you know. Something wrote it through you', Kipling said to Haggard. Certainly, the Victorians went wild over the books, so the 'something' that wrote them was an urge from the British heart. The novels mixed magic, superstition, racialism, and erotic suggestion in about equal amounts and stirred them all up with a generous dollop of hairy-chested adventure; no wonder they made Haggard famous and have supplied the stuff of imitations and films ever since. At the end of the third of those books, several of the characters choose to stay among the white race they have found in the East African heartland, and no better prophecy of racialism could have been made. Like all great trash, the books touched the deepest concerns of their times. They spoke for a mixture of white brashness and white dream.

'*Let us go to Mt Kenia and look for a white race that does not exist.*'

'[I was] always a solitary boy given to living in my dreams. Those dreams, many of them, had been inspired by the late Rider Haggard's adventures.' Haggard's novels 'had a tremendous vogue. The living prototype of Allan Quartermain [*sic*] [was] Frederick Courtney Selous.' 'Like most of my generation . . . I had grown up with the legend of Africa, the danger-legend of the explorer and the white hunter, of Rider Haggard's tales.'

Reduced to the generally accessible, the danger-legend became the safari.

In the hands of Hollywood, that legend underwent another editorial change. Already larger and simpler than life, it was put through the further selective screen of twentieth-century commercialism (that is, vulgarization); what had been a line-drawing became a cartoon. Nowhere is this clearer than in the films of Haggard's books, but, for purposes of the safari's chronology, let us begin with a film about Stanley.

Stanley and Livingstone (1939) was an American film with a partly British cast about an Englishman who became an American and then a Briton again. As history, it is a jumble; you can learn more about Stanley from any children's biography. (Indeed, the children's book is a good analogue for the safari film. It is no accident, for example, that Haggard's novels were 'boys' books'.) It has a concocted story of unrequited love, a sentimentalized Livingstone, and a Stanley who progresses from grit to grandeur under Livingstone's influence. ('You've changed', says the heroine after Stanley's first African journey.)

The film is sexless. Stanley is driven, but never by lust; his impulses are, in the first half, getting Livingstone's story; and, in the second, glorifying Livingstone.

Africa is 'a vast jungle in which you could lose half of America.' Disease and isolation await the white man. There are 'witch-doctors'. 'War drums!' says a white man ominously. 'If we could only tell them that we come in peace', says the anguished, peace-loving Stanley. No organizer of punitive expeditions, he.

Livingstone makes an impassioned plea that Stanley fill in the map of Africa so that whites will come, 'bringing civilization to people who have never heard a word of kindness'. Later, he calls Africans 'these simple people'.

When Stanley returns for his second journey – the film's rousing ending – we see him marching across a map of Africa whose blank spaces are being filled with his name – Stanley Falls, Stanleyville – while 'Onward, Christian Soldiers' provides accompaniment.

Despite the rigours of Africa, Stanley always looks overweight; on the other hand, he does wear correct nineteenth-century safari costume. His safari on the march, although it has only 30 porters and no flag, looks like a safari. However, no indication of safari organization or preparation is given. In fact, the film has no concern for the realities of safari: when he is asked at Zanzibar how he is to get porters, he says matter-of-factly, 'The American consul at Bagomayo is taking care of that'. (This is certainly my own favourite line from the film, except possibly for words uttered when he meets two Africans in the bush: 'Ask them if they know the way to Tanganyika'.)

In other words, this is a Victorian boy's Stanley and a Victorian parent's Africa: terrible country, simple blacks, imposed civilizations, sweet paternalism.

Rider Haggard's *She* was made into films quite a number of times. The 1925 silent version featured titles by Haggard himself, giving it somewhat the air of an authorized version. Yet much of it is far from his novel – film cannot, for once, match his descriptive powers – so that the 'coast of Lybia' looks like Cornwall, the residents of Ayeesha's lost land like troglodytes who have too small a gene pool.

In fact, this *She* is less twentieth-century film than nineteenth-century theatre; even its final spectacle is of the stage rather than the screen. So is the acting. (The film does make one significant contribution to our culture, however. It finds a use for the spiral puttee, which the hero unwraps to make a rope to swing across the final chasm.)

She is a myth of female sexuality. The eroticism of the film is what saves – in fact, explains – it. Betty Blythe as Ayeesha is lushly, frankly erotic in a way that the 1920s rarely allowed; this is no boy in riding costume, but a voluptuous, fleshly woman in costumes of the sort that are now sold through the mail for domestic sex play. When, in the film's (and the novel's) climax, she burns up in the eternal fire, she is as nude as anyone could ask.

Ayeesha – She – drives men mad. She lounges about in long hair and little else; men (white men) roll their eyes and clasp their breasts. They lose their wits, their will, their intellect. The film is Stanley's view of sex – it gets in men's way – raised to nightmarish proportions. When Ayeesha burns up in her own flames (Haggard's metaphor for sexual obsession?), men are freed: the last we see of the three white males, they are profiled against a rock, wind blowing their hair, gazing idealistically into a womanless future. Free at last, free at last!

(It is also a myth of racial purity. The hero can trace his lineage back to the Egyptians and looks exactly like an ancestor of 2000 years ago. *Pace*, Lothrop Stoddard.)

When *She* was remade in 1965 with Ursula Andress, it was placed in Palestine just after the First World War. Andress was an austere, Grecian Ayeesha, less erotic than majestic. But the shift of locale is the film's most significant aspect; made just after *uhuru*, it tells us that Africa is no longer a site for white fantasy.

Of the films of Haggard's other novels, surely the 1950 *King Solomon's Mines* is the outstanding example. Stewart Granger's Quatermain would satisfy any Victorian boy, perhaps rival even Selous himself. The scenes of Africa, especially of African animals, are truly remarkable, still thrilling. (Armand Denis, however, had his name removed from the film, because it showed 'the wrong view of wild life . . . glorifying the hunter and the killing of animals'.) And the changes from Haggard's novel – especially the introduction of the character played by Deborah Kerr – reveal how the safari myth could be manipulated.

The Kerr character exists in the novel as a man, not a woman. The principal action of the novel is to find the fabulous mines of the title; the action of the movie is to find Kerr's husband, who has been looking for the mines. Once Kerr and Granger have connected, this becomes a search to find her husband *dead* so that she can go off with Granger.

The sexual attractiveness of Granger–Quatermain is a given. So is Kerr's inability to resist him; it is the *She* myth in reverse, but in this version the obsession (woman for white hunter) is permissible, in fact desirable. Granger does not burn up in his own flames: he is a man, after all, with important work to do in the world, not a woman who has spent 2000 years lying about in her lingerie.

The Africa of the film is seen ambivalently: on the one hand, as a place of beauty; on the other, as a place of hideous dangers. Snakes turn up underfoot and come slithering down trees. Kerr – silly woman – is always getting the wits scared out of her by Africa – snakes, spiders, leopards, rhino, whatever. Granger spends a lot of his time saving her.

Safari is a male activity. 'A woman on safari? Never!' Granger thunders. And Kerr almost proves him right: she wears the wrong clothes (which he removes); falls, staggers, rips her sleeves constantly. After six weeks of walking, she is still out of condition. 'I can't keep up!' is the female motto. She is never allowed to have a rifle. Safari is a man's game.

Yet the picture of safari itself is superb; clothes, weapons, gear are authentic and convincing (although the locale – Nairobi, 1897 – is a bit of a non-starter). The result is authentic Hollywood flummery – that is, a real film.

This *King Solomon's Mines* inspired a spate of white-hunter-on-safari films: Clark Gable in *Mogambo* (1953); Victor Mature in *Safari* (1956); and Robert Taylor in *Killers of Kilimanjaro* (arguably the worst film of the type ever made, 1959). These are reverse-*She* films in which the male star (and white hunter) is assumed to radiate a sexual attractiveness more potent than that of the firefly in full blaze. Scenes of female sexual frustration are common, most taking place at night under mosquito netting, but the most remarkable being Grace Kelly's full-body anguish in *Mogambo*, which presents sexual obsession as telling as anything in *She*.

The last two of these films added another dimension: black warfare. *Safari* is a film about the horror of Mau Mau, *Killers of Kilimanjaro* supposedly about the building of the Uganda Railway (or something). Both end in pitched battles with modern weapons in which black men are the victims – Mau Mau mowed down by Mature's machine pistol, black men on both sides mowed down by each other as English and German stage a prelude to the First World War. The films anticipate *uhuru* and project a comforting white image: we have the technology, they will do the dying.

The films have one thing in common. In *Safari*, Mature as a white hunter shoots an elephant. In *Killers of Kilimanjaro*, the same elephant rounds the same bush and heads for Taylor. He fires – and over his shoulder in stop-motion, you can see Mature shooting the elephant.

Hemingway's African stories were filmed in this same post-war period, *The Macomber Affair* ('The Short Happy Life of Francis Macomber') in 1946, *The Snows of Kilimanjaro* in 1953. The first is black and white, an African *film noir*; the second is overblown colour, a really dreadful piece of work that Hemingway rightly castigated as 'The Snows of Zanuck', after its producer. Besides Hemingway, the films have Gregory Peck in common; he is a white hunter in one, a dying writer in the other.

Neither was a location film, and neither has the sense of a real Africa that *King Solomon's Mines* gives. Both present an image more Hollywood than Nairobi, from clothes (which are chic and contemporary rather than utilitarian and authentic) to black Africans, who are inevitably played by overweight American blacks.

The Snows of Kilimanjaro is as much about Paris and Spain as Africa, as it traces its gassy way through what purports to be a writer's life. Susan Hayward, as the wealthy wife (for which read, The Bitch Goddess Success) hates Africa and can't understand it, so it is most puzzling when it is she who saves the writer from the infection that Africa has given him. The film's meanings, if it has any, seem to centre around 'love conquers all' but may be as simple as 'Africa is hell'.

The same screenwriter did *The Macomber Affair*, which is largely faithful to the Hemingway story, at least until it becomes necessary to get the female star off the hook at the end. Peck is a taciturn, capable white hunter who says early on, 'Women sometimes make trouble. A woman can muck up a hunt plenty.' Still, he takes Joan Bennett to his camp bed (after, like most women in these films, she lies wide-eyed under her mosquito net). Her husband, played by Robert Preston, loses what manhood he brings with him on safari by funking a lion (clients are wimps, the film tells us) and then gets it back by shooting a buffalo. The wife deals with this by shooting him. This film, too – like Hemingway's story – is a myth of maleness, although the film reduces it to a myth of (romanticized) male sexuality. What it tells us of Africa is that it is a wonderful place to be a man, but don't bring a woman.

Hollywood has given us an Africa and a safari that are heavily weighted to one side of the scale – the male, Victorian, white side. The myth of the irresistible white hunter played right into the Hollywood myth of the irresistible white male star, and the two conflated nicely in Granger, Gable, Mature, and Peck. The myth of the boy-woman on safari (the slender androgyne in riding breeches) did not match Hollywood's myths, however, and so the women of the post-war films are sexually attractive but under wraps; inept; not boyish but not capable, either. They are made to suffer sexually for trespassing on male territory (real physical pain is certainly what is projected by Kelly). Either they are denied male weapons (the gun) or they use them badly – shooting a husband in the back, for example. Contrary to actuality, they do not wear safari clothes, with the exception of Kelly, who is supposed to be British and wears khaki skirts; and Susan Hayward, who wears a bush hat and (always spotless) slacks, with little pastel neck scarves. They wear cute or chic clothes that are 'sporty' but that never get wrinkled, except for Deborah Kerr, who wears full-length nineteenth-century skirts. Ava Gardner wears cinches that emphasize her often-profiled breasts, and her collar is usually turned up, a fashion affectation of the time.

In general, one can say that the men's clothes are more or less authentic, the women's not (they are the outsiders), and that it is the men who are 'sexily' undressed (Gable's bare chest, Granger's and Mature's unbuttoned shirts), while the women unnecessarily cover up their skin (scarves, collars). Breasts, however, remain the movies' principal idea of womanliness, and, although clothed, are much stared at. Be that as it may, these films present a flattering male myth (white-hunter power) in the guise of female sex fantasies.

Blacks in the films are largely absent. Except for personal servants, safari camps seem to run themselves. Nobody seems to have a cook. Blacks speak unintelligible languages – a slow and bad Swahili, in actual fact – that have to be translated for us; they might as well be Martians. Physically, they are usually plump (true of other films as well – e.g., the Tarzan films, Abbott and Costello's *Africa Screams*), but they become wonderfully athletic-looking as *uhuru* nears and Africans become 'real' people. Mostly, they lack individuality and are often shown with complete disregard for ethnological accuracy (e.g., the bone in the nose, the 'war paint', the feathers). They perform dances for white visitors.

They are overawed by magic tricks. (A remarkable exception is the Watusi prince of *King Solomon's Mines*.) Once Mau Mau begins, however, they – 'these simple people', as Cedric Hardwicke's Livingstone calls them – become devious and untrustworthy. Whites, however, never whip them. The kiboko does not sell any more.

These films show that fairly little of the safari myth was invented by Hollywood – perhaps only the reverse-*She* eroticism of the white hunter. We should not be surprised that the rest is nineteenth-century juvenilia – that Hollywood's face, however well made up, looked backward. Except for the white hunter's sexiness, therefore (and perhaps the lack of the whip), the safari myth as it emerged from Hollywood films was mostly a reinforcement of the myth as it had been received from the Victorians: male-dominated, racialist, afraid of Africa. What we are now doing with it is another matter.

Nothing can be done easily now about the gender prejudices of safari or about its racialism; they are part of the excess baggage that we drag into the twenty-first century. Black Africans have at least had *uhuru*, which (as the films so clearly show) wrenched white perceptions of Africans into a new focus. Women have not had their *uhuru*, despite three tries at it since the 1840s, and no matter how many women hunt, photograph, camp, and go on solitary walks in lion country, safari supposedly remains 'no trip for a woman'. This is an aspect that is waiting for a historical shift (as, for example, the shift in sexuality in the twentieth century changed the mythic sexuality of the hunter.)

Another historical shift, however, one that appears to be taking place just now, is affecting our perceptions in another way: just as the myth of white-hunter magnetism played into the culture of commercial movies, so the myth of jungle and danger is playing into the culture of commercial entertainment. The concept of entertainment represented by Disney, a worldwide concept given expression by television, home video, game parks, and zoos, has mated with the safari myth and produced an artificial Africa that seems impervious to fact. At the same time, real jungle and real danger are vanishing at a terrible rate. The results of these changes appear to be combining to affect Africa itself.

A few years ago, I was in Masai Mara with a Kenyan friend. We were sipping beer in camp at day's end as we watched the mini-vans pull through the nearby park gate, many returning from end-of-day game runs, others going into the park to cross it to the lodges before darkness fell. My friend watched the vans coming and going, the green Tusker bottle resting against his chin, then slowly removed the bottle and said, without taking his eyes from the parade of cars, 'Zoo Africa'.

I rejected the image at the time. I thought of the Mara as a wild place, where you can drive and see no other human or vehicle, where you can see the wildebeeste migrate across the Mara River in their frantic thousands as we had just done. And so Masai Mara is.

But it is also a place of half a dozen game lodges; of a kind of non-lethal hunting for the Big Five where what you look for is not so much the animal as the cluster of other vans that surrounds the animal; of campgrounds on the park's edge littered with toilet paper and drying piles of excrement and bits of plastic and cigarette ends; of such pressure that there are car kills on the park roads; of the balloon safaris that sail every morning on the wind.

Zoo Africa.

Zoo Africa is the Africa of the modern myth. It is as if the Western mind, unable to accept the Africa of its Victorian myth (wet, diseased, crawling with snakes) and afraid or unwilling to accept the Africa of fact (open, wild, indifferent to humanity) has created Zoo Africa, which is both a place and a way of looking at it. It is a safe Africa, and a comfortable Africa, and it is an Africa seen in such a way that its earth need never be touched. It is Africa according to Disney.

Ironically, of course, the real Africa that is being rejected is not at all the hell of dank and venom that the myth has made it. The very symbols of that myth – the snake and the insect – suggest how far it has had to reach for its horror. Although the snake and the oversized spider are the cliché of the white language (film, most obviously) that describes Africa, I have in fact seen all of two snakes in months of East Africa safaris, one of them poisonous – a mamba seen from the car. Vivienne de Watteville saw one snake in six months; Philip Percival 'could not recall that he had seen a single case of snake-bite during [the First World War]' despite the thousands of newcomers in the bush. East Africa has snakes, terrible ones, no doubt about it, but the chance of actually encountering one under modern camping conditions is approaching nil.

The spider is pure fantasy; the place to see spiders of real size, in my experience, is North America. On the other hand, East Africa has scorpions (I have actually seen one), malaria mosquitoes, and tsetse flies, none of which is a joke.

The dangers are exaggerated grotesquely. 'The popular idea seems to hold that a stroll through African forest would involve a degree of danger that it would be madness to incur', Abel Chapman wrote. 'That is not the case. Quite as grave a risk would attend a similar ramble in Epping Forest, or even on Hampstead Heath.' This is exaggeration in the other direction, although Taylor said he could walk from Cape to Cairo with nothing deadlier than a walking stick and a knife. Other experienced safarists took Real Africa's dangers almost as lightly: Vivienne de Watteville slept in an open tent in lion country and one night chased a rhino through the bush in her dressing-gown; Louis Leakey slept in the open without a tent and thought trying to keep lions out of camp 'not . . . necessary – or even wise'; Thompson as early as the 1880s reported wryly 'neither desertions, deaths . . . battles, bloodshed, nor other dangers' occurred.

'Wild animals are much less dangerous than automobiles', Clark said in the late 1920s. (He should see the roads today.) Yet animals can be dangerous:

everybody used to be shown the graves of lion victims at Nairobi; everybody
has heard of the man-eaters of Tsavo. Hunters who wounded animals expected
to be attacked, and some were mauled and killed. Armand Denis noted a
tourist who was taken from his tent by a lion in the Serengeti in 1962. Babault
was surprised by a raging grass fire that drove his safari out of a valley. An
acquaintance looked up from contemplating Lake Turkana to see a cobra five
feet away, which spat venom and temporarily blinded one eye.

So potent, however, is the belief in Africa's menace that the inevitable first
question I get from strangers when I talk about African camping is, 'But isn't
it dangerous?' To which the entirely truthful answer is, 'Yes, thank God, just
a little'. For without the spice of danger – the camp in the pile of elephant
dung, the leopard track by the tent door, the scorpion on the bit of firewood
– I would not be in Real Africa. It is the real possibility of danger that gives
the experience depth and honesty, just as an intentional courting of danger
would make it false and pretentious.

Honesty, authenticity of feelings, are a great part of the African safari
experience. That experience, insofar as it includes the animals, means something more than sitting behind glass and steel and looking at them; it means
something more than leaning from a game-viewing hatch and looking at
them through the finder of a camera. It means something more than being
'entertained' by Africa. In fact, I think it means finally something more than
sitting close to animals and watching them, even for long periods. I have not
convinced myself that a relationship with African animals is fully expressed in
watching. It is for this reason that I respect the ethical hunter, for in killing I
think he or she finds a dimension of experience that the mere watcher does
not: the human finds a place among animals by killing, as they kill. But I cannot
defend this idea.

Along with its modest real dangers, Real Africa has its real discomforts. The
trucks for the Vanderbilt safari got lost and left the new Mrs Vanderbilt without
clean clothes, bath, or toilet paper. Teleki and von Hohnel had the safari
dispersed by a swarm of bees. Vivienne de Watteville had to pull one of her
own molars. Barnes lost his camp and walked for 12 hours before he found it
at one in the morning. Livingstone's feet got so sore from walking he had to
go on without shoes. Neumann bathed in a spring and came out covered in
leeches. Everybody who walked on the Athi Plains came out covered with ticks.

But I have had to pick ticks off myself in Texas, remove chiggers in South
Carolina. I have encountered more poisonous snakes in two days' fishing in
Georgia (one rattlesnake, one mocassin) than in months in East Africa. The
12-foot alligator I saw while canoeing in South Carolina would have done well
in the Ewaso Nyiro. The number of tourists taken by lions is probably less
than the number taken by American grizzlies.

Yet no amount of comparing Real Africa with the Africa of the white
unconscious will remove the fears. The fact is that at the end of the twentieth

century, what most people in the world seem to want – and I mean most people, including Japanese and Europeans and Americans and even some Africans – is Zoo Africa. They do not want Real Africa at all. While the safari has come crawling toward them through the grass, shedding skins, adapting to new technology and new conditions, they have been changing, more radically and more quickly, inside their own skins. The safari is connected to the nineteenth century and even to the ninth and the first; the modern human is connected only to the twentieth century and the twenty-first and wants, not authentic experience, but comfortable experience; not extended experience in depth, but compressed experience at the surface. Not, in fact, experience at all, but entertainment. Not Real Africa, but Zoo Africa.

In the mid-1980s, I had a few days in Kenya and took a lodge tour. In the van was a 15-year-old girl with her parents. She spent the whole five days listening to her cassettes, Real Africa shut out by earphones, eyes averted. She was bored. Perhaps in a sense, reality was not artificial enough for her. It was not 'real', that is, easily comprehended. It went on for too long. It was not thrilling. It was not packaged properly.

The San Diego Zoo is the pride of the city and one of the great zoos of the world. Its varied habitats, masked from each other and sited to take advantage of the terrain, are as carefully planned and as beautifuly executed as stage sets, and they seek, as honestly as possible, to recreate something of the primal world they represent.

Yet, as we stood in the long line that snaked down to the Guided Bus Tour, and later as we stood in the shorter line to take the Skyfari aerial tramway, something niggled at me. I couldn't identify it until my companion said, 'Disneyland. It's like Disneyland – it's mostly waiting in lines, isn't it?'

And that, of course, was it. The zoo experience was, in fact, mostly one of seeing other humans – shuffling in lines, sitting in the bus, pushing along the crowded pavements towards the gift shop and the Peacock and Raven Deli. And more than that, it was the creation of a human experience whose analogue and model is the amusement park. Wild animals are thus turned into an 'amusement'; the modern zoo takes for its ideal not wilderness, but a theme park. And it perpetuates that other durable aspect of the safari myth, the dominion of humans over animals: we own them and they exist for our amusement.

This shift from experience to amusement I take to be a fundamental and probably inescapable one, part of the shift in human sensibility that marks the change from the industrial-atomic to the electronic age. Increasingly, as Zoo Africa is imposed on Real Africa, safari will become a form of amusement rather than a form of experience. It has been undergoing compression of time since the nineteenth century; however, compression now must move toward the one-hour mark, preferably even less, and compression has to come hand-in-hand with hyper-stimulation – less time, more thrill.

The day after the San Diego Zoo I visited that institution's Wild Animal Park, an 1800-acre expanded habitat in the hills east of San Diego, where wild breeding stock are kept. You see the Park by monorail (for which, of course, you stand in line). A very pleasant and knowledgeable guide told us where we were and what we were seeing: 'Now we're coming into East Africa – we'll visit East Africa three times this morning – there's a black rhinoceros'. What niggled me now? Disneyland again! Its boat safari down the Nile, Congo, and Amazon, all in one 'attraction' of less than an hour's length. So, here, the monorail tour through East, South, and North Africa; India; the Mountain Terrain.

But of course it is not East Africa. It is nothing like East Africa. It is an amusement-park 'ride', in which we glide in our spaceship across the face of some curious place, looking down at the fauna. It is instant safari, instantly here, instantly gone. It is *amusement*.

When I left the San Diego Wild Animal Park, I noticed a large sign advertising that day's animal and non-animal attractions. Several animal 'shows' were listed in several animal theatres. The biggest amphitheatre, however, featured Dick Dale and the Del Tones.

Coincidentally, the San Diego Zoo and Animal Park a few days later switched its advertising agency. Its four-million-dollar account was moved to an agency that understood the Zoo's 'marketing goals', it was reported. 'We'll present the zoo more as living theatre', a spokesman for the new agency was quoted as saying.

The traditional safari was a comedy of manners and a tragedy of race and gender. Its comedy made it endearing, even made it possible to ignore its dark side. Viewed from inside the bubble of white male privilege, it looked like a wonderful thing and it was made the stuff of a wonderful popular myth, which movies exploited. During the years when it had glamour, it was part of a world about which we of the industrialized West now feel great nostalgia: the world of Cunard liners, of Fred Astaire, of Ivor Novello and Happy Valley and Hispano-Suizas. It is perhaps remarkable, then, that although those other things have vanished, the safari continues.

The dark side cannot now be ignored. That the traditional safari, with its two white faces at the head of 100 black ones, was one of the paramount symbols of racialism, is something that whites can now admit. That paternalism and male superiority were also part of it, and that they persist in images of it, cannot be dodged.

Whether Real Africa will give way utterly to Zoo Africa remains to be seen. Pressures that at first glance seem unconnected all work to that end: population increase, poaching, industrialization, the spread of modern weapons. Perhaps all of these things, and the sensibility that wants amusement rather than experience, are parts of one whole, the emergence of the next human self-definition. (Or perhaps they are part of the human DNA's celebration of its planetary victory: Disneyland as biological status symbol.)

Is it unthinkable that a guided tour monorail run through the Masai Mara instead of the mini-vans? I think not. In fact, there are probably sound ecological arguments for such a thing. Is it unthinkable that all hunting will become restricted to fairly small (a few hundred thousand-acre) fenced areas? I think not. Is it unthinkable that what is left of Real Africa will become the wilderness lands of Huxley's *Brave New World*? No; we are almost there.

Will the safari disappear? Not, I think, so long as there are people who would rather touch the earth than ride above it. And not so long as there are wild animals in habitats big enough to give them complete ecological play. The vehicles may change; the campgrounds and the lodges may change. The colour of the human skins may change; perhaps one day we will have black clients and white cooks. But, so long as the earth and some of the animals remain, so will safari.

NOTES

Rather than disfigure the text with numbers, the references are simply listed under chapter in the order they appear.

Short title references are to the Bibliography.

CHAPTER ONE
Moorehead's *White Nile* was essential to much of the chapter, as were Spear's *Kenya's Past* and Coupland's *Exploitation of East Africa.*
● *two or three Arab merchants* ... : Coupland, 136–7. ● *from its traditional* ... : Spear, 135.● *could only be prevented* ... : Coupland, 131. ● *the conquest of Africa* ... : Rhodes, quoted in Strage, 111. ● *half-mystical ... divine pattern* ... : Moorehead, 113. ● *through the jungle like a scourge* ... : ibid., 209. ● *Stanley Africanus* ... : letter, 8 May 1886 [?], Knox, May French Sheldon papers, Library of Congress. ● *the Bagdad, the Ispahan* ... : Stanley, *How I Found Livingstone*, 5. ● *too narrow ... rose as we passed*: Grant, *Walk*, 11. ● *what a ship must have* ... : Stanley, *How I Found Livingstone*, 33. ● Safari supply list: von Hohnel, vol. i, 29. ● *beads stand for copper* ... : Stanley, *How I Found Livingstone*, 25. ● *fine wire* ... : von Hohnel, vol. i, 13. ● *provided ammunition for two years* ... : Burton, 10. ● *enough guns, powder, and ball* ... : Stanley, *How I Found Livingstone*, 33. ● *old flintlock muskets*: Petherick, 430. ● *my little bush-piece* ... : Peters, 75. ● *One of Speke's* ... : Stanley, *How I Found Livingstone*, 27. ● Thomson on Chuma: Thomson, *To the Central African Lakes*, 31–2. ● *bad drinking habits*: ibid., 33–4. ● *Mauna Sara* ... : Thomson, *Through Masai Land*, 9. ● *the celebrated Muhina Sara*: Jackson, 104. ● *not a first-rate caterer*: von Hohnel, vol. i, 36. ● *proficient ... in many languages* ... : Neumann, 272. ● *practically a race of professional porters* ... : Stigand, *The Game of British East Africa*, 190. ● *frank and amiable*: Grant, 43. ● *After the terrible loss of life* ... : Thomson, *To the Central African Lakes*, 67. ● Neumann on Juma: Neumann, 227, 336. ● Speke and Grant figures: Grant, 22–3. ● Stanley figures: Stanley, *How I Found Livingstone*, 72. ● Thomson figures: Thomson, *To the Central African Lakes*, 83–4. ● Teleki figures: von Hohnel, vol. i, 19. ● Willoughby figures: Willoughby, 39. ● Wolverton figures: Wolverton, 9. ● *I have heard* ... : Neumann, 135. ● *quiet, decent, well-conducted creatures*: Grant, 43. ● *beginning to bargain with us* ... : von Hohnel, vol. i, 51. ● *trashy bazaar ... ludicrous squabbling*: Grant, 20–4. ● *None were satisfied* ... : Thomson, *To the Central African Lakes*, 81–2. ● *their captain* ... : Grant, 24. ● *Back to the brown mounds* ... : pre-colonial 'hunting and caravan song' in K. Jackson, 'The Dimensions of

Kamba Pre-Colonial History', in Ogot (ed.), 229. • Thomson's safari's start: Thomson, *To the Central African Lakes*, 86–8. • *riff-raff of the bazaars*: Foran, *African Odyssey*, 39. • *a loss to be counted on*: Jackson, 316. • von Hohnel and the deserters: von Hohnel, vol. i, 52–7. • *a bathroom attached* . . . : Sir Frederick Jackson, 'East Africa', in Phillipps-Wolley, 162. • *obscene or topical songs* . . . : Stigand, *The Game of British East Africa*, 202–3. • *cheery salutation* . . . : Wolverton, 6. • *the cry of 'Haya safari*!: von Hohnel, vol. i, 434. • *more weary and worn* . . . : ibid., 41. • *What we assuaged* . . . : Neumann, 71. • *A picturesque and pleasing sight* . . . : Peters, 79. • *over-hauled every bale*: von Hohnel, vol. i, 172. • *comfort of the camp . . . any dinner*: Neumann, 89. • *except in the most extreme cases* . . . : ibid., 367. • *corpses thrown in the river*: Peters, 105. • *laid in chains* . . . : ibid., 63. • *the only possible way* . . . : Stanley, *How I Found Livingstone*, 344. • *if I did not succeed* . . . : ibid. • *a white man never* . . . : ibid., 312. • *completely devoid of all serious motive*: Burger, *My Forty Years in Africa*, 181. • *primarily for 'news'*: Coupland, *The Exploitation of East Africa*, 122. • *hampered at every turn* . . . : ibid. • *my knives and forks* . . . : Stanley, *How I Found Livingstone*, 425. • *Masai agricultural groups* . . . : J. E. G. Sutton, 'The Kalenjin', in Ogot (ed.), 44. • *The Kikuyu produced food* . . . : G. Muriuki, 'The Kikuyu in the pre-Colonial Periods', in Ogot (ed.), 107. • *took to raiding the countryside* . . . : Spear, 130. • *fighting between the Kikuyu and the foreigners* . . . : G. Muriuki, 'The Kikuyu', in Ogot (ed.), 135. • *the right of self-preservation* . . . : Peters, 88. • *the only means of making* . . . : von Hohnel, vol. i, 337. • *rather unpleasant* . . . : Buxton, letter to Roosevelt dated 8 August 1908. • '*Stanley . . . shoots negroes . . .*' and Bumbrie Islands: in Coupland, *The Exploitation of East Africa*, 324–8. • *men [who] fell* . . . : Rainsford, 22. • Delamere's 1896 caravan: Huxley, *White Man's Country*, vol. i, 28. • *tea, sugar, coffee, bread* . . . : Grant, 366. • *picturesque sight* . . . : Neumann, 433. • *dry, scrub-covered plains*: Huxley, *White Man's Country*, vol. i. 59.

CHAPTER TWO

Where observation did not suffice, I relied on *The Cambridge Encyclopedia of Africa* and a variety of maps and guidebooks. Again, Spear's *Kenya's Past* was invaluable. • *Everything was localized* . . . : Spear, 72. • *destined to play a part*: von Hohnel, vol. i, 351. • *cowardly and treacherous . . . well-behaved and intelligent*: J. H. Patterson, *The Man-Eaters of Tsavo*, 270–1. • *unambitious, weak* . . . : White, *The Land of Footprints*, 168. • *At one and the same moment* . . . : Thomson, *Through Masai Land*, 154, 158. • *lances, hoes* . . . : Petherick, 395–6. • *crowds of Embe women*: Neumann, 82–3. • *from men like Kivui*: Jackson, 'Dimensions', in Ogot (ed.), *Kenya*, 227. • *Swahilis and slave trade*: Spear, 'The Mijikenda', in Ogot (ed.), ibid., 280. • *a number of camping places* . . . : Spear, 129. • *a caravan road* . . . : Patterson, *The Man-Eaters of Tsavo*, 161. • Trade figures: Spear, 117, and P. T. Dalleo, 'Somali Role in Organized Poaching, 1909–1939', *International Journal of African History Studies*, 12, 3, 414. • *an unequal exchange*: Spear, 135. • *A black, swampy stretch* . . . : Preston, 172. • *a dreary windswept plain*: 'Diary of a Foreman Platelayer', the *Globetrotter*, 1907. • *A brand-new town* . . . : Buxton, *Two African Trips*, 38.

CHAPTER THREE

• *splendid ferocity*: White, *The Land of Footprints*, 29. • *blaze of amazing light*: Lorimer, 7. • *like having breakfast* . . . : de Watteville, *Speak to the Earth*, 122. •

To get back . . . thousand dangers: Schillings, vol. ii, 666–7. ● *the first-comers . . .* :
Chapman, *Retrospect*, 93. ● *shooting expedition*: Godwin (?), letter to the *Field*, 17
February 1906. ● *both the caravan . . .* : Roosevelt, *African Game Trails*, 20. ●
safarist: Page, 185 and elsewhere. ● *a very nice English club . . .* : Younghusband,
19. ● *I had to take my own bedding . . .* : Lorimer, 12. ● *Perfection is said to be . . .* :
D. Benbow, letter to the *Field*, 30 October 1903. ● *embedded in red clay . . . most
wonderful and interesting railway journey in the world*: Kirkland, 62. ● *wait patiently
. . .* : Foran, *A Cuckoo in Kenya*, 67. ● *after all, an Indian show*: Jackson, 321. ●
Indian statistics: Trzebinski, *The Kenya Pioneers*, 15. ● *the first mosque*: Preston,
Oriental Nairobi, 38; early Indian traders from ads in same. ● *settled in the district*:
Kenya National Archives, DC/FH 6/1, 'History of Fort Hall', 5. ● *indispensability
of Asian traders*: Ghai, 101. ● police records: Foran, *The Kenyan Police*, 20. ●
Nairobi population: 1903 figure, Trzebinski, *The Kenya Pioneers*, 51; 1907 figures
from Colonial Office, 'Flogging', 1; 1909 census from Preston, *Oriental Nairobi*,
2. ● *the only shop*: Meinertzhagen, 9. ● *many undesirable . . .* : Foran, *The Kenyan
Police*, 21. ● *Tinville*: Jessen, 386. ● *beds of violets . . . rest of his life*: F. H. Blockley,
letter to the *Field*, 2 February 1907. ● *beautiful and most interesting*: Rainsford, 417.
● *ne rappelle en rien . . .* : Babault, 8. ● Reactions to Nairobi: in order, from
McCutcheon, 45; Lloyd-Jones, 22; Roosevelt, *African Game Trails*, 173; Hepburn,
30; Stigand, *The Land of Zinj*, 193. ● *its large native quarter . . .* : Roosevelt, *African
Game Trails*, 173. ● *Almost with the first . . .* : Holman, 41. ● Boustead, Ridley &
Co: Purvis, *Handbook to British East Africa and Uganda*, 61. ● Buxton's safari:
Buxton, *Two African Trips*, 4. ● *agents . . . energy . . .* : A.H.B., letter to the *Field*,
23 September 1905. ● Smith, McKenzie, Boustead, Grand Hotel: letter from M.
to the *Field*, 13 February 1904. ● *several agents*: Yzbashi, letter to the *Field*, 30
April 1904. ● *enormous . . . extremely casual . . .* : F.L.T., letter to the *Field*, 15
April 1905. ● Newland and Tarlton businesses: Trzebinski, *The Kenya Pioneers*,
83. ● *The preliminary arrangements . . .* : Cranworth, *Kenya Chronicles*, 96–7. ● N
& T 'fell' into the business: Akeley, *In Brightest Africa*, 149. ● *Lord and Lady
Cranworth . . .* : East African Standard, 14 December 1907. ● *1908 witnessed the
arrival . . .* : Riddell, 'Boma', 261. ● *Captain Riddell, M.V.O. . . .* : B.J.L., letter to
the *Field*, 7 March 1908. ● *Geoffrey Archer . . .* : Riddell, 'Boma', 267. ● *buccaneering
flavor*: Trench, 'Why a Greek', 52. ● Boma Trading details: *East African Standard*,
advertisements, various dates; and the *Leader*, various dates. ● Other competition:
ibid. ● *Valhalla*: Bronson, 59. ● Delamere and 'white hunter:' see, for example,
Bull, 203. ● *When you arrive . . .* : McCutcheon, 50. ● *one director said*: Cranworth,
Kenya Chronicles, 106. ● Evaluation of Cuninghame and Judd: Silberrads memo,
enclosure in letter from Pease to Roosevelt, 7 October 1908. ● *who afterward proved
to be . . .* : Rainsford, 75. ● *the army of porters and tents . . .* : Roosevelt, *African
Game Trails*, 22. ● *The English rule . . . a protectorate*: ibid., 120, 4, 2. ● *the spirit
of daring adventure*: ibid., 42. ● *I had never been with . . .* : Pease, *Half a Century of
Sport*, 280. ● *perseverance and common sense*: Pease, ibid., 280. ● *army Springfield,
.30-calibre . . .* : Roosevelt, *African Game Trails*, 28. ● *a craft, a pursuit of value . . .* :
said of Buxton by Roosevelt, ibid., 382. ● *There was much . . .* : ibid., 42. ● *We
might be off . . . dying twilight*: ibid., 66. ● *Our night ride . . .* : Roosevelt to Tarlton,
28 December 1918. ● *the devastation that is done . . .* : Cranworth, *A Colony in the
Making*, 236. ● *Every Briton . . .* : *The Illustrated Sporting and Dramatic Times*, 8
October 1910, 222. ● *One must regret . . .* : H. A. Bryden, letter to the *Field*, 9

November 1910. ● *a matter of great regret* . . . : Jackson, 381. ● *an abominable habit*: John G. Millais, letter of December 1918, quoted in Lyell, *African Adventures*, 103. ● *subsidized in part* . . . : Wilson, *Theodore Roosevelt, Outdoorsman*, 177. ● *one is to do it yourself* . . . : Barnes, *Babes in the African Wood*, 20. ● *a smattering of* . . . *jumble sale*: ibid., 23. ● *cut and dried*: 'Mauser', letter to the *Field*, 24 July 1909. ● *very rich men*: Colville, letter to the *Field*, 28 August 1909. ● *surprisingly large figures*: Hepburn, 106–7. ● Government wage figures: *Blue Book*, 1914. ● *One couple who organized their own safari*: Younghusband, 148 ff. ● *professional porters*: Barnes, *Babes in the African Wood*, 48. ● *the benighted custom* . . . : Rainsford, 12–13. ● White and the porter 'villages': White, *African Camp Fires*, 134–8. ● *is attractive to them* . . . : Roosevelt, *African Game Trails*, 95. ● *struggling against the advent* . . . : Cranworth, *Kenya Chronicles*, 96–7. ● *Rising before daylight* . . . : Buxton, *Two African Trips*, 8. ● *Up at 4* . . . : Bronson, 58–9. ● *The whole joy* . . . : Chapman, *On Safari*, 112. ● *I counted fourteen tents* . . . : Rainsford, 32. ● *the pile of camp baggage* . . . : ibid., 52. ● *a long drink* . . . *sponge and towel*: Chapman, *On Safari*, 114. ● Numbers of safaris: Hindlip, letter to the *Field*, 21 January 1905, 98; Bronson, 3; McCutcheon, *In Africa*, 50; Governor's report in the *Field*, 23 April 1910, 731; Roosevelt responding to Tarlton, 28 June 1911. ● Rainsford's departure: the *Leader*, 1 March 1913. ● *the Coy's business* . . . : Tarlton, letter to Roosevelt, 11 November 1915. ● *virtually ceased to exist*: Ofcansky, 'History of Game Preservation', 34.

CHAPTER FOUR

May French Sheldon's *Sultan to Sultan* and Mary Hall's *A Woman's Trek From Cape to Cairo* were essential for this chapter. ● Fears of rape, etc: Huxley, *White Man's Country*, ii, 14. ● *The leaders wheeled* . . . : Sheldon. Unless otherwise noted, quotations in this section are from this work. ● *To study women and children* . . . : *Woman of the Century*, Sheldon. ● *An American lady litterateur* . . . : Stanley, letter dated 16 January 1891. ● *an accomplished writer* . . . *to the full*: Stanley, letter dated 15 January 1891. ● *for historical purposes*: Blaine, letter dated 26 January 1891. ● *the English Parliament* . . . : Williams, 'White Queen'. ● *Let me tender you my honest advice* . . . : Stanley, letter dated 15 January 1891. ● *Difficulty in marching* . . . : Sheldon, manuscript list, Library of Congress collection. ● *A great deal depended* . . . : *The Times* (London), 25 August 1891. ● *Exploration is not the forte* . . . : Williams, 'White Queen', 342. ● *Africa reveals* . . . *never lulled into forgetfulness*: Sheldon, typed MS, Library of Congress collection. ● *mentally substituting* . . . : Hall, *A Woman's Trek From Cape to Cairo*. Unless otherwise noted, quotations in this section are from this work. ● C. G. Buxton: the *Field*, 23 July 1910, 162. ● *Gonera* . . . : Stanley, *How I Found Livingstone*, 75. ● *the houses in which* . . . *young wives*: Peters, 64. ● Women porters: *Nairobi News*, 1 March 1905; and White, *The Land of Footprints*, 242. ● *practically unknown* . . . *civilization*: Dane, 74–5. ● *Smart black women* . . . : Rainsford, 5. ● *In a community* . . . : Trzebinski, *The Kenya Pioneers*, 66. ● *Masai and other* . . . : Foran, *Cuckoo in Kenya*, 81. ● *slept with one or two* . . . : Meinertzhagen, *Kenya Diary*, 34. ● *Every railway official* . . . : ibid., 12–23. ● *loyal co-operation* . . . : KNA MC/2 BAR/11, Enclosure B. ● *white men* . . . : Gunther, 329. ● Being asked to pimp for clients: Allen, 267. ● *One woman in a party* . . . : Young, 25. ● *They're best left at home* . . . : Wykes, 144. ● *No trip for a woman*: Osa Johnson, *I Married Adventure*, 208. ● *She has the brains and knowledge* . . . : Undated letter to May

French Sheldon's husband, indecipherable signature. • [*Hers*] *was the voice of a boy* . . . : Young, 25. • Stanley on sex: *How I Found Livingstone*, 316, 313, 292. • *expedition of 180 men* . . . : Davis, 'American in Africa', 634.

CHAPTER FIVE

• Black conscription and casualties: Hodges, 'African Manpower Statistics', 113–14; Greenstein, 'Africans in European War', 265. • *during which it is estimated* . . . : KNA DC/FH 6/1. 'History of Fort Hall', 20. • Population figures: Perham, 14 (note). • *far more*: Percival, *Game Ranger on Safari*, 291. • *killed off most of the rhinos*: Blayney Percival to Martin Johnson, in Johnson, *Camera Trails*, 118. • *Nairobi was the heart* . . . : Hunter, *Hunter*, 111. • *a fine town* . . . : Dugmore, *The Wonderland of Big Game*, 11. • *ridiculous looking dudes* . . . : Frederick Patterson, 57. • *Nairobi was largely peopled* . . . : Perham, 24. • *One of the shabbiest* . . . : ibid., 24. • *the Paris* . . . : Farson, *Behind God's Back*, 285. • *the old stone hostel* . . . : Mary L. Akeley, 20. • *dirty and inefficient* . . . : Perham, 24. • *agonizing day-in day-out* . . . : Gunther, 406. • *a grass plain* . . . : White, *The Rediscovered Country*, 16–17. • *that most perfect* . . . : Clark, *Trails of the Hunted*, 131. • *someone who has no pity* . . . : Szechenyi, 123. • *the Africa that was*: Mary L. Akeley, 40. • *the Cook's of big game* . . . : Gandar Dower, 65. • *commercialization of big-game* . . . : Perham, 190. • *transport over almost all* . . . : A. T. A. Ritchie, 'Kenya', in Maydon (ed.), 257. • *My trophies represent* . . . : Gandar Dower, 64. • Hunting licence figures: Kenya Colony and Protectorate Game Department, *Annual Report*, various years. • *'thing to do'* . . . : Clark, *Good Hunting*, 97. • *Silas K. Vanderoil* . . . : Davis and Robertson, 67. • *meaningful contact* . . . : Elias Mandala, Foreword, in Eastman, *Chronicles of a Second Trip*, xiv. • Tarlton to Marsabit: Tarlton, letter to Evans, 29 November 1923, Library of Congress (Roosevelt Collection). • *Packard with safari body*: Appel, 132. • *4 Albion lorries . . . King Solomon's Mines*: Chalmers, 107. • Vanderbilts: Vanderbilt, 45. • Szechenyi: Szechenyi, 59. • *sometimes we had to send* . . . : Clark, *Good Hunting*, 99. • *You may scrape* . . . : Chalmers, 107. • *the best way to ruin* . . . : Clark, *Trails of the Hunted*, 158–9. • *They did not walk* . . . : Stoneham, *Wanderings in Wild Africa*, 135. • *The old safari days are gone* . . . : Tarlton, letter dated November 1926, in Lyell, *African Adventures*, 69. • *The motor-car has destroyed* . . . : Tarlton, letter of January 1927, in Lyell, ibid., 72. • *aid to the week-end sportsman*: Kearton, *In the Land of the Lion*, 17. • Incident of the girl: Moore, *Serengeti*, 13. • *not the vehicle* . . . : Percival, *A Game Ranger on Safari*, 245. • *the Southern Masai Reserve* . . . : Dyer, *The East African Hunters*, 23. • Flying to Arusha for the newspaper: Szechenyi, 136. • *much easier than driving* . . . : Vanderbilt, 59. • *I have never* . . . : Mary L. Akeley, 170. • *taking care of* . . . : Frederick Patterson, 26. • *Old Kitchener* . . . : Finch Hatton to Kermit Roosevelt, 27 January 1919. • *filter-and-water safari* . . . : Ritchie, 'Kenya', in Maydon (ed.), 258. • Stoneham on expense: Stoneham, *Wanderings in Wild Africa*, 10. • *Each tent* . . . : Allen, 36. • *called at half-past four* . . . : Curtis, 22. • *Scores of servants* . . . : Stoneham, *Wanderings in Wild Africa*, 10. • *38 boys* . . . : Vanderbilt, 48. • *the largest safari*: Martin Johnson, *Camera Trails in Africa*, 282. • Egyptian prince: letter from Martin Johnson to Daniel Pomeroy, 26 February 1925. • *one of the most spectacular*: Hunter and Wykes, *Hunter's Tracks*, 212–15. • *to keep the safari in asparagus* . . . : Davis and Robertson, 69–71. • First Eastman safari: see Eastman, *Chronicles of an African Trip*. • *Chicago Tinned Can Museum*: Davis and Robertson, 67. • Martin and Osa Johnson: see Martin Johnson, *Camera Trails in Africa* and *Safari* and Osa Johnson, *I Married Adventure* and *Four Years in Paradise*. • *Eighteen guns* . . . : Osa Johnson, *I Married Adventure*, 208. • *pleasure fleet* . . . : Mary L. Akeley, 92. • *the price of all Kenya's principal exports* . . . : Huxley, *White Man's County*, vol. ii, 305. • *liquidations . . . axeing of labour*: Szechenyi, 1. • *Cancellation of Safaris*: clipping, undated and unascribed. • licence figures: Ugandan, Kenyan, and Tanganyikan Game Department annual reports, various years. • *fewer visitors* . . . : East Africa Protectorate, *Financial Report*, various years. • an estimate of $22,000: Carlos Baker, 289. • *practically non-existent*: Allen, 155. • *Because of this goddam war* . . . : Denis, 139.

CHAPTER SIX

• *lassoo, a trap or from a balloon*: Cranworth, *A Colony in the Making*, 234. • *No more lion-sticking* . . . : Meinertzhagen, *Kenya Diary*, 96–7. • *an elaborate tin castle*: the *Leader*, 15 May 1909. • *wonderful tin castle . . . workmanship*: the *Leader*, 22 May 1909. • *Unique Idea* . . . : *Blade*, 19 June 1909. • *Mr Boyce in England* . . . : *Blade*, 14 August 1909. • *Famous Guide* . . . : *Blade*, 28 August 1909. • *the first woman* . . . : McCutcheon, *In Africa*, 64. • *fashionably dressed . . . march through the city*: ibid., 55. • *a grotesque conception* . . . : Jackson, 382. • *It is scarcely possible* . . . : ibid. • *showed us something* . . . : Burger, *Horned Death*, 300. • Charles S. Bird: Easton and Brown, 175. • *Tarpon Dick*: Binks, 103. • *forty splendid ponies*: Burger, *Horned Death*, 296. • *he truly believed* . . . : Easton and Brown, 183. • *collars and belts* . . . : Scull, 13. • *the English Lords* . . . : Jones, in Easton and Brown, 167. • *Lord Delmar*: Easton and Brown, 188. • *special train* . . . : Scull, 3. • Capture of the lioness: *New York Times*, 28 May 1910, and Easton and Brown, 188–98. • *At last a cablegram* . . . : Charles S. Bird, quoted in Kersey, 7. • *They astonished the world* . . . : Pease, *Book of the Lion*, 253. • *Buffalo Jones and his two cowboys* . . . : Roosevelt, *African Game Trails*, 552. • *but he was brutally cruel* . . . : Clark, *Good Hunting*, 34. • *big game hunter, naturalist* . . . : Fortiss, 'Paul Rainey', 746–9. • *despised his hunting methods*: Cuninghame, letter to Kermit Roosevelt dated 14 September 1912. • *this person* . . . : Cuninghame, letter of 1924, in Lyell, *African Adventure*, 47. • *If my hounds* . . . : Rainey, 'Royal Sport', 131, 146. • *It was a great sport* . . . : ibid., 137–8. • *Rainey's chief interest . . . lions as game animals*: Heller, letter to Roosevelt, 18 June 1911. • *a feat unparalleled* . . . : anon., 'Champion Lion-Killer', 616. • *I shot several times . . . the future*: *New York World* interview, quoted ibid., 618. • *The same effect* . . . : White, *The Land of Footprints*, 144. • *circus stunt*: White, 'Archery in Africa', 33. • *uncertainty of the feat . . . we did it*: Young, 'African Lions and the Longbow', July 1926, 11. • *in the large muscles . . . flesh wounds*: ibid., 13. • *American-style archers* . . . : Denman, *Animal Africa*, 57. • *the game wardens very rightly* . . . : Wykes, 195. • *the long bow* . . . : White, 'Archery in Africa', 34.

CHAPTER SEVEN

• *large game*: Gunther, 385. • *Nairobi is the safari capital* . . . : Moorehead, *No Room in the Ark*, 68. • *. . . safari capital of the world*. Gunther, 322. • *Everyone in Nairobi* . . . : Cloete, 8. • *come unstuck*: Farson, *Last Chance in Africa*, 176. • *90 per cent increase* . . . : Ghai, 'Economic Survey', in *Portrait of a Minority*, 91. • *five* *and a half million* . . . : Gunther, 319. • comparison with apartheid: John Karmali, quoted in Lamb, 157. • *infinitely, beyond calculation* . . . : Gunther, 425. • *most visitors want* . . . : Kenya Colony and Protectorate Game Department, *Annual Report*, 1950, 12. • *licensed hunting has now reached* . . . : ibid., 1956–7, 9. • *In the 1930s* . . . : Holman, 218. • *a big game safari as now* . . . : Kenya Colony and Protectorate Game Department, *Annual Report*, 1950, 12. • *now these percentages* . . . : Gunther, 391. • *The great majority are Americans* . . . : Glenn Cottar, quoted in Holman, 236. • *fishing and hunting trips: Washington Post*, 29 November 1987, H8. • *[At the new Stanley bar]* . . . : Cloete, 2. • *The first outdoor magazine* . . . : Rae (ed.), 226. • *up to £1,000* . . . : Kenya Colony and Protectorate Game Department, *Annual Report*, 1956–7, 9. • *with every luxury possible*: Moorehead, *No Room in the Ark*, 69. • Uganda Wildlife, Ltd: Page, 219. • Game Department figures: Republic of Kenya, *Estimates of Revenue for the Year Ending 30th June 1978*. • Kenya government salary figures: Colony *Staff List*, 1957. • *One of the most delightful* . . . : Rainsford, 43. • *being reborn* . . . : Farson, *Last Chance in Africa*, 295; Dickinson, 176. • Eric Rundgren: quoted in Holman, 216. • East African Professional Hunters Association figures: from the Membership List (excluding non-professional, honorary, and undated members) in Dyer, *The East African Hunters*, 123–31. • *very private little club*: Allen, 74. • *The White Hunter racket* . . . : Taylor, *Pondoro*, 213. • *positively unscrupulous.* Hirsch, 230–1. • *All-motorized* . . . : Bell, *Bell of Africa*, 226. • 11 miles an hour: Farson, *Last Chance*, 269. • Muthaiga Club: Lovell, *Straight on Till Morning*, 279. • *elephant-hair bracelets* . . . : Holman, 216. • *astonishing luxury* . . . : O'Connor, 'Lions Don't Come Easy', 227. • *parties in the field*: Morden and Morden, *Our African Adventure*, 119. • Ernest Hemingway: Carlos Baker, 653–9. • Dates of parks: Ofcansky, 'History of Game Preservation', 197, 205. • *selvaggia* . . . : Disertori, 16. • *tickly job*: Farson, *Last Chance in Africa*, 293. • Itigi, Ngorongoro, Ngulia, Ol Tukai: East Africa Tourist Association, *Hotels* (1953).

CHAPTER EIGHT

• *like one of Walt Whitman's poems*: Streeter, *Denatured Africa*, 99. • *We had so much 'kag'* . . . : ibid., 95. • *with the tail tips* . . . : Hunter, 23. • Bowker's hat, *many settlers*: Trzebinski, *The Kenya Pioneers*, 127. • *Ellwood's patent* . . . *shapeless pulp*: Jackson, 'East Africa', in Phillipps-Wolley, 160. • Lugard on the hat: Lugard, 33. • *when the solar topee* . . . : Bell, *Bell of Africa*, 2. • *deadly tropical sun*: Kirkland, 42. • *the protection of helmet* . . . : White, *The Land of Footprints*, 408. • *brown Spanish hat*: Perham, 159. • *struck dead*: Farson, *Last Chance*, 264. • *Kharki Norfolk jackets* . . . : Willoughby, 41. • Jackson on safari clothes: Jackson, 'East Africa', in Phillipps-Wolley, 158–60. • *could almost carry* . . . : Farson, *Behind God's Back*, 184. • *comfortable and cool*: Stigand, *Hunting the Elephant*, 307. • *It was cooler*: Streeter, *Denatured Africa*, 157. • *yellow Turkish boots* . . . : Petherick, 28. • *the most useful things* . . . : Younghusband, 99. • *silly little skirt*: Herbert, 38. • *wool is the watchword* . . . : Purvis, *Handbook to British East Africa*, 59. • spinepads: White, *Land of Footprints*, 431–6. • *unspeakably slim* . . . : Young, 167. • *Peter Pan existence* . . . : de Watteville, *Speak to the Earth*, 244. • *The clothing question* . . . : A. C. Knollys, 'Uganda', in Maydon (ed.), 272. • *I took with me* . . . : Neumann, 63. • Jaeger blankets, etc: Rainsford, *The Land of the Lion*, 442. • *camping rugs, blankets* . . . : McCutcheon, *In Africa*, 9. • *and built to pitch* . . . *golden syrup*: White, *The*

Rediscovered Country, 12, 318. ● *Abercrombie and Fritz*: Bennett, 264–5. ● *canvas comfort station* . . . : Cloete, 11. ● Hindlip on water: Hindlip, 161. ● *nitrous, and nearly the price* . . . : Grant, 29. ● *This improved the taste* . . . : von Hohnel, vol. ii, 98, 104. ● *to endure* . . . : Sutherland, 169. ● *a vile cook* . . . : Barnes, 69. ● *hanging his pots* . . . : Hoefler, 60. ● *a real Swahili ruffian*: Finch Hatton to Kermit Roosevelt, 27 January 1919. ● *we had to live* . . . : Barnes, 154. ● *flatly refused to look* . . . : de Watteville, *Out in the Blue*, 87. ● *The menu was* . . . : ibid., 86. ● One *Field* correspondent: H. A. Bryden, the *Field*, 17 August 1907. ● *though sweet, requires* . . . : Grant, 33–4. ● Menus, in order: Bronson, 31; Younghusband, 127–8; Patterson, *African Adventures*, 22; Chapman, *On Safari*, 115; Johnson, *Lion*, 66. ● Sundowners: Wells, 147. ● Jugged Lion: Lake, 126–7. ● *A sportsman* . . . : Dane, 172. ● *the party went* . . . : Chalmers, 173. ● *Calomel and julep* . . . : Grant, 26. ● *no quinine should be taken* . . . : Stanley, *How I Found Livingstone*, 594. ● *doomed to extinction*: the *Field*, 14 March 1908. ● *miasma* . . . : Jackson, 'East Africa', in Phillipps-Wolley, 163. ● *Wounds which might contain poison* . . . : quoted in Binks, 70. ● *a medical outfit with which* . . . : Patterson, *African Adventures*, 30.

CHAPTER NINE

● *The hunter is a* . . . : Ortega y Gasset, 101. ● *that glorious madness* . . . : de Watteville, *Out in the Blue*, 34. ● *The English seasons* . . . : Huxley, *White Man's Country* 25. ● *big-game hunting* . . . : A. T. A. Ritchie, in Kenya Colony and Protectorate Game Department, *Annual Report*, 1932–4. ● *not an elevating* . . . : McCutcheon, 65. ● *dark survival* . . . : Rainsford, 87. ● *lust to acquire beauty* . . . : Farson, *Last Chance in Africa*, 137. ● Three qualities of hunting: Page, 202. ● *forego the shot*: Herbert, *Dianas*, 97. ● *a sort of madness*: Page, 190. ● *a nice gong* . . . : Younghusband, 196. ● *Beautiful souvenirs . . . inkstands*: White, *The Land of Footprints*, 70. ● *glee for killing*: Moorehead, *No Room in the Ark*, 22. ● *they wanted to kill* . . . : Stoneham, *Wanderings in Wild Africa*, 135. ● *prince from Central Europe*: Moorehead, *No Room in the Ark*, 178. ● *appeared to give me permission* . . . : Streeter, *Denatured Africa*, 85. ● *whatever they were* . . . : Bronson, 41. ● *the twelve* . . . : White, *The Land of Footprints*, 278. ● *one or two specimens* . . . : Hindlip, 183. ● *armed tourists* . . . : Kearton and Barnes, 2. ● *The killing of the animals* . . . : Letter from J. P. W. Onege, *East African Standard*, 13 June 1977. ● *looking as perfect* . . . : Grant, 35. ● Muzzle-loaders in Tanganyika: Cloudsley-Thompson, 83; Tanganyika Territory Game Department, *Annual Report*, 1954. ● Stanley on guns: Stanley, *How I Found Livingstone*, 62. ● *Express Train*: Taylor, *African Rifles*, 3. ● Paradox for tiger: Russell, 29. ● *laughed at*: Neumann, 121. ● *wonderful* and use of glove: Neumann, letter to Millais, 20 July 1902, in Millais, 149. ● *the unromantic fact* . . . : Carmichael, 335. ● *as my right cheek and bone* . . . : Baldwin, 385. ● Selous's shooting: Burger, *African Adventures*, 154. ● *dared use no other . . . nasty words* and headache: Neumann, 336, 214, 218, 182. ● *the blast* . . . : Roosevelt, *African Game Trails*, 304. ● Barnes on recoil: Barnes, 350. ● *a very inferior weapon*: Selous, letter to Roosevelt, 24 May 1908. ● *rather out of fashion . . . in reserve*: Buxton, letter to Roosevelt, 24 May 1908. ● *the presumption* . . . : McCutcheon, 8–9. ● *thoroughly unsuitable and unsportsmanlike*: Sutherland, 171. ● *though a firm believer*: Percival, *Game Ranger's Notebook*, 194–5. ● *tremendous* recoil: Rice, 87. ● Game Department advisory: Game Department, *Hunt Management Program, Kajiado District* (Nairobi, 1973). ● *for a springing* . . . : Stigand, letter of September 1905,

in Lyell, *African Adventures*, 34. ● *It is far better* . . . : Burger, *Horned Death*, 325. ●
Nyoka: the *Field*, 17 April 1909. ● *stripped out* . . . : Carmichel, 336. ● *one-gun
safari* . . . : Page, 211–12. ● 1980s gun prices: Fjestad. ● biggest tusks: Capstick,
Death in the Long Grass, 73. ● *his first ten* . . . : von Hohnel, vol. ii, 85. ● Elephant
kills, in order: Huxley, *White Man's Country*, vol. i, 47; Neumann, 198, and letter
dated 8 December 1904 in Millais, 153; Bronson, 275–6; Taylor, *Pondoro*, 288. ●
the moment the abdominal wall . . . : Bronson, 162. ● *The death of a lion* . . . : White,
Land of Footprints, 129. ● *The rhinoceros will probably* . . . : Selous, 'Hunting
Grounds of Africa', xxv. ● *shot on sight*: Rainsford, 307. ● *roughly handled*: Roosevelt,
African Game Trails, 272. ● Peter Capstick estimated: Capstick, *Death in the Long
Grass*, 245. ● *one of the most deplorable* . . . : Capstick, ibid., 244. ● *Who wants* . . .
getting married: Barnes, 76. ● *become as extinct* . . . : Judd, the *Field*, 27 January
1906. ● *It sounded ridiculous* . . . : Streeter, *Denatured Africa*, 300. ● *one should never
fire* . . . : Dickinson, 29. ● *a very long shot* . . . *10 or 12 paces*: Taylor, *Big Game*,
43, 71. ● *too far back* . . . *give him up*: Hindlip, 144. ● *I was reluctantly compelled*
. . . : ibid., 169. ● *I was heartbroken* . . . *more like him*; Jordan: Bronson, 53, 52,
153 ff. ● *some distance* . . . *too late to follow him*: von Hohnel, vol. i, 125, 216. ●
Bernard de Watteville: de Watteville, *Out in the Blue*, 186–7, 67, 32, 29, 28. ●
crippled . . . *very sick*: Chapman, *On Safari*, 98, 70. ● *imprudent* . . . *stiffened* . . . :
Bronson, 55. ● *half of his own front leg*: Perham, 217. ● Franklin Russell on politics:
Russell, 54–6. ● *it was not until* . . . : Cloudsley-Thompson, 51. ● *the game is
doomed* . . . *game survive*: Lee, 217. ● *as long as natives* . . . : Selous, 'Hunting
Grounds of Africa', xxv. ● Capstick on hunting ban: Capstick, *Safari*, 16. ●
Carmichel on Bell: Carmichel, 346. ● *In the early 1900s* . . . : Lieberman, 'The
Ivory Trade', 17. ● *Game Department Black List*: KNA, *Miscellaneous Correspondence*,
1926. ● J. S. Finnie: the *Leader*, 4 December 1912. ● *sportsmen*: KNA MC/19,
ELGM/10, *Elgeyo Marsabit Miscellaneous Correspondence*, 1914–30. ● *in Uganda
. . .* : G. Graham, the *Field*, 17 September 1910. ● *written requests from army officers*
. . . : Kajanja, 'Uganda National Parks', 11. ● *Between 1880 and 1910* . . . :
Cloudsley-Thompson, 87. ● *Uganda's 90 percent* . . . *threat*: Kajanja, 'Uganda
National Parks, 17–18. ● *The outcome* . . . : Redmond, 'Islands of Elephants', 19.
● Rhino estimates: Dyer, *Classic East African Animals*, 31. ● Aerial rhino survey:
EcoSystems Ltd, 9. ● Rhino population, Mara: *Swara*, January/February 1987,
32. ● Rhino population, Selous: *Swara*, September/October 1986, 23. ● *The real
threat* . . . : Cloudsley-Thompson, 179. ● *the octopus of population* . . . : Page, 255.
● [*Efforts to conserve*] . . . : Ortega y Gasset, 79.

CHAPTER TEN

● *speaks Swahili* . . . : Cranworth, *A Colony in the Making*, 234. ● *runs the safari
. . .* : 'Nyoka', the *Field*, 17 April 1909. ● Millais on Neumann: the *Field*, 15 June
1907. ● *a white man* . . . : B.J.L., letter to the *Field*, 7 March 1908. ● *each with his
attendant* . . . : Chapman, *On Safari*, 111. ● *marked element of the theatrical* . . . : K.
Jackson, 'Dimensions of Pre-Colonial History', in Ogot (ed.), 226. ● *Gentleman
with unique* . . . *personal expenses*: the *Field*, 28 May 1898. ● India and South Africa:
the *Field*, 25 June 1898. ● *Big Game Shooting* . . . : the *Field*, 25 February 1905.
● *Men who know the Game*: the *Globetrotter*, 4 July 1906. ● *the most colorful group
. . .* : Hunter, 23. ● *a first-class shot* . . . : Roosevelt, letter to Selous, 19 August
1908. ● *as if I were being personally conducted* . . . : Roosevelt, letter to Buxton, 20

August 1908. • *I should want it distinctly understood* . . . : Roosevelt, letter to Buxton, 12 September 1908. • *what trade goods I would require*: ibid. • Selous, Pioneer Column: Strage, 73–4. • *If Mr Selous* . . . : Rainsford, letter to Roosevelt, 25 December 1908. • *arranged a lion hunt*: Riddell, 'Boma', 260. • Hoey, Cockburn's elephant: *East African Standard*, 4 January 1908. • Bull on first white hunter: see Bull, 205. • Madeira and Cuninghame: Roosevelt to Selous, 19 August 1908. • *teach him to hunt* . . . : Carl Akeley, 153. • *Cuninghame accompanied* . . . : ibid. • J. H. Patterson: Patterson, letter to Roosevelt, 15 January 1908; and Patterson, *In the Grip of the Nyika*. • *offering his services* . . . : Edmund Lechmere, letter to the *Field*, 15 April 1906. • *a good shot* . . . : Silberrads memo, enclosure in letter from Pease to Roosevelt, 7 October 1908. • *lean, sinewy* . . . : Roosevelt, *African Game Trails*, 26. • *collègue* . . . : Babault, 2. • *I am fairly fit* . . . : Cuninghame to Kermit Roosevelt, 27 July 1914. • *a huge safari* . . . : Cuninghame to Roosevelt, 19 December 1914. • *fishing for wounded*: Tarlton to Roosevelt, 11 November 1915. • *mysterious mission* . . . : Jessie Tarlton to Roosevelt, 25 April 1916. • *such that I cannot see* . . . : Cuninghame to Kermit Roosevelt, 23 July 1924. • *Probably the most experienced* . . . : Bronson, 1. • *celebrated . . . a good* . . . : Jackson, 369–70. • *trading store*: Millais, 191. • *killed by an elephant*: Dyer, *The East African Hunters*, 9. • *I've had enough* . . . : McCutcheon, 153. • *Mrs Safari*: Tarlton to Roosevelt, 13 November 1910. • *The financial depression* . . . : Tarlton to Kermit Roosevelt, 24 November 1933. • Black was born in 1886: Trzebinski, *The Kenya Pioneers*, 137. • *hunter friend of Judd's*: Dane, 78. • *name might as well* . . . : White, 'You Never Can Tell', 26. • *Percival junior*: the *Leader*, 1 January 1910. • *an old Australian* . . . : Bronson, 1. • *of these an Austrian* . . . : Jackson, 368. • Seth Smith: *Standard*, 10 April 1909. • Lydford: Kearton and Barnes, 2. • James Clark: Clark, *Good Hunting*, 35–6, 99. • *they all drew the same* . . . : Jackson, 370. • *carefully avoid* . . . : Stigand, the *Field*, 2 April 1910. • *the demand just now* . . . : 'Nyoka', the *Field*, 17 April 1909. • *several professional hunters . . . your weapon*: Rainsford, 417, 25. • *relieved of all camp worries* . . . : Millais, 192. • *A white hunter* . . . : Unidentified Nairobi resident, quoted in Hoefler, 293–4. • *He was white* . . . : Davis and Robertson, 66. • *made Africa a playground . . . risky profession*: Perham, 110. • *this racket . . . stop it*: Taylor, *Pondoro*, 214. • *a group of good* . . . : Dyer, *The East African Hunters*, 18. • *better-known hunters* . . . : Stoneham, *Wanderings in Wild Africa*, 139. • *men like Pat Ayre* . . . : ibid., 139. • *not Allan Quartermaine* . . . : Gandar Dower, 65–6. • *my wife's lover* . . . : Lovell, 97. • Blixen's income: from Holman, quoted in Lovell, 98. • *never missed a chance* . . . : Allen, 122. • *one of the first* . . . : ibid., 5. • *just happened* . . . : Frederick Patterson, *African Adventures*, 9. • *fearless . . . popular* . . . : ibid., 20. • Beryl Markham on Finch Hatton's sexuality: Lovell, 365n. • *brilliant* . . . : ibid., 94. • *Suggest you cancel* . . . : ibid., 100. • 3 pounds a day: B.J.L., the *Field*, 7 March 1908. • £250 a month: Cranworth, 107. • *gradually raised* . . . : Hunter, 57. • *the big names* . . . : Holman, 200. • Duties of a hunter: Hunter, 116 ff. • *He has been called upon* . . . : Cranworth, 107. • Source of '*Short Happy Life*': Carlos Baker, 363–4. • *Of course I made love* . . . : Lovell, 151. • *Some of the younger* . . . : Colony and Protectorate of Kenya Game Department, *Annual Report*, 1950, 12. • *like a goddam butler*: Robins, 112. • *rather be a men's room attendant*: Heminway, 272. • *Clients tend to see* . . . : ibid., 61. • *Within a few years* . . . : Dyer, *The East African Hunters*, 40–1. • *African full member*: ibid., 127. • *where the hunting ban* . . . : Robins, 108.

CHAPTER ELEVEN
● *Mr Roosevelt will* . . . : Bronson, 183. ● *les indigènes* . . . *for yourself*: Babault,
51–2. ● *As for punishment* . . . : White, *Land of Footprints*, 169. ● *in front of Nairobi*
. . . : *Daily Mail*, 15 March 1907. ● *they disregarded* . . . : Great Britain Colonial
Office, *Flogging*, 2. ● *heard the sounds* . . . : ibid., 5. ● *simple hurt . . . considerable*
period: ibid., 32. ● *typical example* . . . : Hunter and Mannix, *African Bush Adventures*,
32. ● *There were many young men* . . . : ibid., 46. ● *anti-Asian, anti-Semitic* . . . :
Trzebinski, *The Kenya Pioneers*, 156. ● *As it has always . . . warning to the natives*
. . . *white lady*: Great Britain Colonial Office, *Flogging*, 2, 32, 33, 26. ● *the Boer*
method . . . : Grogan, 231, quoted in Jablow, 'Image', 211. ● *repugnant to the instincts*
. . . : the *Field*, 23 March 1907. ● *medically condemned* . . . : Great Britain Colonial
Office, *Flogging*, 4. ● *roared for mercy*: Grant, 32. ● Stanley and the whip: Stanley,
How I Found Livingstone, 140, 108, 314, 276, 345, 398–9, 126. ● Other Europeans,
in order: Decle, 459; von Hohnel, vol. i, 50; Lorimer, 3; Babault, 51; Bronson,
381. ● *sundry other persons* . . . : Hindlip, 187. ● *nearly sick . . . bleeding horribly*:
Meinertzhagen, 11. ● *very little need*: Barnes, 58. ● *If this great* . . . : Grant,
'Introduction', in Stoddard, *The Rising Tide*, xxix. ● *When I say* . . . : Stoddard,
ibid., 157. ● *The black race* . . . : ibid., 100. ● *the decay of ideals* . . . : ibid., 167. ●
Asia, in the guise . . . : Grant, op. cit., xxxi. ● *clean, virile, genius-bearing* . . . :
Stoddard, 305. ● *having no past* . . . : ibid., 92. ● *the race-heritage* . . . : ibid., 226.
● Racial quotations: Mary L. Akeley, 43; Dickinson, 182; Barnes, 141; Neumann,
155; Bronson, 184; Martin Johnson, *Lion*, 63; White, *Land of Footprints*, 123;
Appel, 149; Martin Johnson, *Lion*, 233; Rainsford, 341; Barnes 192; Clark, *Trails*
of the Hunted, 153; Martin Johnson, *Camera Trails*, 137–8; White, *Land of Footprints*,
221; de Watteville, *Out in the Blue*, 44; Lorimer, 64; Streeter, *Denatured Africa*, 81;
Younghusband, 32, 174; Chapman, *On Safari*, 96; Dickinson, 40; Young, 32. ●
The white race . . . : quoted in Perham, 112. ● *the white man* . . . : quoted in
Meinertzhagen, 60. ● White and the two thermometers: White, *Land of Footprints*,
440. ● *it will be quite impossible* . . . : Courtney, 34. ● *appears in all the fiction*:
Jablow, 'Development of Image', 282. ● Uses of racial language: Preston, *The*
Genesis of Kenya Colony, 8; the *Field*, 19 August 1905; Hepburn, 14; Young, 329;
de Watteville, *Out in the Blue*, 217; Taylor, *African Rifles*, photo caption, 176–7;
Carl Akeley, *In Brightest Africa* 149; de Watteville, *Speak to the Earth*, 9. ● *at least*
part . . . : Roosevelt, *African Game Trails*, 9. ● white claims: Trzebinski, *The Kenya*
Pioneers, 93. ● statutory White Highlands: Gunther, 319. ● *Our own people . . .*
favourite phrases: Huxley, *White Man's Country* vol. i, 131. ● *form of white supremacy*
. . . : ibid., vii. ● *simple mind* . . . : ibid., vol. ii, 80. ● *had not even reached* . . . :
ibid., vol. i, 73. ● *the Uasin Gishu and Laikipia* . . . : Huxley, ibid., 73. ● Recent
historians: see, for example, J. E. G. Sutton, 'The Kalenjin', in Ogot (ed.). ● *he*
intends to confine . . . : Meinertzhagen, 31. ● Frederick Selous . . . Mark Strage:
quoted in Strage, 104. ● *His fortune, his home* . . . : Rainsford, 350. ● *Africans are*
rapidly being spoilt . . . : Edward Lechmere, the *Field*, 15 April 1908. ● *the increased*
prosperity . . . : East African Protectorate, *Financial Report*, 1908–9, 5. ● Hut tax
figures: East African Protectorate, *Financial Report*, 1908–9, 3. ● Conscription in
WWI: Hodges, 'African Manpower', 103. ● *weeping, mourning . . . recruited*: ibid.,
115, 113. ● WWI death statistics: Greenstein, 'Africans in a European War', 265.
● No pensions: ibid., 216. ● Black drivers' school: ibid., 125. ● *without safaris* . . . :

Frederick Patterson, 26. • *Before the whites came . . . :* Cloudsley-Thompson, 62. • *Price manipulations . . . :* Spencer, 'Settler Dominance', 508. • *apartheid was very strong . . . :* Lamb, 157. • Nairobi airport: Gunther, 328. • *if my porters . . . :* Peters, 86. • *the mainstay . . . :* Percival, *Game Ranger on Safari*, 1. • *many a hunter . . . :* Cotlow, 350. • *The niggers do all . . . :* quoted in Taylor, *Pondoro*, 214. • *The white man's . . . :* Farson, *Last Chance in Africa*, 12. • 1954 wages by race: East African High Commission, *Reported Employment and Wages in Kenya*, 1954.

CHAPTER TWELVE

• *always a solitary boy . . . :* Taylor, *Pondoro*, xvii. • *novels had a tremendous vogue*: Riddell, 'Boma', 258. • *Like most of my generation . . . :* Moorehead, *No Room in the Ark*, 16. • *the wrong view of wild life . . . :* Denis, 254. • *could not recall . . . :* Curtis, 98. • *The popular idea . . . Hampstead Heath*: Chapman, *Memories of Fourscore Years*, 139. • *not necessary or even wise*: Leakey, 55. • *neither desertions . . . dangers*: Thomson, *To the Central African Lakes*, vii. • *Wild animals . . . automobiles*: Clark, *Trails of the Hunted*, 3. • *marketing goals . . . living theatre: Los Angeles Times*, 9 August 1988.

BIBLIOGRAPHY

Books

ABRAHAMS, R. G., *The Nyamwezi Today* (Cambridge: Cambridge University Press, 1981).

AKELEY, CARL ETHAN, *In Brightest Africa* (Garden City: Doubleday, 1923).

AKELEY, MARY L. JOBE, *Carl Akeley's Africa* (New York: Blue Ribbon Books, 1929).

ALLEN, IAN 'BUNNY', *First Wheel* (Clinton, NJ: Amwell, 1983).

AMES, EVELYN, *A Glimpse of Eden* (Boston: Houghton Mifflin, 1967).

APPEL, JOSEPH H., *Africa's White Magic* (New York: Harper, 1928).

BABAULT, GUY, *Chasses et Recherches Zoologiques en Afrique Orientale Anglaise, 1913* (Paris: Librairie Plon, 1917).

BAKER, CARLOS, *Ernest Hemingway: A Life Story* (New York: Avon, 1980 [1968]).

BAKER, CARROLL, *To Africa With Love* (New York: Fine, 1986).

BALDWIN, WILLIAM CHARLES, *African Hunting and Adventure*, 3rd edn (London: Richard Bentley, 1894).

BANNERMAN, FRANCIS, SONS, *The Bannerman Catalog* (Blue Point, Long Island: authors, 1966).

BARNES, RONALD GORELL, *Babes in the African Wood* (London: Longman, Green, 1911).

BARNS, T. ALEXANDER, *Across the Great Craterland to the Congo* (London: Benn, 1923).

BEARD, PETER HILL, *The End of the Game* (New York: Viking, 1965).

BEATON, KEN DE P., *A Warden's Diary* (Nairobi: East African Standard, 1949).

BELL, WALTER DALRYMPLE MAITLAND, *Bell of Africa* (London: Spearman & Holland, 1960).

—, *Wanderings of an Elephant Hunter* (New York: Scribner's, 1923).

BENNETT, EDWARD, *Shots and Snapshots in British East Africa* (London: Longman, Green, 1914).

BINKS, H. K., *African Rainbow* (London: Sidgwick & Jackson, 1959).

BLIXEN-FINECKE, BROR VON, *African Hunter*, trans. F. H. Lyon (New York: Knopf, 1938).

BRONSON, EDGAR BEECHER, *In Closed Territory* (Chicago: A. C. McClure, 1910).

BULL, BARTLE, *Safari* (New York: Viking, 1988).

BURGER, JOHN F., *African Adventures* (London: Hale, 1957).

—, *Horned Death* (Huntington, WV: Standard, 1947).

—, *My Forty Years in Africa* (London: Hale, 1960).

BURRARD, SIR GERALD, *Notes on Sporting Rifles*, 3rd edn (London: Edward Arnold, 1932).

BURTON, RICHARD F., *The Lake Regions of Central Africa* (New York: Harper, 1860).

BUXTON, EDWARD NORTH, *Two African Trips* (London: Stanford, 1902).

BUXTON, M. ALINE, *Kenya Days* (London: Edward Arnold, 1927).

CAPSTICK, PETER HATHAWAY, *Death in the Dark Continent* (New York: St Martin's, 1983).

—, *Death in the Long Grass* (New York: St Martin's, 1977).

—, *Safari: the Last Adventure* (New York: St Martin's, 1984).

CARMICHEL, JIM, *The Book of the Rifle* (New York: Outdoor Life Books, 1985).

CHALMERS, PATRICK R., *Sport and Travel in East Africa* (London: Allan, 1934).

CHANLER, WILLIAM ASTOR, *Through Jungle and Desert* (New York: Macmillan, 1896).

CHAPMAN, ABEL, *Memories of Fourscore Years Less Two: 1851–1929* (London: Gurney & Jackson, 1930).

—, *On Safari: Big-Game Hunting in British East Africa* (London: Arnold, 1908).

—, *Retrospect* (London: Gurney & Jackson, 1928).

CHASE, ILKA, *Elephants Arrive at Half-Past Five* (Garden City: Doubleday, 1963).

CHURCHILL, WINSTON S., *My African Journey* (Toronto: Briggs, 1908).

CLARK, JAMES L., *Good Hunting* (Norman, OK: University of Oklahoma Press, 1966).

—, *Trails of the Hunted* (London: Chatto & Windus, 1929).

CLOETE, REHNA, *The Nylon Safari* (Boston: Houghton Mifflin, 1956).

CLOUDSLEY-THOMPSON, J. L. *Animal Twilight – Man and Game in East Africa* (Chester Springs, PA: Dufour, 1967).

COTLOW, LEWIS, *Zanzabuku* (New York: Rinehart, 1956).

COTTON, P. H. G. POWELL, *A Sporting Trip Through Abyssinia* (London: Ward, 1902).

—, *In Unknown Africa* (London: Hurst & Blackett, 1904).

COUPLAND, REGINALD, *East Africa and Its Invaders* (New York: Russell & Russell, 1965 [1938]).

—, *The Exploitation of East Africa* (Evanston, IL: Northwestern University Press, 1967 [1939]).

COURTNEY, ROGER, *Claws of Africa* (London: Harrap, 1934).

COWIE, MERVYN, *East Africa: Gateway to Safari* (Nairobi, 1970).

—, *I Walk with Lions* (New York: Macmillan, 1961).

CRANWORTH, BERTRAM F. G., *Kenya Chronicles* (London: Macmillan, 1939).

—, *A Colony in the Making* (London: Macmillan, 1912).

CURTIS, CHARLES PELHAM, AND RICHARD CARY CURTIS, *Hunting in Africa East and West* (Boston: Houghton Mifflin, 1925).

DANE, SIR RICHARD, *Sport in Asia and Africa* (London and New York: Melrose, 1921).

DAVIS, ALEXANDER AND H. G. ROBERTSON, *Chronicles of Kenya* (London: Palmer, 1929).

DECLE, LIONEL, *Three Years in Savage Africa* (New York: Mansfield, 1898).

DENIS, ARMAND, *On Safari* (London: Collins, 1963).

DENMAN, EARL, *Animal Africa* (London: Hale, 1957).

DE WATTEVILLE, VIVIENNE, *Out in the Blue* (London: Methuen, 1927).

—, *Speak to the Earth* (New York: Smith & Haas, 1936).

DICKINSON, FRANCIS A., *Big Game Shooting on the Equator* (New York: Lane, n.d. [1907]).

DINESEN, ISAK [KAREN BLIXEN], *Out of Africa* (New York: Vintage, 1985 [1937]).

—, *Shadows on the Grass* (New York: Random House, 1961 [1938]).

DISERTORI, BEPPINO, *Cronaca di un Safari* (Venice: Nevi Pozza Editore, 1967).

DONALDSON SMITH, A., *Through Unknown African Countries* (New York: Greenwood, 1969 [1897]).

DUGMORE, ARTHUR RADCLYFFE, *Camera Adventures in the African Wilds* (New York: Doubleday, Page, 1910).

—, *The Wonderland of Big Game* (London: Arrowsmith, 1925).

DYER, ANTHONY, *The East African Hunters* (Clinton, NJ: Amwell, 1979).

—, *Classic East African Animals* (New York: Winchester, 1973).

East Africa Women's League, *Silver Jubilee Bulletin, 1917–1942* (Nairobi: Boyd, 1942).

—, *They Made It Their Home* (Nairobi: East African Standard, 1962).

East African Tourist Travel Association, *The Hotels, Safari Lodges, and Restaurants . . .* (Nairobi: author, 1953).

EASTMAN, GEORGE, *Chronicles of an African Trip* (Privately printed, 1928).

—, *Chronicles of a Second African Trip*, ed. Kenneth M. Cameron (Rochester, NY: Friends of the University of Rochester Libraries, 1987).

EASTON, ROBERT OLNEY, AND MACKENZIE BROWN, *Lord of Beasts, the Saga of Buffalo Jones* (Tucson: University of Arizona Press, 1961).

EcoSystems, Ltd, *Livestock, Wildlife, and Land Use Survey, Arusha Region, Tanzania: Final Report* (1980).

FARSON, NEGLEY, *Behind God's Back* (New York: Harcourt, Brace, 1941).

—, *Last Chance in Africa* (New York: Harcourt, Brace, 1950).

FJESTAD, S. P., *Blue Book of Gun Values*, 9th edn (Minneapolis: Investment Rarities, Inc., 1988).

FLETCHER, COLIN, *The Winds of Mara* (New York: Knopf, 1972).

FORAN, WILLIAM ROBERT, *A Cuckoo in Kenya* (London: Hutchinson, 1936).

—, *African Odyssey* (London: Hutchinson, 1937).

—, *The Kenyan Police, 1887–1960* (London: Hale, 1962).

GANDAR DOWER, KENNETH C., *The Spotted Lion* (London: Heinemann, 1937).

GHAI, DHARAM P. (ed.), *Portrait of a Minority: Asians in East Africa* (Nairobi: Oxford University Press, 1965).

GORDON-BROWN, A. (ed.), *Year Book and Guide to East Africa* (London: Hale, 1958).

GRANT, JAMES AUGUSTUS, *A Walk Across Africa* (Edinburgh: Blackwood, 1864).

GREENER, W. W., *The Gun and Its Development*, 9th edn (New York: Bonanza, n.d. [1910]).

GREGORY, J. R. [BURKITT, R. W.], *Under the Sun* (Nairobi: Gregory, 1977 [1951]).

GUNTHER, JOHN, *Inside Africa* (New York: Harper, 1955).

HAGGARD, H. RIDER, *Three Adventure Novels* [*King Solomon's Mines, She, Allan Quatermain*] (New York: Dover, 1951).

HALL, MARY, *A Woman's Trek from Cape to Cairo* (London: Methuen, 1907).

HANLEY, GERALD, *Warriors and Strangers* (New York: Harper & Row, 1971).

HARDY, RONALD, *The Iron Snake* (New York: Putnam's, 1965).

HEADLEY, JOEL TYLER, AND WILLIS FLETCHER JOHNSON, *H. M. Stanley's Wonderful Adventures in Africa* (New York: Excelsior, 1890).

HEMINGWAY, ERNEST, *Green Hills of Africa* (New York: Collier, 1987 [1935]).

—, *The Snows of Kilimanjaro and Other Stories* (New York: Macmillan, Collier Books, 1986).

HEMINWAY, JOHN, *No Man's Land: The Last of White Africa* (New York: Dutton, 1983).

HEPBURN, ALONZO BARTON, *The Story of an Outing* (New York: Harper, 1913).

HERBERT, AGENES, *Two Dianas in Somaliland* (London and New York: Lane, 1908 [1907]).

HIBBEN, FRANK C., *Hunting in Africa* (New York: Hill & Wang, 1962).

HILLABY, J., *Journey to the Jade Sea* (New York: Simon & Schuster, 1964).

HINDLIP, CHARLES ALSOPP, *Sport and Travel: Abyssinia and British East Africa* (London: Unwin, 1906).

HIRSCH, PETER, *The Last Man in Paradise* (Garden City: Doubleday, 1961).

HOEFLER, PAUL L., *Africa Speaks* (Chicago: Winston, 1931).

HOLMAN, DENIS, WITH ERIC RUNDGREN, *Inside Safari Hunting* (New York: Putnam's, 1970).

HULME, KATHRYN, *Look a Lion in the Eye* (Boston: Little, Brown, 1974).

HUNTER, J. A., *Hunter* (New York: Harper, 1952).

—, AND DANIEL MANNIX, *African Bush Adventures* (London: Hamilton, 1954).

—, AND DANIEL MANNIX, *Tales of the African Frontier* (New York: Harper, 1954).

—, AND ALAN WYKES, *Hunter's Tracks* (London: Hamilton, 1957).

HUTCHINSON, HORACE G. (ed.), *Big Game Shooting* (London: Country Life, 1905).

HUXLEY, ELSPETH, *The Flame Trees of Thika* (New York: Morrow, 1959).

—, *White Man's Country*, 2nd edn (London: Chatto & Windus, 1953 [1935]).

JACKSON, SIR FREDERICK J., *Early Days in East Africa* (London: Dawson, 1969 [1930]).

JESSEN, BURCHARD HEINRICH, *W. N. McMillan's Expeditions* (London: Privately printed, 1906).

JOHNSON, MARTIN, *Camera Trails in Africa* (New York: Grosset & Dunlap, 1924).

—, *Lion* (New York: Blue Ribbon, 1929).

—, *Safari* (New York: Putnam's, 1928).

JOHNSON, OSA, *Four Years in Paradise* (Garden City: Garden City Publishing, 1941).

—, *I Married Adventure* (New York: Lippincott, 1940).

JOHNSTON, HARRY H., *The Kilima-Njaro Expedition* (Farnborough: Gregg International, 1968 [1886]).

JORDAN, JOHN ALFRED, 'as told to George Leith', *The Elephant Stone* (London: Kaye, 1959). [Incorporates material from Bronson, *In Closed Territory*.]

KEARTON, CHERRY, *In the Land of the Lion* (London: Arrowsmith, 1929).

—, AND JAMES BARNES, *Through Central Africa from East to West* (London & New York: Cassell, 1915).

KENYATTA, JOMO, *Facing Mount Kenya* (Nairobi: Heinemann, 1978 [1938]).

KERSEY, RALPH T., *Buffalo Jones* (Garden City, KA: Elliott, 1958).

KIRBY, F. VAUGHAN, *Sport in East Central Africa* (London: Ward, 1899).

KIRKLAND, CAROLINE, *Some African Highways: A Journey of Two American Women to Uganda and the Transvaal* (London: Duckworth, 1908).

KITTENBERGER, KALMAN, *Big Game Hunting and Collecting in East Africa, 1903–1926* (New York: Longman, Green, 1929).

LAKE, ALEXANDER, *Hunter's Choice* (Garden City: Doubleday, 1954).

LAMB, DAVID, *The Africans* (New York: Random House, 1982).

LEAKEY, L. S. B., *Kenya – Contrasts and Problems* (Cambridge, MA: Schenkman, 1966 [1937]).

LEATHAM, A. E., *Sport in Five Continents* (Edinburgh: Blackwood, 1912).

LEBRETON, F. H., *Up-Country Swahili Exercises* (Richmond: Simpson, 1964 [1936]).

LEE, ROBERT, M., *Safari Today* (Harrisburg, PA: Stackpole, 1960).

LIVINGSTONE, DAVID, *Last Journals* . . . (London: Murray, 1874).

LLOYD-JONES, WILLIAM, *Havash!* (London: Arrowsmith, 1925).

LORIMER, NORMA, *By the Waters of Africa* (London: Robert Scott, 1917).

LOTHROP, RUTH, *East African Safari* (New York: Exposition, 1973).

LOVELL, MARY S., *Straight on Till Morning* (New York: St Martin's, 1987).

LUGARD, F. D., *The Rise of Our East African Empire* (Edinburgh: Blackwood, 1893).

LYELL, DENIS, D., *African Adventures* (London: Murray, 1935).

—, *Memories of an African Hunter* (London: Unwin, 1923).

MARKHAM, BERYL, *West with the Night* (San Francisco: North Point Press, 1983 [1942]).

MARSHALL, EDISON, *The Heart of the Hunter* (New York: McGraw-Hill, 1956).

MAXWELL, MARIUS, *Stalking Big Game with a Camera* (New York: Century, 1924).

MAYDON, HUBERT CONWAY (ed.), *Big Game Shooting in Africa* [Lonsdale Library vol. XIV] (London: Seeley Service, 1932).

MCCULLOUGH, DAVID, *Mornings on Horseback* (New York: Simon & Schuster, Touchstone, 1981).

MCCUTCHEON, JOHN T., *In Africa* (Indianapolis: Bobbs-Merrill, 1910).

MCELROY, C. J. (ed.), *SCI Record Book of Trophy Animals* (Tucson, AR: Safari Club International, 1987).

MEINERTZHAGEN, RICHARD, *Kenya Diary, 1902–1906* (London: Oliver & Boyd, 1957).

MIDDLETON, DOROTHY, *Victorian Lady Travellers* (Chicago: Academy, 1982 [1965]).

MILLAIS, JOHN G., *Wandering and Memories* (London: Longman, Green, 1919).

MILLER, CHARLES, *The Lunatic Express* (New York: Macmillan, 1971).

MOORE, AUDREY, *Serengeti* (London: Country Life Ltd, 1938).

MOOREHEAD, ALAN, *The White Nile* (New York: Dell, 1962 [1960]).

—, *No Room in the Ark* (New York: Harper, c.1959).

MORDEN, WILLIAM AND IRENE, *Our African Adventure* (London: Seeley Service, 1954).

MOWBRAY, J. H., *Roosevelt's Marvelous Exploits in the Wilds of Africa* (Philadelphia [?]: 1909).

NEUMANN, ARTHUR A., *Elephant Hunting in East Equatorial Africa* (London: Ward, 1898).

OGOT, B. A. (ed.), *Kenya Before 1900* (Nairobi: East African Publishing House, 1976).

OLIVER, ROWLAND, AND MICHAEL CROWDER (eds) *The Cambridge Encyclopedia of Africa* (Cambridge: Cambridge University Press, 1981).

ORTEGA Y GASSET, JOSÉ, *Meditations on Hunting*, trans. Howard B. Wescott (New York: Scribner's, 1972).

Oxford History of East Africa. Oxford: University Press.

PAGE, WARREN. *One Man's Wilderness* (New York: Holt, Rinehart, & Winston, 1973).

PATTERSON, FREDERICK B., *African Adventures* (New York: Putnam's, 1928).

PATTERSON, JOHN HENRY, *In the Grip of the Nyika* (New York: Macmillan, 1909).

—, *The Man-Eaters of Tsavo* (New York: Macmillan, 1927 [1907]).

PEASE, SIR ALFRED EDWARD, *The Book of the Lion* (London: Murray, 1914).

—, *Half a Century of Sport* (London: Lane, 1932).

—, *Travel and Sport in Africa* (London: Humphreys, 1902).

PERCIVAL, A. BLAYNEY, *A Game Ranger on Safari* (London: Nisbet, 1928).

—, *A Game Ranger's Note Book* (New York: Doran, 1924).

PERHAM, MARGERY, *East African Journey, 1929–30* (London: Faber & Faber, 1976).

PETERS, CARL, *New Light on Dark Africa*, trans. H. W. Dulcken (London: Ward Lock, 1891).

PETHERICK, JOHN, *Egypt, the Soudan, and Central Africa* (Edinburgh: Blackwood, 1861).

—, AND KATHERINE PETHERICK, *Travels in Central Africa . . .* (London: Farnborough, Gregg, 1869).

PHILLIPPS-WOLLEY, CLIVE (ed.), *Big Game Shooting* (London: Longman, Green, 1895).

PRESTON, R. O. *The Genesis of Kenya Colony* (Nairobi: Colonial Printing Works, n.d. [1953?]).

—, (ed.), *Oriental Nairobi* (Nairobi: Colonial Printing Works, 1938).

PRINGLE, HENRY I., *Theodore Roosevelt* (New York: Harcourt, Brace, 1931).

PURVIS, JOHN B. *Handbook to British East Africa and Uganda* (London: Swan Sonnenschein, 1900).

—, *Through Uganda to Mount Elgon* (New York: American Tract Society, 1909).

RAE, WILLIAM E. (ed.), *A Treasury of Outdoor Life* (New York: Harper & Row/Outdoor Life, 1975 [1954]).

RAINSFORD, WILLIAM S., *The Land of the Lion* (New York: Doubleday, Page, 1909).

RICE, F. PHILIP, *The Outdoor Life Gun Data Book* (New York: Outdoor Life, 1986 [1975]).

ROBINS, ERIC, *Secret Eden* (London: Elm Tree, 1980).

ROOSEVELT, KERMIT, *A Sentimental Safari* (New York: Knopf, 1963).

ROOSEVELT, THEODORE, *African Game Trails* (New York: Scribner's, 1910).

RUARK, ROBERT C., *Horn of the Hunter* (Garden City, NJ: Doubleday, 1953).

RUSSELL, FRANKLIN, *The Hunting Animal* (New York: Harper & Row, 1983).

SCHILLINGS, G. C., *With Flashlight and Rifle . . .* trans. Frederic Whyte (London: Hutchinson, 1906).

SCOBIE, ALEXANDER, *Women of Africa* (London: Cassell, 1960).

SCOTT, ROBERT, L., JR., *Between the Elephant's Eyes* (New York: Dodd, Mead, 1954).

SCULL, GUY H., *Lassoing Wild Animals in Africa* (New York: Stokes, 1911).

SHELDON, MAY [MARY] FRENCH, *Sultan to Sultan* (Boston: Arena, 1892).

SIEDENTOPF, A. P., *The Last Stronghold of Big Game* (New York: McBridge, 1946).

SIMPSON, DONALD H., *Dark Companions* (New York: Barnes & Noble, 1976).

SPEAR, THOMAS T., *Kenya's Past* (London: Longman, 1981).

SPEKE, JOHN HANNING, *Journal of the Discovery of the Source of the Nile* (London: Dent, 1969 [1863]).

STANLEY, HENRY MORTON, *The Exploration Diaries of H. M. Stanley* . . . (New York: Vanguard, 1961).

—, *How I Found Livingstone* (New York: Scribner's, 1899 [1874]).

—, *Through the Dark Continent* (New York: Harper, 1878).

Stanley's Story, or Through the Wilds of Africa (Chicago: Thompson & Thomas, 1890).

STEINDLER, R. A., *The Firearms Dictionary* (Harrisburg, PA: Stackpole, 1970).

STIGAND, CHAUNCEY HUGH, *The Game of British East Africa* (London: Cox, 1909).

—, *Hunting the Elephant in Africa* (London: Macmillan, 1913).

—, *The Land of Zinj* (London: Constable, 1913).

—, *To Abyssinia* (New York: Negro Universities Press, 1969 [1910]).

—, AND N. Y. N. STIGAND, *Cooking for Settler and Trekker* (London: Field Press, 1915).

STOCKLEY, CHARLES H., *African Camera Hunts* (London: Country Life, 1948).

STODDARD, LOTHROP, *The Rising Tide of Colour Against White World-Supremacy*, introduction by Madison Grant (Westport, CT: Negro Universities Press, 1971 [1921]).

STONEHAM, CHARLES T., *Africa All Over* (London: Hutchinson, 1934).

—, *From Hobo to Hunter* (London: Long, 1956).

—, *Hunting Wild Beasts with Rifle and Camera* (London: Nelson, 1933).

—, *Wanderings in Wild Africa* (London: Hutchinson, 1932).

STRAGE, MARK, *Cape to Cairo: Rape of a Continent* (New York: Harcourt, Brace, Jovanovich, 1973).

STREETER, DANIEL W., *Camels!* (New York: Putnam's, 1927).

—, *Denatured Africa* (Garden City: Garden City Publishing, 1926).

SUTHERLAND, JAMES, *The Adventures of an Elephant Hunter* (London: Macmillan, 1912).

SUTTON, RICHARD L., *An African Holiday* (St Louis, MO: Mosby, 1924).

SZECHENYI, ZSIGMUND, *Land of Elephants* (London: Putnam, 1935).

TAYLOR, JOHN, *African Rifles and Cartridges* (Georgetown, SC: Small Arms Technical Press, 1948).

—, *Big Game and Big Game Rifles* (London: Jenkins, 1948).

—, *Pondoro – Last of the Ivory Hunters* (New York: Simon & Schuster, 1955).

THOMSON, JOSEPH, *Through Masai Land*, 3rd edn (London: Cass, 1968 [1885]).

—, *To the Central African Lakes and Back*, 2nd edn (Boston: Houghton Mifflin, 1881).

TOMKINSON, MICHAEL, *Kenya: A Vacation Guide* (New York: Scribner's, 1972).

Travellers' Guide to East Africa, 4th edn (London: Thornton Cox, 1972).

TRUESDELL, S. R. *The Rifle: Its Development for Big Game Hunting* (Harrisburg: Military Service Publishing, 1947).

TRZEBINSKI, ERROL, *The Kenya Pioneers* (London: Heinemann, 1985).

—, *Silence Will Speak* (London: Heinemann, 1977).

VANDERBILT, LUCILLE P., *Safari: Some Fun! Some Fun!* (Privately printed, 1936).

VON HOHNEL, LUDWIG, *Discovery of Lakes Rudolf and Stephanie* . . . , trans. Nancy Bell (London: Longman, Green, 1894).

WALDECK, THEODORE J. *On Safari* (London: Harrap, 1946).

WALKER, ERIC SHERBROOKE, *Treetops Hotel* (London: Robert Hale, 1962).

WARD, H. F., AND J. W. MILLIGAN, *Handbook of BEA, 1912–1913* (London: Sifton and Praed, *c.*1913).

WELLS, CARVETH, *In Coldest Africa* (New York: McBride, 1931).

WHITE, STEWART EDWARD, *African Camp Fires* (Garden City: Doubleday, Page, 1913).

—, *The Land of Footprints* (New York: Doubleday, 1913).

—, *The Rediscovered Country* (Garden City: Doubleday, Page, 1915).

WILLOUGHBY, SIR JOHN C., *East Africa and Its Big Game* (London: Longman, Green, 1889).

WILSON, ROBERT L. *Theodore Roosevelt, Outdoorsman* (New York: Winchester, 1971).

WOLVERTON, LORD, *Five Months' Sport in Somali Land* (London: Chapman & Hall, 1894).

WYKES, ALAN, *Nimrod Smith . . .* (London: Hamilton, 1961).

YOUNG, FRANCIS BRETT, *Woodsmoke* (New York: Dutton, 1924).

YOUNGHUSBAND, ETHEL, *Glimpses of East Africa and Zanzibar* (London: Long, 1910).

Government publications

Colony and Protectorate of Kenya, Game Department, *Annual Report*, various years, 1950–1962, Nairobi.

East Africa High Commission, *Reported Employment and Wages in Kenya*, various years, 1948–1960.

East Africa Protectorate, *Annual Report of Game Warden, 1913–14* (Nairobi, 1915[?]).

—, *Blue Book*, various years, 1913–1916 (Nairobi).

—, *Handbook, 1912–1913* (Nairobi).

East Africa Protectorate, Customs Department, *Annual Report*, various years, 1910–1921 (Nairobi).

East Africa Protectorate, Game Department, *Annual Report*, various years, 1913–1915 (Nairobi).

East Africa Protectorate, Treasury Department, *Financial Report, 1908–09* (Nairobi, 1909).

Great Britain, Colonial Office, *East Africa Protectorate, Correspondence, 1912–1914* (London: HMSO, 1915).

—, *East Africa Protectorate, Correspondence Relating to the Flogging . . .* (London: HMSO, 1907).

—, *East Africa Protectorate, Letters Relating to Offices . . .* (London: HMSO, 1908).

Great Britain, Foreign Office, *Correspondence Relating to the Preservation of Wild Animals in Africa* (London, 1906).

—, *Further Correspondence Relating to the Preservation of Wild Animals in Africa* (London, 1909).

Great Britain, Geographical Section of the Naval Intelligence Division, *A Handbook of Kenya Colony and the Kenya Protectorate* (London: HMSO, 1920).

Great Britain, Overseas Settlement Office, *General Information as to the East Africa Protectorate* (London: HMSO, 1919).

Kenya Colony and Protectorate, *Staff List as at September 1st 1957* (Nairobi, 1958[?]).

Kenya Colony and Protectorate, Game Department, *Annual Report*, various years, 1925–1950.

Republic of Kenya, *Estimates of Revenue for the year ending 30th June 19--*, various years.

Republic of Kenya, Game Department, *Annual Report*, 1963–1965.

Republic of Kenya, the National Assembly, *Official Report*, by sessions, various years.

Republic of Kenya, Game Department and UNDP/FAO Wildlife Management Project, *Hunt Management Programme, Kajiado District* (Nairobi, 1973).

Tanganyika Territory, Game Preservation Department, *Annual Report*, various years (Dar es Salaam: Government Printer).

Uganda Protectorate, Game Department, *Annual Report*, various years.

Unpublished dissertations

CASADA, JAMES ALLEN, 'The Imperialism of Exploration: British Explorers and East Africa, 1856–1890' (Vanderbilt University, 1972). DDJ73-14501.

GREENSTEIN, LEWIS J., 'Africans in a European War: The First World War in East Africa . . .' (Indiana University, 1975). DDJ76-11365.

JABLOW, ALTA, 'The Development of the Image of Africa in British Popular Literature, 1530–1910' (Columbia University, 1963).

KELLEY, NORA, 'In Wildest Africa – the Preservation of Game in Kenya, 1895–1933' (Simon Fraser University, 1979). 40/09A.

MCCARTHY, MICHAEL J., 'Africa and America: A Study of American Attitudes Toward Africa and the Africans During the Late Nineteenth and Early Twentieth Centuries' (University of Minnesota, 1975). DDJ75-27215.

OFCANSKY, THOMAS P., 'A History of Game Preservation in British East Africa, 1895–1963' (West Virginia University, 1981). DDJ81-27827.

Articles

'Champion Lion-Killer', *Literary Digest*, 23 March 1912.

DALLEO, P.T., 'Somali Role in Organized Poaching, 1909–1939', *International Journal of African History Studies*, Vol. 12, No. 3, pp. 472–82 (1979).

DAVIS, RICHARD HARDING, 'An American in Africa', *Harper's*, March 1893.

FORTISS, GEORGE, 'Paul Rainey, Sportsman', *Outing*, Vol. 58, pp. 746–9 (September 1911).

HANNINGTON, J., 'A Missionary's Letter to the Youngsters at Home', *Frank Leslie's Sunday Magazine*, Vol. 17, pp. 25–32 (January 1885).

HODGES, G. W. T., 'African Manpower Statistics for the British Forces in East Africa, 1914–1918', *Journal of African History*, Vol. 19, No. 1, pp. 107–16 (1978).

KANJANJA, F. I. B., 'The Uganda National Parks', *Swara*, Vol. 9, No. 5 (September/October 1986).

LAND, T., 'Kenya Escalates the War on Poaching', *Contemporary Review*, Vol. 235, pp. 24–5 (July 1979).

LIEBERMAN, SUSAN J., 'The Ivory Trade', *Humane Society News*, Vol. 33, No. 2, pp. 16–19 (Spring, 1988).

MANDALA, ELIAS, 'Foreword'. See Eastman, *Chronicles of a Second African Trip*.

O'CONNOR, JACK, 'Lions Don't Come Easy', reprinted in Rae, William E. (ed.), *A Treasury of Outdoor Life* (New York: Harper & Row/Outdoor Life, 1975 [1954]).

PETHERICK, MRS JOHN [KATHERINE], 'Mrs Petherick's African Journal', *Blackwood's Magazine*, Vol. 91, pp. 673–701 (1862).

RAINEY, PAUL J., 'The Royal Sport of Hounding Lions', *Outing*, Vol. 49, No. 2 (November 1911).

—, 'The Capture of the "Silver King"', *Scientific American Supplement*, 18 March 1911.

REDMOND, IAN, 'Islands of Elephants', *Swara*, Vol. 10, No. 2 (March/April 1987).

RIDDELL, JACK, 'The Boma Trading Company', *Blackwood's Magazine*, April 1943.

—, 'The Duke's Safari', *Blackwood's Magazine*, July 1943.

SELOUS, F. C., 'The Hunting Grounds of Africa', the *Field*, Supplement, pp. xxiii–xxv, 30 July 1910.

SPENCER, IAN, 'Settler Dominance, Agricultural Production and the Second World War in Kenya', *Journal of African History*, Vol. 21, pp. 497–504 (1980).

TRENCH, CHARLES CHENEVIX, 'Why a Greek? An East African Frontier in 1905', *History Today*, Vol. 15, No. 1, pp. 48–56 (1965).

WILLIAMS, F. C., 'A "White Queen" in Africa', *Chautauquan*, Vol. 18, No. 3, pp. 324 ff (December 1893).

WHITE, STEWART EDWARD, 'Archery in Africa', *Saturday Evening Post*, 23 January 1926.

—, 'Lion Hunting', *Saturday Evening Post*, 24 October 1925.

—, 'Lions with the Bow and Arrow', *Saturday Evening Post*, 17 October 1925.

—, 'You Never Can Tell About Lions', *Saturday Evening Post*, 2 January 1926.

YOUNG, ARTHUR, 'African Lions and the Long Bow', *Field and Stream*, July–September 1926.

Periodicals consulted (various dates)

East African Standard
Field, The
Field and Stream (New York)
Globetrotter, The (Nairobi)
Leader, The (Nairobi)
Petersen's Hunting Magazine (New York)
Saturday Blade (Chicago)
Swara
Times of East Africa, The (Nairobi)

Manuscript collections

Richard J. Cuninghame, private collection.

George Eastman, Department of Rare Books and Special Collections, University of Rochester, Rochester, NY.

Moreton Frewen, Library of Congress, Washington, DC.

Martin Johnson, American Museum of Natural History, New York.

Kenya National Archives, Microfilm Collection, Arents Research Library, Syracuse University, Syracuse, NY.

Kermit Roosevelt, Library of Congress, Washington, DC.
Theodore Roosevelt Collection, Library of Congress, Washington, DC.
Roosevelt Collection, Widener Library, Harvard University, Cambridge, MA.
May French Sheldon, Library of Congress, Washington, DC.

Films

Africa Screams, Abbott and Costello (1949).
Africa Speaks, Paul Hoefler (1930).
African Natives ('Military Drill of Kikuyu Tribes') (c.1909–1913).
George Eastman in Africa, non-commercial? (1927).
Jungle Queen, serial (c.1944).
Killers of Kilimanjaro (1960).
King Solomon's Mines (1950).
The Macomber Affair (1947).
Mogambo (1953).
Paul Rainey in Africa (c.1913).
Safari (1956).
She (1925).
She (1965).
Simba, Martin Johnson (1928).
Simba (1955).
The Snows of Kilimanjaro (1953).
Stanley and Livingstone (1939).
Theodore Roosevelt in Africa, Cherry Kearton (1910).

INDEX

Abbott and Costello, 190
Abdulla Ashur, 22
Abercrombie, David, 50
Abercrombie & Fitch (New York),
    50, 122–3, 124
Abercrombie & Kent, 114, 115
Aberdares (mountains), 38, 41
aeroplane, 85–6
    travel, 106
Africa, European image of, 28, 32,
    83, 185–96; and 'amusement',
    191–6; and film, 186–91
Africa Screams (film), 190
African Guides (company), 81
Africans, black, white idea of, 177–8;
    and film, 190–1; and language,
    179
Aga Khan, 46
Aggett, Boyce, 61
Akeley, Carl, 47, 54, 149, 162, 163,
    179
Akeley, Mary Jobe, 75, 86, 178
Akeley, Mrs (first), 96–7
Allen, Ian ('Bunny'), 111, 167, 168,
    169
Amad, Meghi, 44
American Museum of Natural
    History, 88, 165
Andress, Ursula, 188
animals on safari, 23, 24, 28, 29, 36,
    57
animals, wild, 40, 147–51
    'Big Five', 82, 146, 192
    effects of wars on, 79–80, 105–6
    image of, 93, 94
    kills, 51, 55–6, 147, 148, 149

wounded and left, 152–3
    see also under individual species
anti-Semitism, 44
Appel, Joseph, 178
Arabs, 15, 18, 19, 20, 21, 28, 30, 37,
    39, 63, 77, 81, 175
Archer, Geoffrey, 48
Army and Navy Stores, 45, 48
Artz, Simon, 45
Arusha, 41, 80, 81, 123
askaris, 16, 19, 21–2, 46, 73
Astaire, Fred, 195
Athi Plains, 35, 41, 61, 95, 193
    River, 41
Ayre, Pat, 167

Babault, Guy, 45, 163, 168, 173,
    175, 193
Bagamayo, 21, 24, 25, 30, 187
Baker, Samuel, 17, 30, 137, 139
baksheesh see tribute
Baldwin, William C., 135, 141, 161
Barnes, James, 136
Barnes, Ronald G., 56, 59, 131–2,
    141, 151, 152, 175, 178, 193
Barns, T. Alexander, 81, 83
Bean, L. L. (company), 122
Belgian Congo, 31, 32, 70, 71, 91
Bell, W. D. M. ('Karamoja'), 119,
    135, 140, 142, 147, 154
Bennett, Joan, 190
Bird, Charles S., 99
Bisley, John, 115, 116, 150, 172
Black, Alan, 49, 118, 162, 164, 167,
    169
Black, Tom Campbell, 85

black cotton soil, 35
Blaine, James E., 64–5
Blixen, Bror (von), 86, 88, 167, 169–70
Blixen, Karen (Isak Dinesen), 39, 75, 167, 168, 182
Blythe, Betty, 187
Boma Trading Co., 48, 52, 53, 57, 58, 61, 90, 99, 161, 164, 165
Bombay, Sidi, 20, 22, 77
Boustead, Ridley & Co., 46
Bowker, Russell, 118
Boyce, W. D., 96–8, 103
British Museum, 146, 162, 163
Bronson, Edgar, 57, 60–1, 127, 136, 147, 152, 153, 164, 173, 175, 178
Brookes, Clifford, 162
Buck, Frank, 91, 95
buffalo, 34, 56, 90, 126, 144, 146, 150, 157, 171
Bull, Bartle, 161–2
Bulpett, Charles, 51
Burberry's, 120, 124
Burton, Richard F., 16, 17, 18, 19, 20, 21, 29, 77
Burundi, 31, 33
Bushbuck (company), 115
Buxton, C. G. (Ms), 75
Buxton, Edward North, 29, 46, 50, 51, 52, 55, 61, 75, 105, 137, 141
Buxton, M. Aline (Ms), 84

Cameron, Lovett, 17, 20
camps, 54, 68, 73, 114
'Cape-to-Cairo', 16, 70, 77, 173
Capstick, Peter Hathaway, 154
Carmichel, Jim, 140, 154
cartridge, development of, 138, 139, 143–4
    'magnum', 143–4
Chanler, Astor, 18, 77
Chapman, Abel, 152, 159, 178, 192
Chuma, 20
Churchill, Winston, 53, 161
Clark, James, 81, 82, 84, 100, 147, 152, 165, 178, 192
cloth, 15
clothes, 117–23, 190

Cloudsley-Thompson, J. L., 155–6, 157, 183
Cockburn, N. C., 47, 147, 161
Cole, Berkeley, 61
Collier's, 56
Colonial Office, 39, 76
Colt (gun), 19
Colville, Arthur, 57
'concubinage' see sexual exploitation
Congo, River, 31
Connaught, Duke of, 48, 53, 164, 165
cook (as safari worker), 26, 90, 125–6
Cook, Thomas, 91, 160
Corn, C. K., 47
Cotlow, Lewis, 183
Cottar (family), 167
Cotton, P. H. G. Powell, 46, 141, 151
Cowie, Mervyn, 113
Cranworth, Lady, 47
Cranworth, Lord, 47, 55, 59, 95, 149, 158, 168
Cuninghame, R. J., 52, 53, 54, 81, 101, 119, 124, 141, 161, 162, 163, 165, 168, 169, 172, 173

Dale, Dick (and the Del Tones), 195
Dar es Salaam, 17
DaSilva, M. A., 52, 53, 160, 162, 165
Dassji, Shankar, 44
Decle, Lionel, 132, 175
de Crispigny, 95
Delamere, Lord, 18, 22, 29, 30, 35, 42, 47, 49, 90, 95–6, 99, 133, 147, 180
Denis, Armand, 94, 188, 193
Depression, Great, 82, 92, 106, 166, 183
de Watteville, Bernard, 152
de Watteville, Vivienne, 42, 75, 83, 111, 122, 126–7, 132, 133, 134, 152, 157, 178, 179, 192, 193
de Winton, Francis, 64
Dickinson, F. A., 110, 151, 178

disease, 30, 34, 35–6, 71
  bilharzia, 27
  malaria, 35–6, 130, 131
  sleeping sickness, 35, 36
Disney (company), 191, 192
Disneyland, 185, 194, 195
Donaldson Smith, Arthur, 18, 35,
  82, 88, 90, 127, 136
Downey, Sydney, 167
Dugmore, Arthur, 83, 89, 165
duka, 44, 61, 127, 181
Dyer, Anthony, 156, 164, 166–7

East Africa Professional Hunters
  Association, 77, 85, 111, 164, 167,
  171, 172
East African Standard, 44, 48, 50, 145,
  161, 164
Eastman, George, 82, 84, 85, 88–92,
  122, 124, 126, 130, 135, 136, 142,
  147, 148
Egypt, 34, 36, 71
elephant, 32, 33, 34, 41, 55, 85, 90,
  91, 113, 126, 139, 144, 146–8,
  152, 155–6, 157, 170
Eliot, Sir Charles, 181
Embu, 36
Emin Pasha, 17, 64
Enfield (gun), 19
Engelbrecht (car service), 83
Ethiopia, 31, 35
Evans (gun), 144
Ewaso Nyiro, River, 39, 41, 91, 193

Fabrique National (gun), 145
Farson, Negley, 110, 112, 114, 120,
  121, 133, 134, 183
Ferraragi, 90
Field, The, 46, 47, 48, 57, 126, 131,
  151, 158, 159, 162, 174, 179, 181
Fiennes, Celia, 70
Finch Hatton, Denys, 86, 126, 132,
  167, 168, 170, 172, 183
Finnie, J. S., 155
Fitch, Ezra, 50–1
Fletcher, W. A. L., 47
Flower, W., 47
food allowance (safari workers'), 26

Foreign Office, 38
Fourie, Ben, 167
Frewen, Moreton, 127, 162, 181

Gable, Clark, 189, 190
game departments, 62, 92, 107, 108,
  109, 110, 144, 153, 155, 171
Gametrackers (Kenya), 115, 172
Gandar Dower, Kenneth, 82
Gardner, Ava, 190
Gibbs (gun), 144
Gethin & Hewlett, 81
Globetrotter, The, 61, 74, 162, 165,
  177
Gondwana, 32
Gonera, 75
Granger, Stewart, 107, 112, 118,
  169, 188, 190
Grant, James, 16, 18, 21, 23, 26, 30,
  89, 125, 131, 175
Grant, Madison, 176
Great Ruaha Rufiji, River, 34
Greener, W.W. (gun), 138, 139
Griffin & Howe (gun), 144
Grogan, Ewart, 70, 77, 127, 173–4,
  179, 184
gunbearer (safari worker), 20, 22
guns, 16, 19–20, 22, 25, 42, 51,
  54–5, 91, 134, 137–46
  bolt-action, 140
  cost, 145–6
  double, 140, 141
  'express', 138, 140, 141
  'high-velocity', 138, 140, 141, 142
  'magnum', 142–4
  'Paradox', 138, 139, 141–2
Gunther, John, 76, 108, 183

Haggard, H. Rider, 37, 42, 69, 161,
  169, 185–6, 187, 188
  Allan Quatermain, 186
  King Solomon's Mines, 186
  She, 169, 186
Hall, Mary (Miss), 70–4, 77, 89, 113,
  121
  smallness of safari, 72
'Happy Valley', 79, 167, 195
Hardwicke, Cedric, 191

hats and headgear, 45, 51, 118–20
Hayward, Susan, 189, 190
headman (safari worker), 20–1, 23, 25, 28, 30, 59, 72
Heller, Edmund, 53, 54, 101
Hemingway, Ernest, 76, 82, 93–4, 105, 107, 112–13, 134, 137, 142, 151, 167, 169, 170, 185
    Green Hills of Africa, The, 76, 93–4, 129
    Short Happy Life of Francis Macomber, The, 93, 150, 169, 189
    Snows of Kilimanjaro, The, 93, 189
Hemingway, Mary, 113
Hemingway, Patrick, 171
Heminway, John, 171
Henry (gun), 19
Hepburn, Alonzo, 59, 179
Herbert, Agnes, 75, 134
Heubner & Co., 46
Heyer, Charles & Co., 48
Hill, Clifford, 165
Hill, Harold, 149, 165
Hinde, Hildegarde, 127
Hindlip, Lord, 60, 125, 131, 136, 152, 175
Hoefler, Paul L., 126
Hoey, A. C., 53, 147, 161, 163, 164, 167
Holden, William, 105
Holland & Holland (gun), 138, 139, 144, 146
    .375 magnum cartridge, 143, 145, 148
Hollywood (and safari), 94, 118, 169, 186, 189, 190–1
Holman, Dennis, 46, 79, 109, 168, 169
hongo see tribute
Hunter, J. A., 81, 88, 109, 148, 149, 155, 161–2, 167, 168, 169
hunting, 133–7, 151–3; and Africans, 136; ban, 110, 154; cost, 150; de-emphasis of, 108; ethic, 134–6, 151–2; and politics, 153–4; trophies, 134–5; see also poaching
Husquvarna (gun), 145

Huxley, Aldous, 196
Huxley, Elspeth, 133, 180

Imperial British East Africa Company (IBEA), 29, 64, 65, 66
Indians, 15, 18, 30, 39, 43, 44, 45, 46, 61, 75, 106, 181, 184
independence see uhuru
International Monetary Fund, 110
Ismay, C. Power, 47

Jackson, Frederick, 18, 20, 21, 22, 25, 51, 52, 56, 98, 119, 120, 164, 165
Jaeger (company), 123–4,
Jeevanjee, S. A. M., 44
Jeffery (gun), 138, 144, 145
Jerramani, 90
Jetha, Karman, 44
Jocelyn (gun), 19
Johnson, Martin, 88, 89–92, 119, 124, 125, 141, 148, 149, 178
Johnson, Osa, 88, 89–92, 124, 126, 127, 130, 141, 149
Johnston, H. H., 18, 21, 64, 68
Jones, Charles Jesse ('Buffalo'), 98–100, 103, 165
Jordan, John Alfred, 152
Judd, Will, 52, 53, 54, 61, 96, 136, 151, 152, 160, 161, 162, 163–4
Juma, 22
Jungle Queen (film), 122

Kamba (people), 39, 134, 149, 154
Kapiti Plains, 41, 43, 53
Kearton, Cherry, 85, 89, 99, 100, 119, 136
Kelly, Grace, 189, 190
Kenya, 31, 32, 33, 34, 35, 36, 37, 38, 39, 79, 81, 92–3, 105, 106–7, 108, 109, 110, 113, 114, 115, 127, 154, 156, 158, 170, 171, 172, 173, 180, 184, 194
Kenya, Mt, 16, 33, 34, 38, 41, 42, 54, 84, 122, 127
Ker, Donald, 167
Ker, Downey (& Selby), 109, 115
Kerr, Deborah, 169, 188, 190

Kibiego, Henry, 171–2
Kikuyu (people), 29, 37, 38, 58, 59,
    60, 76, 106, 180, 181, 182, 183
Kilimanjaro, Mt, 16, 20, 21, 32–3,
    37, 39, 41, 65, 68, 69, 70, 77, 80,
    93, 148, 162
Killers of Kilimanjaro (film), 189
King Solomon's Mines (film), 107,
    118, 169, 188–9, 191
kipande (worker's pass card), 86, 182
Kipling, Rudyard, 186
Kirkwood, J. A. C., 165
Kirparam, 44
Kitchener, H. H., General, 86
Kithusi, 39
Kivui, 39, 159
Klein, Al, 84, 94, 148, 165, 167

laibon, 38
Lake, Alexander, 129
Lakes
    Albert, 71, 74
    Baringo, 20, 34
    Eyasi, 33
    Kivu, 32, 33
    Manyara, 33
    Mobutu Sese Seku, 33
    Naivasha, 33
    Nakuru, 33
    Natron, 33
    Nyasa, 33, 71
    Paradise, 90, 92
    Ritunzige, 33
    Tanganyika, 16, 17, 33, 34, 71
    Turkana (Rudolph), 18, 30, 33,
        35, 36, 125
    Victoria, 16, 30, 33, 34, 36, 71, 74,
        75
Lamu, 15
Lawn & Alder, 48, 51, 52
Leader, The, 61, 96, 97–8
Leakey, Louis, 192
    family, 36
LeBreton, F. H., 175
Lee-Metford (gun), 139
Lee-Enfield (gun), 144
leopard, 113, 144, 146, 148, 149–50,
    157

licence, game, 57, 81–2, 87, 92–3,
    107–8, 154
lion, 32, 55, 84, 85, 99–100, 101–2,
    103–4, 107, 113, 144, 146, 148,
    152, 157, 171
Livingstone, David, 16, 17, 20, 22,
    27, 28, 186–7, 193
London, Jack, 89
Longden, G. G., 47
Lorien Swamp, 34, 41
Lorimer, Norma, 175, 178
Loring, J. Alden, 53, 54
Loveless, Marshall, 98–100
Lucy, Jack, 167
Lugard, F. D., 17–18, 27, 119, 122
Lydford, S. H., 165

Mabruki, 21
McCutcheon, John T., 54, 57, 61,
    96, 97, 124, 133, 142
machila, 72
Mackenzie, George S., 64, 66
McMillan, William Northrup, 96,
    136
Macomber Affair, The (film), 118,
    189–90
McQueen, 179, 181
Madeira, Percy, 47, 162
Maji Maji (rebellion), 40, 71
Mandala, Elias, 83
Mandara, 69
Mannlicher (gun), 140, 144
Mara, River, 38, 164
Markham, Beryl, 86, 112, 168, 170
Marsabit, 30, 33, 35, 38, 48, 90, 91,
    92, 147
Martin, James, 160, 162
Martini-Henry (gun), 139
Masai (people), 16, 20, 29, 33, 37–8,
    39, 40, 41, 48, 53, 64, 68, 70, 74,
    75, 76, 77, 97, 130, 180
Masai Mara, 41, 80, 97, 101, 155,
    191–2, 196
Mature, Victor, 189, 190
Mau Mau, 36, 38, 106–7, 108, 189,
    191
Mauser (gun), 144, 145
Mbatian, 33

Mbuu, 39
Means, Ambrose, 98–100
Mearns, Edgar A., 53, 54
meat, 22–3, 26
medicines, 69, 130–2
Meinertzhagen, Richard, 76, 95, 175, 179
Mhogo, 20
Millais, J. G., 158
Mnyamiri, 21
Mogambo (film), 189
Mombasa, 17, 30, 39, 42, 43, 44, 46, 48, 53, 65, 66, 67, 80, 86, 106, 115, 120, 181
Moorehead, Alan, 106, 109, 135
mosquito boots, 60, 87, 123
motor car, 61, 80, 81, 83–5, 112, 115
  effect on clothes, 123
  effect on safari, 84–5, 87, 112
Mount Kenya Safari Club, 105
Mozambique, 17, 31
Muinyi (Mauna) Sera, 20

Nairobi, 40–1, 42, 43, 44–6, 47, 58, 61, 74, 80, 81, 95, 99, 106, 112, 115, 123, 145, 165, 166, 173, 179, 183, 189
  animals in, 45
  hotels, 45, 80
  population, 44–5, 106
  prostitution, 76
'Nairobi flogging incident', 173–4, 186
Nandi (people), 38, 40, 71
Nazareth Brothers, 48
Ndorobo (Wanderobo) *see* Okiek
Neumann, Arthur, 17, 21, 22, 23, 27–8, 30, 35, 39, 117, 123, 136, 139, 141, 144, 147, 158, 161, 178, 181, 193
Newland, V. M., 47, 61, 62
Newland & Tarlton, 47–8, 49, 52, 53, 57, 58, 59, 61, 81, 158, 159, 160, 161, 164
Ngong, 39, 40
Ngorongoro, 33, 80–1, 114
Nile (River), 16, 17, 34, 36, 41, 70, 71, 74, 91, 185

Norfolk Hotel, 45, 56, 61, 80
Norfolk Stores, 47
Norma (cartridge), 143, 145
Novello, Ivor, 195
Nthiwa wa Tama, 39

O'Connor, Jack, 112
Okiek, 38, 134, 154
Ol Doinyo Sabuk, 41
Olenana (Lenana), 38
Ortega y Gasset, Jośe, 133, 157
Out of Africa (film), 123
Outram, George Henry, 127, 164

Page, Warren, 42, 134, 135, 145, 151, 157
parks, national, 113
Patterson, F. B., 132, 168, 182
Patterson, J. H., 30, 38, 39, 50, 57, 90, 162, 163, 165
Pease, Sir Alfred, 50, 51, 52, 54, 100, 121, 141
Peck, Gregory, 118, 189, 190
Pembe, 15
Percival, A. Blayney, 23, 78, 85, 89, 91, 140, 142, 164, 183
Percival, Philip, 91, 93, 112, 121, 147, 164, 167, 169, 172, 192
Perham, Margery, 152, 166, 167, 168, 179
Peters, Carl, 17, 18, 20, 27, 28, 29, 54, 60, 75, 183
Petherick, John, 19, 39, 75, 131
Petherick, Katharine, 75, 119, 121
photography, 89–92, 95–8
Pickford, Mary, 89
Pike, Sam, 43
poaching, 154–7
Pomeroy, Daniel, 88, 127
Pope, Saxton, 102–3, 142
porterage, porters, 15, 18, 21, 22, 23, 24, 28, 42–3, 57–8, 58–9, 83, 84, 86
  desertion of, 25, 58
posho, 26
Powell, Anthony, 79
Preston, R. O., 179
Preston, Robert, 190

prostitution, 24, 76
punishment, corporal, 27–8, 68,
    173–6
Purdey (gun), 138

racialism, white, 28, 37, 44, 48–9,
    106, 173–84, 188, 191; and
    hunting, 153–4; and wages,
    183–4; and white hunter,
    159–60, 163, 170, 172
raiding, European, 29, 36
Railway, Uganda, 30, 37, 40, 43, 59,
    60, 66, 74, 189
Rainey, Paul J., 101–2, 103, 134,
    136, 137, 164
'rains, the', 34, 35
Rainsford, W. S., 26, 29, 42, 45, 50,
    52–3, 56–7, 59, 60, 61, 76, 110,
    123–4, 131–2, 133, 149, 151,
    161, 163, 166, 178, 181
Rattray, 149
recoil (gun), 141
Remington (gun), 145
rhinoceros, 55, 56, 91, 100, 113, 126,
    144, 148–9, 150, 152, 156, 157
Rhodes, Cecil, 16, 70, 161, 173
Rhodesia, 16
ricksha(w), 72
Riddell, Captain (Jack), 48, 51, 52,
    57, 58, 161, 164–5, 168
Ridley, Mervyn, 47
Rift (Valley, Great), 32, 33, 37, 41,
    71
Rigby (gun), 139, 144, 146
Ritchie, Archie, 86, 111, 120, 133,
    149
Roosevelt, Kermit, 50, 51, 52, 53,
    54, 55, 161, 164, 168
Roosevelt, Theodore, 42, 47, 49–56,
    57, 59, 60, 61, 62, 65, 68, 81, 82,
    83, 89, 93, 94, 96, 98, 99, 100,
    101, 103, 105, 112, 117, 119, 120,
    121, 122, 124, 134, 136, 141, 147,
    149, 158, 160–1, 162, 163, 164,
    170, 173, 176, 179–80
Ross, C. J. (Major, DSO), 165
Royal Geographical Society, 65, 70
Royal Zoological Society, 163

Rundgren, Eric, 111, 149, 170
Russell, Franklin, 138, 153
Rwanda, 31, 33, 34, 71, 75

Safari (film), 107, 189
'safari' (word), 42, 49
safari
    cost, 56, 56–8, 65, 86–7, 109–10,
        114
    day, 26, 55, 60, 68, 87
    food, 125–30
    goals, 69, 77, 78
    image, 93–4, 107, 169, 185–6;
        change in, 82
    leader (European), 27, 48–9,
        51–3
    length, 59, 110
    lodges, 114–15
    luxury, 82, 88
    march, 25, 68
    mishaps, 67, 188
    organization of, 25, 50–1, 66, 72
    outfitters, 44, 46–9, 81, 109, 115
    political and racial overtones, 108
    return, 29–30
    season, 59
    setting out, 24–5
    size, 23, 90
'safariland', 30, 31–41, 106, 115
Safarilands (company), 81, 86, 109,
    164
Sako (gun), 145
Samburu (people), 38
San Diego Zoo, 185, 194, 195
    Wild Animal Park, 195
Sanderson, Arman, 160, 162
Schauer, Konrad, 48
Schillings, Carl G., 42, 89
Scott, McKenzie & Co., 44, 46
Scribner's Magazine, 56
Sedgley (gun), 144
Selous, Frederick Courtney, 50, 51,
    52, 53, 54, 57, 81, 102, 120, 121,
    135, 141, 149, 154, 160, 161, 163,
    169, 181, 186, 188
Serengeti, 41, 80, 81, 84, 90, 156,
    193
servants, personal, 21, 60, 182

Seth Smith (Donald?), 165, 167
settlers, 39
Sewell, W. G., 48, 99
Seymour (safari guide), 47
sex, 24, 187–8, 189
  and safari, 75
sexism, 76–7, 190, 191
sexual exploitation (white male, of
  black female), 76
She (film), 187–8, 189
Sheldon, May (Mary) French, 18,
  46, 64–70, 72, 73, 74, 77, 78,
  113, 121, 125, 131, 155, 175
Shindelar, Fritz, 165, 167, 172
Simson, Leslie, 85, 102, 124, 148
slavery (and porterage), 21, 39
Smith, G. E., 149
Smith-Lorien, General, 163
Snider (gun), 19, 22
Snows of Kilimanjaro, The (film), 189
Somali (people), 38, 39, 48, 52, 58
Somalia, 23, 30, 31, 35
South Africa, 36, 40, 45, 159, 172,
  183
  South Africans, 45
Speke, John Hanning, 16, 17, 18, 19,
  20, 21, 22, 23, 29, 30, 42, 77
Springfield (gun), 54–5, 91, 141, 144
Stairs, William, 67, 68
Stanley, Henry Morton, 17, 18, 19,
  20, 21, 22, 23, 26, 27, 28, 29, 30,
  42, 54, 56, 60, 64, 65, 66, 67, 70,
  72, 73, 75, 77, 78, 82, 93, 95, 98,
  119, 131, 137, 155, 175, 185,
  186–7
Stanley and Livingstone (film), 186–7
Starr (gun), 19
Stigand, Chauncey Hugh, 30, 121,
  145, 165
Stoddard, Lothrop, 176, 177
Stoneham, C. T., 87, 167
Strage, Mark, 181
Streeter, Daniel, 84, 117, 121, 136,
  147, 151, 178
Sudan, 19, 30, 31, 34, 36, 37, 39,
  71, 172
Susi, 20
Sutherland, James, 125, 142, 147

Sutton, Richard L., 83
Swahili (people and language), 15,
  16, 18, 21, 30, 37, 39, 43, 48, 58,
  59, 87, 158, 159, 166, 172, 174,
  190
Szechenyi, Zsigmund, 84

Taft, William Howard, 49
Tana (River), 34, 38, 41
Tanganyika, 31, 32, 35, 37, 38, 41,
  46, 69, 71, 74, 79, 80, 81, 92, 93,
  106, 107, 108, 114, 137
Tanzania, 17, 31, 32, 34, 36, 109,
  110, 115, 156, 171, 172
Tarlton, Henry, 47
Tarlton, Leslie, 47, 48, 49, 53, 54,
  55, 57, 61, 62, 81, 83, 85, 144, 158,
  161, 163, 164, 167, 172
Tarn, H. Holmes, 162, 163
Tarzan films, 190
Taylor, John, 151–2, 166, 179
Taylor, Robert, 189
Teleki, Count, 17, 18, 19, 20, 21,
  23, 24, 25, 27, 29, 35, 88, 125, 147,
  193
tents, 26, 50–1, 59, 73–4, 87, 124
  Edgington, 45, 124
  porters', 59
Thomson, Joseph, 17, 18, 19, 20, 21,
  22, 23, 25, 26, 27, 29, 37, 40, 42,
  60, 75, 77, 95, 124, 155, 160, 192
Thuku, Harry, 183, 186
Times of East Africa, The, 174
toilets (safari), 87, 114, 124–5
toto, 24
Tracy, Spencer, 119
trade, non-European, 29, 38, 39
trade goods, 19, 160
transport, 61
Treetops (lodge), 115
tribute, 18, 19, 20, 26, 30, 69
trout (Kenya), 127
Trzebinski, Errol, 180
tsetse, 36; and horses, 36
Turkana (people), 39

ugali (maize meal), 26
Uganda, 31, 32, 33, 34, 37, 41, 71,

72, 74, 79, 81, 91, 92, 106, 107, 109, 110, 113, 115, 124, 155, 156
Uganda Wildlife Development Ltd, 109
uhuru, 38, 92, 106, 108, 109, 153, 171, 172, 175, 184, 188, 189, 190, 191
Ujiji, 15, 17, 18
Ulyate, Ray, 99, 100, 165
United Touring Company (UTC), 115

Valibhai, Hasham & Co., 48
Vanderbilts, Mr and Mrs, 84, 88, 193
Vandermeyer (storekeeper), 61
Virgee, Suliman, 44
Visram, A. A., 44
von Hohnel, Ludwig, 18, 19, 23, 25, 27, 29, 38, 88, 125, 138, 152, 175, 193

wages, safari workers' *see* workers
Wales, Prince of (HRH), 82, 84, 85, 88, 105, 167
Wanyamwezi (people), 21, 25, 43, 59
Ward, H. F., 48
Ward, Herbert, 64
Ward, Rowland (company), 48, 134
wars, world
    First, 62, 63, 79–80, 121, 142, 182
    Second, 81, 94, 105–6, 183
Warwick, Earl of, 162, 181
water, 27, 68, 73, 125
Watson, H. G., 47
Waugh, Evelyn, 124
Weatherby (gun), 143, 150
Wells, Carveth, 128
Werndl (gun), 19
Westley Richards (gun), 144, 145, 148
White, Billy (Mrs S. E.), 122
White, Stewart Edward, 38, 49, 58, 80, 102, 103, 119, 122, 124, 136, 137, 141, 148, 149, 151, 163, 164, 178
'White Highlands', 34, 38, 44, 106, 180, 186

'white hunter' (term), 48–9
white hunter (safari position), 51–3, 72, 77, 111–12, 131, 158–72
    cost, 57, 86, 168
    danger to, 170–1
    ethics, 165, 166–7, 170
    image, 82, 167, 191
    sex and, 169–70, 190
White Hunters, Ltd, 109
'white man's country', 180–1; and safari, 180
William, Prince of Sweden, 163
Willoughby, John C., 18, 23, 46, 88, 120, 160, 162
Wilson, Maitland, 47
Winchester (gun), 19, 54, 137–8, 141, 145
    .458 magnum cartridge, 143, 145, 150
    Model 70, 144–5
Wodehouse, Lord, 47
Wolverston, Lord, 23
women
    African; as porters, 23–4, 66, 75; with male porters, 23–4, 75; position of, 63, 75, 177
    European, on safari, 63–75, 76–7, 190, 191
    and hunting, 137
    'safari wives', 21, 75
workers, safari, 15, 16, 30, 38, 58, 83, 183
    changed relationship, 111
    'villages', 59
    wages, 22, 58, 86, 181–4
    see also under specific occupations
World Bank, 110

York, Duke and Duchess of, 81, 82
Young, Arthur, 102–3, 142
Young, Francis Brett, 169, 178, 179
Younghusband, Ethel, 121, 178

Zaire, 31
Zanzibar, 15, 16, 17, 18, 19, 20, 23, 25, 31, 42, 58, 65, 66, 120, 163
Zanzibar, Sultan of, 15, 17, 18, 20, 22, 25, 27, 61, 66, 72